food file

food file

Geoffrey Cannon, Sue Dibb, Maurice Hanssen,
Colin Spencer and Amanda Ursell

Edited by Eleanor Stephens

BOXTREE

in association with Channel Four Television

First published in Great Britain in 1994 by Boxtree Limited

The Food File series on which this book is based is produced for Channel Four Television by Stephens Kerr.

1 2 3 4 5 6 7 8 9 10

Cover and text designed by Geoff Hayes
Printed and bound in Finland by WSOY for

Boxtree Limited
Broadwall House
21 Broadwall
London SE1 9PL

A CIP catalogue entry for this book is available from the British Library.

ISBN 1 85283 498 6

PICTURE ACKNOWLEDGEMENTS

Front cover photograph by © Anthony Blake Photo Library
Back cover photograph by © Caroline Marden
Plate section: pp.1,3 - © Phil Davis; pp.2, 4, 8 - © Caroline Marden; p.5 - © Steffan Hill; p.6 - © Laurent Fasano; p.7 - © Warwick Bedford. Back cover and text line drawings: © Peter Richardson

contents

introduction

If diet in the 1970s, when I was growing up, was characterized by starch-reduced breads advertised by girls in hot-air balloons, diet in the '90s has got its feet firmly on the ground. At long last, instead of being told to cut back on this and avoid that, we now know that eating for a healthy life actually means having more of certain foods, not less. We also recognize that eating well is not just about nutrients or calories; it is about enjoying good food which stimulates the senses as well as nourishing the body.

In this book, we look at recent research which has led us to this way of thinking. For example, there is now little doubt that the nutrients in fruit and vegetables have a protective effect against some of the biggest killers of our times, including heart disease and some cancers. It seems likely that the key lies in the antioxidant vitamins they contain. By meeting *Food File's* 'Take Five' challenge and eating at least five portions of fruit and vegetables a day, we really can improve the quality and perhaps the length of our life. The good news does not stop there. Enjoying a diet richer in starchy carbohydrates like bread, potatoes, pasta and rice has a wide variety of benefits too. We explain why these foods, which were out of fashion 20 years ago, are now here to stay.

More and more of us want to know what goes into the food on our plate and how it has been grown, produced, stored or preserved. Information is power and we need to know what we are buying in order to make the choices which are right for us. While eating should be one of life's pleasures, it can be a pressure: eating problems seem to be on the increase and food intolerance and allergies can also make life miserable for some. All these practical issues and more are tackled by leading experts and *Food File* contributors in the 'A-Z Guide to Eating Well'. In true *Food File* fashion, we provide the facts and opinions, you decide how to use them.

Recipes from the popular 'World in a Stew' strand of the programme feature in the second half of the book. Devised by Eliza Stephens and Robert Muir, this section is packed with delicious and unusual recipes, most of which I have been lucky enough to have cooked for me by different families from around the world, now living in the UK. Simple to make and very economical, these recipes are well worth tasting and each section contains fascinating details about each country's food history and culture.

Amanda Ursell

Editor's Note

Each contributor to this book brings specialist experience and wisdom and, where appropriate, gives personal opinions on what are sometimes controversial subjects. In the 'A-Z Guide to Eating Well', each entry is marked with the contributor's initials so that the reader may know whose voice is speaking. Inevitably, this section cannot be completely comprehensive, but it reflects the same wide range of subjects, with areas of special interest, as the *Food File* programmes. Names and addresses of organizations relevant to the 'A-Z' are listed at the end of the book.

I wish to thank all those who have contributed both to this book and to the television series. Special thanks to all the *Food File* team, particularly Pat Llewelyn, Jo Azzopardi, Rupert Parker and my partner Jean Kerr, also to Sue Shephard and Sandy Holton at Channel Four and the editors at Boxtree.

Eleanor Stephens
January 1994

The Contributors

Geoffrey Cannon is Chairman of the National Food Alliance, the representative body for British national non-governmental organizations concerned with food and agriculture policy. As such he is a member of the government's national Nutrition Task Force, set up to advise Ministers on how to achieve the nutrition targets set in the White Paper, 'The Health of the Nation'. He is the co-author of *Dieting Makes you Fat* and *The Food Scandal*, and author of *Fat to Fit*, *The Politics of Food* and *Food and Health: the Experts Agree.*

Sue Dibb is a researcher and contributor on Channel Four's *Food File* programme, and its sister programme *Eat Up*. She is co-director of the Food Commission and co-edits its *Food Magazine*. She is also a member of the School Meals Campaign, co-ordinator of the National Food Alliance Working Party on Advertising and author of *Children: Advertiser's Dream, Nutrition Nightmare?* She is also a regular contributor to magazines and books, which have included *The Safe Food Handbook*.

Maurice Hanssen's interest in food and cooking began in childhood, continued through a stint in the Army, and led to a first career in product research, development and marketing. In 1975 he became a freelance writer and adviser. He is now involved with the National Association of Health, Guild of Food

Writers, European Health Product Manufacturers Federation, Health Food Manufacturers Association and the Natural Medicines Society. His many publications include the *E for Additives* series, and several books in the *Country Kitchen Recipes* series.

Colin Spencer has written a regular food column for the Guardian for the last 13 years, and over a dozen cookery books. He is also a novelist, playwright and painter. His last book, *The Heretic's Feast*, was a historical survey of the ideological reasons for people to abstain from meat since the earliest times. His next book is a 'Vegetable Guide', which looks at the history, cultivation and cuisine of every vegetable that is grown and eaten today. His many other books include *Cordon Vert* and *Vegetable Pleasures*. He is Vice-President of the Guild of Food Writers.

Amanda Ursell is a State Registered Dietitian, and a member of the British Dietetic Association, the Nutrition Society, Register of Accredited Nutritionists, British Diabetic Society and the Guild of Food Writers. In the spring of 1992 she appeared on the first two programmes in the first series of *Food File*, and in 1993 presented the 'World in a Stew' slot in the second series; she will be presenting the third series of *Food File*, in spring 1994. She also works as a freelance nutritionist and journalist, contributing to the *Daily Mail, Guardian, Daily Mirror, BBC Good Food* and *Here's Health* among other publications.

Eleanor Stephens is series editor of Channel Four's *Food File* series. She trained as a psychologist and counsellor before entering television. With her company, Stephens Kerr, she has produced many series, including *The Survivors' Guide, Sex Talk and Love Talk*, and she was editor of *Cook It*, a young person's guide to cooking skills which was published in conjunction with the *Eat Up* television series. She is author of *Compulsion* and *Love Talk* and is a member of the Guild of Food Writers.

Eliza Stephens and **Robert Muir** are *Food File's* cookery consultants and authors of *Cook It – Cooking for Beginners*.

A-Z Guide to Eating Well

a

A.C.E. – antioxidants

The health-promoting and disease-preventing properties of antioxidants are one of the most exciting discoveries of recent years. Oxygen is vital to life but the process of oxidation in our bodies can be harmful. Scientists link it to ageing and degenerative diseases like arthritis, cataracts, some cancers and heart disease. Antioxidant nutrients, which include beta-carotene and vitamins C and E, neutralize this oxidation.

When our cells are oxidized they become leaky and attract free radicals. These are molecules with a spare electron, like dancers desperately searching for a partner. This makes them highly reactive and antioxidants are needed to mop up these free radicals before they damage our cells.

The ideal intake of antioxidants is not yet established but fortunately they are very safe, so it would be hard to overdose on them. The body turns beta-carotene into vitamin A as needed, so you do not need to take excessive amounts of vitamin A which could be harmful. A good daily intake, in addition to that consumed in the diet, would be 150 mg vitamin E, 15 mg beta-carotene and 150 mg vitamin C. To this can be added up to 800 µg vitamin A and 100 µg selenium. The main reason we are urged to increase our fruit and vegetable consumption to at least five portions a day is to increase our intake of antioxidant nutrients. (See Vitamins.) *MH*

Abattoir

(See Slaughterhouse)

Additives

The E number coding was devised to show the consumer that additives had been tested and to allow them to be identified. A very large proportion are safe and useful, but some of the most widely used allow cheap rubbish to be passed off as good food. There are too many unnecessary additives with potentially adverse side-effects for sensitive people. As yet there is no equivalent coding and list for the 5,000 or so flavouring substances, but these are expected within the next five or six years.

Some manufacturers faced with using additives which they know are not popular with the public, tend to avoid the E number and use the proper name in the hope that no one will be able to remember what it is. It should be mandatory to use the E numbers even if the proper name is also given.

It is a general principle of food law that food should be safe in the quantities likely to be consumed. This does not give comfort to the one in a hundred or one in a million who may be sensitive to E102 tartrazine or, for that matter, peanuts. So we need a full declaration to permit choices to be made.

Additives exist to fill an identifiable need. This does not mean that if additives are not present the consumer will have food that is unfit to eat or awful to taste and look at, but that manufacturers have demonstrated a technical requirement which in the case of colours, for example, is purely cosmetic.

The EC is engaged in harmonizing the additives used within the European Union in order to allow the free movement of goods. It is likely that conclusions across the whole spectrum will not be reached before 1995, but there is now a common position on the vast majority of proposals.

The Scientific Committee for Foods produced the data upon which decisions could be made, but frequently politics have ridden roughshod over science when the needs of an industry and indeed national cultures are at stake. MAFF (Ministry of Agriculture, Fisheries and Food) hailed its negotiations as a triumph when colours were retained in sausages, thus ensuring the continuation of British bangers, notorious for their high fat content and low proportion of meat as the consumer would understand it (see Sausages). You need to question why you can buy sausages, a product requiring a considerable investment in production and materials, at 60p per lb, while meat that you would enjoy costs far more. In France, Germany and Italy sausages typically cost more than meat.

The categories of additives are:

1. Colours (see Colours).
2. Preservatives, which prolong the shelf-life of foodstuffs by protecting them against deterioration caused by micro-organisms.
3. Antioxidants, which prolong the shelf-life by preventing deterioration caused by oxidation such as fat rancidity and colour changes.
4. Carriers, including carrier solvents, which are used to dissolve, dilute or disperse or otherwise physically modify a food additive without altering its technical function in order to facilitate its handling or use.
5. Acids, which increase the acidity of a foodstuff (often for the preservative effect) or
6. Acidity regulators, which control the acidity or alkalinity.
7. Anti-caking agents, which reduce the tendency of individual particles to stick together, for example, in salt and icing sugar.
8. Anti-foaming agents.
9. Bulking agents, substances other than excipients which contribute to the volume of food without increasing its available energy value. This enables you to

use very small quantities of the required food easily.

10. Emulsifiers, which allow oil and water to be mixed together, as when egg yolk or lecithin is used to produce mayonnaise.
11. Emulsifying salts, which convert the proteins in cheese into a form which allows them to become a smooth and creamy mixture with the fat and water present.
12. Firming agents, which either work with gelling agents to increase their effect or keep the tissues of a fruit or vegetable firm, for example as when canning pears.
13. Flavour enhancers, which enhance the existing smell or taste.
14. Foaming agents, which ensure an even distribution of bubbles.
15. Gelling agents, which provide texture and 'mouth feel' as in some soya milks.
16. Glazing agents, which give a protective or shiny coating as with vitamin tablets or some confectionery.
17. Humectants, which stop foods drying out, for example, sorbitol in filled chocolates.
18. Modified starches, which have been changed either physically, for example by heat, or by enzymes, to make them easier to handle, as in packaged soups and desserts.
19. Packaging gases, which are gases other than air introduced into the container to prevent deterioration. For example, nitrogen prevents the oxidation of fish or nuts.
20. Propellants, which are gases other than air for making an aerosol work. Environmentally friendly substances such as carbon dioxide can now often be used.
21. Raising agents which liberate gas to help dough rise, such as bicarbonate of soda.
22. Sequestrants, which prevent unwanted reactions such as off-flavours in processed fruits and vegetables and discolouration in fish.
22. Stabilizers, which help maintain the physical state of a product as manufactured throughout its shelf-life, so preventing the oil coming out of salad cream or water from mint jelly, for example.
23. Thickeners, which increase viscosity.
24. Flour treatment agents, which are said to improve baking quality.
25. Sweeteners are a separate category (see Sweeteners).

The immense volume of legislation going through still leaves many scandals untouched. We have the right to know what the ingredients, however unexpected, are in everything that we consume. Although legislation is scheduled, we need a full disclosure on the substances added to alcoholic drinks; no manufacturers seem to have taken a lead with a voluntary disclosure. Medicines only have to carry information on their active ingredients, and even though producers agreed in principle more than ten years ago that they would disclose colours, preservatives and other potential problem ingredients for some sensitive people, nothing has happened.

If you buy wrapped bread or packaged cake you know what they are made from, but remove the packaging and the disclosure is not required. Yet every momma and poppa baker in Sicily puts the list of ingredients on the price ticket; why not us?

Take-aways and fast food restaurants routinely use colours to which many are sensitive - a single portion of fish in batter can contain the total acceptable daily intake of tartrazine. And if you think that tandoori chicken is bright red because of some herbal ingredient, think again!

I want to see total ingredient disclosure when anything is added that a good cook would not use in the kitchen, or that could give rise to an adverse reaction. Action for food honesty should start right now. *MH*

Adulteration of food

The passion for very white flour in the Victorian era led to one of the major scandals of food history in which white lead was used to improve the colour, with fatal consequences. Fredrick Accum wrote his treatise on the *Adulterations of Food and Culinary Poisons* in 1820 and so began a revolution in attitudes to food safety, which gained legal status with the Adulteration of Food and Drink Act 1860, prohibiting the sale of food to which materials or ingredients injurious to health had been added, and of impure food.

Today we are faced with ever more sophisticated and often legally-condoned adulteration. Irradiation and genetic engineering (see these sections) may or may not be fine and there is a Novel Foods Committee overseeing our welfare. Nevertheless, choices are being taken away from us because information is restricted. I would like to see a full and frank disclosure of whether or not food has been treated in any way which could be considered adulteration, in that it did not occur in nature.

The European Community's single market means that the checks and limits normally available at ports of entry are now denied us, so produce adulterated by pesticides and growth stimulants can enter the UK unchecked. Additives incorporated into ingredients which do not have an effect on the total product are exempt from declaration. For example, your muesli which claims to be free from additives could be made with dried fruits which have been sulphited, to which an asthmatic may have an adverse reaction. *MH*

Advertising

Food advertising is big business, worth over £600 million every year, but many health campaigners argue that it does little to encourage healthy eating. Chocolate manufacturers top the league of big spenders on advertising, with sauces, pickles and salad creams, crisps and snacks, sugary confectionery and biscuits all in the top ten, making a pretty unhealthy selection of foods.

Surveys of children's commercial television have found that over 80 per cent of the foods advertised between programmes are ones that do little to encourage healthier eating. A child bombarded by adverts for confectionery, pre-sweetened cereals, fast food, fizzy drinks, crisps and ice-cream, using cartoons or films of kids having fun, accompanied by exciting music and sound effects, may be less likely to find that wholesome 'real' food holds the same appeal. Small wonder that so many family dinner tables are battlefields. *SD*

Agribusiness

If what we want is cheap food, and in particular if what we want is cheap meat and milk as everyday staple food, what we get is agribusiness. This means modern intensive agriculture that exploits the countryside and farm animals as commodities, and eventually exhausts the earth's resources.

The devastation, squalor and degradation created by agribusiness is now widely deplored by relatively well-off people who care about the environment, health and animal welfare. Intensive agriculture, more ruthlessly practised in the UK than elsewhere in Western Europe, has uprooted much of the British landscape; raises poultry, pigs and cattle in abominable conditions; and uses methods that are unsustainable in the long term. British farming is in crisis.

So are British farmers. For they are victims too. British agribusiness is above all the creation of governments which, after the Second World War, pursued a policy of national self-sufficiency. The mission was plenty of cheap food for everybody. Farmers were given massive financial incentives to rip up woods and hedges, replace workers with machines, use chemicals that kill birds, bees and butterflies, and turn their farms into factories for the mass manufacture of animal products.

Companies whose profits depend on agribusiness claim that such methods are necessary to sustain a rapidly growing world population. This is probably true. The counter-argument, is that the global population explosion, itself a result of intensive agriculture, is unsustainable, and that the traditional farming systems which have now almost vanished from Britain and are threatened in Africa and Asia, should be preserved and protected.

Meanwhile, if you deplore agribusiness, put your money where your mouth is. If you continue to consume cheap meat and animal products as staples, you are like those who tut-tut about energy conservation while driving big cars. Don't buy cheap animal products, and say why. Better still, shift your whole diet and that of your family so that it is vegetable-based: eating meat only occasionally or not at all is good for the planet, and good for you, too. *GC*

Air

Air and water are magic ingredients for the food manufacturer, harmless, tasteless and not terribly expensive. It must have been a blow when labelling regulations required that water should be included in the descending order by weight of ingredients.

Mr Whippy ice-cream, developed by an inspired team of food scientists including Margaret Thatcher before she became Prime Minister, was and is a temptingly light creation because of the air cunningly extending the fats and sugars with which it is made.

Good bread requires good oxidation, which is why the Aerated Bread Company (ABC) flourished in the 1930s. A light loaf depends upon the correct combination of a good yeast and flour with a high gluten (protein) content to form the elastic matrix to give you the holes which make for lightness in bread, plus the right fat. The Chorleywood Process revolutionized bread-making, enabling continuous production of a product with a high volume in relation to the weight. You can replicate the idea at home by adding a crushed 200 mg vitamin C tablet to the bread mixture, allowing it to prove once, and then baking. This is how the mass bakers have made wholemeal bread popular in an ever- growing market.

Those of you who have never tried making bread in the traditional way, vigorously knocking it up to stretch the gluten, allowing it to rise and then repeating the process, have missed a combined therapeutic and gastronomic experience which any good cook book will show you how to rectify. *MH*

Alcohol

There is a crucial difference between heavy drinking and light drinking. Heavy drinking is dangerous. Half of all murders are committed by drunken people. One-third of all car accidents involve a driver over the legal limit. Drinking is involved in two-thirds of all suicides, one-fifth of child abuse cases, and one-third of domestic accidents. Heavy drinking eventually ruins the liver and pancreas, and is an important cause of heart attacks and cancers of the mouth, throat and gullet.

What is 'heavy drinking'? Women are affected by alcohol faster than men. A man who usually drinks a bottle of wine or four pints of beer a day, or more, is certainly a heavy drinker. For a woman half this amount is liable to be dangerous. Regular social drinkers are well advised usually to avoid alcohol when at work, and to abstain occasionally for a week or a month. Anybody who drinks throughout the day and never takes a break from alcohol is in great danger of alcoholism. Even the alcohol industry warns against heavy drinking.

It is commonly supposed that moderate drinking is positively good for you. This is probably not true. The Health Education Authority proposes a 'safe' upper average limit of three drinks a day for men, and two for women. (A 'drink' is half a pint of medium-strength beer, a glass of wine, or a single shot of spirits.) Most people will probably come to no harm if they keep under this limit and also abstain from time to time. But never drink and drive. And never drink when planning to have a child and during pregnancy; alcohol is a 'teratogen'; literally, a creator of monsters.

There is some evidence that light drinking, especially of red wine, protects against coronary heart disease. But to protect yourself against stroke and cancers, the evidence is that the less alcohol you drink, the better. Also, just like sugar, alcohol is 'empty calories'; regular drinkers are liable either to get fat or else to be short of some nutrients. Light drinking, which is to say a drink or two a day, is one of life's pleasures for most people, but it's unlikely that alcohol generally does you any good, apart from cheering you up. (See Diet; Smoking; Wine.) *GC*

Allergies

(See Food Intolerance.)

Anaemia

Anaemia is caused when the level of haemoglobin, the oxygen carrier in red blood cells, is below what is expected for an individual's age and sex. Anaemic people suffer symptoms such as breathlessness on light exercise, fatigue, palpitations, dizziness, dimness of vision, headaches and insomnia. Anaemia can occur due to non-dietary factors such as blood loss and excessive destruction of red blood cells. It can also be caused by inadequate production of normal red blood cells, in which diet plays a role.

Iron deficiency is the most usual dietary cause of anaemia and is the most common cause of anaemia world-wide. Iron deficiency is caused either by a lack of iron in the diet or by its presence in a non-absorbable form. In the Western world, teenagers on restricted diets, pregnant women and the elderly are most at risk from iron-deficiency anaemia. A lack of vitamin B12 and another B vitamin, folic acid, can also affect red blood cell formation. Strict vegetarians and vegans can be at risk because it is mostly animal foods that contain B12. Non-animal sources include miso (fermented soy bean products) brewer's yeast, sea kelp and Guinness. If in doubt, foods fortified with B12 or supplements should be taken.
AU

Animal welfare

Concern about the rearing of livestock, taking into account the natural demands made by the animals' metabolism, has a long history; writers of antiquity (Plutarch, Seneca and Ovid, to name but a few) often deplored the rearing methods used in their own time. The tenets of animal welfare were enshrined in the ten mandates of the government-funded Brambell Committee which sat in 1965. All the following simple and humane recommendations have been ignored by government legislation ever since.

1. Movement - freedom from permanent tethering, stalling and caging.
2. Daily exercise.
3. Rest - access to a clean bedded area or clean pasture.
4. Access to a clean supply of water.
5. Regular adequate food suitable to the species: roughage for ruminants over two weeks of age.
6. Environment - shelter if outside and temperature and ventilation control if inside.
7. Plenty of daylight - window area to be between one-tenth and one-fifteenth of the total floor area.
8. Freedom from mutilation and castration.
9. Transportation for purposes of sale no more than once in any period of eight weeks. No transportation of over 60 miles for slaughter.

10. Slaughter to be carried out only by the most painless methods.

There is increasing consumer concern about animal welfare, particularly among young people, and both the RSPCA and the Soil Association are campaigning to improve standards. (See Abattoirs; Factory farming.) *CS*

Anorexia nervosa

Anorexia is the word used to describe the loss or deficiency of appetite. Anorexia nervosa is the obsessional aversion to food fuelled by the aim to lose more and more weight. It is a serious psychiatric disorder, particularly prevalent in teenage girls and young women, and requires specialist treatment. (See Eating disorders.) *AU*

Antibiotics in food

Much of the food that makes up any diet eaten in industrialized countries is contaminated with traces of toxic substances. Modern intensive farming depends on the systematic use of pesticides, herbicides and other chemicals, some of which are known to be carcinogenic or else to damage the nervous system of animals and therefore probably of humans.

Are the minute residues of such contaminants found in food dangerous? Most independent scientists say no, or probably not, and believe that the occasional media 'scare stories' about food contamination are irresponsible. The honest answer is that nobody really knows for sure. A reasonable guess is that pesticides are a significant problem usually only to farm workers and people living in the country who are exposed to spray and spray-drift.

Intensive rearing of animals depends on regular use of antibiotics, for any and all of three purposes: to treat bacterial infections; to prevent infections inevitable when animals are overcrowded; and also to accelerate the growth of young chickens, pigs and cows. It is unclear why antibiotics promote growth, and thereby enable farmers to market animals faster, but they do. Traces of antibiotics can be found in meat and other animal products, notably milk.

Like any potent drug, antibiotics are toxic: that is to say, they can be a cause of illness as well as being effective against bacterial infection. For example, penicillins, the most extensively used antibiotics, are a cause of allergic-type reactions, ranging from skin rashes to the rare, potentially fatal anaphylactic shock. Very young babies, old and/sick people, pregnant women, and other 'at risk' groups, are unusually sensitive, sometimes even to small doses of antibiotics.

Could some people become ill as a result of consuming tiny traces of antibiotics in food? As with pesticides, most scientists think this is unlikely, and in well-regulated countries like Britain antibiotic residues in meat and milk are carefully monitored. Prudent mothers may wish not only to avoid feeding cows' milk to their babies, but also themselves to avoid taking antibiotics, as these pass into breast-milk.

The main problem with antibiotics, as now systematically used in agriculture, is that they breed mutant strains of bacteria that may cause dangerous drug-resistant diseases. Scientists have proved beyond reasonable doubt that such 'superbugs' can and do cause disease in animals and then in humans. But that is another story. *GC*

Aphrodisiac foods

The idea that certain foods stimulate the erogenous zones of the body and provoke sexual activity goes far back into pre-history. As a well-nourished body includes healthy and active sexual organs capable of vigorous expression, we could say that a well-balanced diet is indeed a stimulus to sexuality.

But there is no physiological proof that certain foods have a particular effect. It is best to remember that aphrodisiacs are sought by males who fear impotency and whose main aim is to stimulate an erection and maintain it. There are two substances that do this, and neither is a food: cantharides and yohimbene both stimulate the genito-urinary tract and are dangerous - the latter contains strychnine.

Certain foods have sexual associations because of their sensual appearance, flavour or texture - oysters, fresh figs, asparagus, for example. And the delights of good food and drink may well encourage and act as a prelude to sexual pleasure. *CS*

Appetite

Life can be dominated by a perpetual battle between the factors which stimulate appetite - hunger, delicious food aromas and the sight and expectation of good food - and a desire to maintain a weight somewhere around normal.

The chief centre for appetite control in the brain is called the hypothalamus. Eating fat causes the intestine to produce cholecystokinin, which suppresses the appetite: this is why fatty foods are so satisfying.

Natural appetite control is not just a chemical response to food, however; it is also strongly psychological. If you are used to eating a lot at every meal then you feel unsatisfied with less. The converse is equally true (see Eating disorders).

The elderly often lose interest in food and should stimulate their appetite by, for example, taking a moderate glass of wine or a little consomme. Frequent small meals can also be more appetizing than great platefuls. (See Elderly.) *MH*

Apples

The temperate fruit of the species Malus, which originated in central Asia, apples were certainly cultivated as far back as 2500 BC and were prized in the ancient world. Pliny mentions twenty different varieties. Apples refreshingly combine acid and sugar and in Britain we distinguish between dessert and cooking apples, generally Bramleys, which dissolve easily into a puree - good for some dishes but not others.

There are hundreds of varieties of apples, many of them with fragrant and distinct flavours. One of the most popular and widely available is Cox's Orange Pippin. There is growing interest in traditional varieties, a number of which are sold in season by some supermarkets, individually labelled. Ones to look out for are Egremont Russet (golden-brown skin and white, nutty flesh); Jonagold (large, golden-red with very sweet, white, full-flavoured flesh); James Grieve (small, golden-red with good sweet/acid balance); Orleans Reinette (large russet and gold with very sweet juicy flesh); Worcester Pearmain (bright red with white flesh with slight hint of strawberry).

Apples have fewer nutrients than one might think. They do contain essential acids like malic acid, and minerals such as potassium, sodium, calcium, magnesium and phospherous, which are all found within the skin. But their vitamin C content is quite low and further loss takes place if the apple is processed, peeled, pureed, frozen or juiced. *CS*

Apricots

This fragrant, plump and juicy fruit originated in China where it was written about in documents over 2000 years ago. Apricot trees were transported through the Middle East from where the Arabs eventually brought them to the Mediterranean, in particular to southern Spain. The apricot tree continued its migration as the Romans spread throughout Europe, finally reaching England.

The orangy-yellow colouring of fresh apricots indicates the presence of beta-carotene, a plant pigment and important antioxidant (See Beta-carotene). Apricots also provide some vitamin C and fresh ones are quite low in calories, with a 100 g (4 oz) portion providing only 31 calories. Most of this energy is from carbohydrate. If canned in syrup the calories double, and for semi-dried apricots shoot up to 158 for 100 g (4 oz).

Whilst the fruit itself is succulent and tasty, the kernels should on no account be eaten. They contain a substance called laetrile, a cyanide compound which can cause death if taken in repeated doses. *AU*

Artificial and other sweeteners

In a number of food uses, sugar is uniquely useful. Nutritionally, though, sugar is pure energy with no other value. (It is sometimes described as consisting of empty calories.) The secret is therefore to find products which do not provide the calories but have at least some of sugar's other attributes. They can be used to sweeten drinks as part of a calorie-controlled diet.

E950 Acesulfame-K : 200 times sweeter than sugar
Made from sulphamic acid, it has a distinct after-taste. It appears to pass through the body unchanged.

E951 Aspartame : 200 times sweeter than sugar
A combination of two amino-acids (proteins), at recommended intakes very safe indeed. Should not be used by those who have the inherited condition of phenylketonuria (PKU). To my mind the most acceptable of all intense sweeteners.

E952 Cyclamates : 30 times sweeter than sugar
Currently banned in the US and the UK, there is nevertheless pressure from some countries such as Germany to reintroduce it through Europe. Because it is heat-stable it works better than saccharin in processed foods. I have not seen enough information to convince me that it is safe.

E953 Isomalt : half as sweet as sugar
Isomalt has many of the sensory properties of sugar but is only half as sweet. A sugar alcohol, 30 g (1 oz) or more per day has a laxative effect.

E954 Saccharin : 300 times sweeter than sugar
Chemically synthesized in 1879, some saccharin is thought to be absorbed and accumulated in the bladder, and very high doses, equivalent to 2000 cans of sweetened drink a day, have been proved to cause bladder cancer. In the USA, saccharin carries a health warning. Has a bitter after-taste and a typically metallic taste in the mouth. MAFF has warned against regular heavy usage.

E957 Thaumatin : 2000 times sweeter than sugar
Made from two proteins from a West African plant, it has a liquorice after-taste. Little safety data available.

E959 Neohesperidine (DHC) : 1500 times sweeter than sugar
Produced from naturally occurring bio-flavonoids. There is a lingering after-taste. Little used. Xylitol : as sweet as sugar First produced from birch bark and helps to prevent tooth decay. It is therefore useful in chewing-gum. Safe.

E966 Lactitol : one-third as sweet as sugar
Produced from whey, a by-product of cheese production. Does not increase the blood sugar and is useful (see Isomalt) because it is technically usable for many products.

E965 Maltitol : almost as sweet as sugar, with the same bulking effect. Prepared by hydrolyzing starches such as glucose. Laxative at high levels, probably safe.
MH

b

Baby foods

Feeding babies is no small business. Over 80 per cent of babies are fed commercial baby foods regularly, with less than 40 per cent offered home-made baby foods. The enormous range on offer can encourage parents to believe that commercial foods are better than the foods they may make at home. But food and health advisers are concerned about the nutritional quality of some of these foods.

In a 1991 survey the Food Commission found that many commercial baby foods were so diluted with added thickeners, bulking agents and water that they were failing to provide babies with the recommended nutrients.

Many baby drinks are high in sugar and can thus cause decay to developing teeth and encourage a sweet tooth at an early age. Parents whose children's teeth have been damaged by sugary baby drinks are taking legal action against manufacturers.

Baby cereals, puddings and rusks also often contain added sugar - in fact many rusks contain a higher percentage of sugar than a doughnut.

Now some companies are introducing sugar-free baby drinks and better-quality baby foods, but the best advice is still to prepare the food yourself. It may take a little longer but at least you will know what you are giving your baby. *SD*

Baking

To cook with dry heat in an oven. Slow baking means that the food is put into a covered dish and cooks at a low temperature. Some dishes using this method, such as baked beans, can be left in the oven overnight. Making bread was one of the earliest uses of baking, converting raw grains into a staple food. *CS*

Bananas

We consume around 60 million bananas a week in Britain. After apples they are our most popular fruit. Bananas originated from tropical areas and were named from the Arabic word ***banan***, meaning finger. They are often accused of being fattening, but nothing could be further from the truth: filling, medium- sized fruit provides only 80 - 90 calories. Most of this energy comes from carbohydrate making them an excellent food for healthy eating plans and sports people. They are also rich in the mineral potassium as well as fibre, and have some vitamin C. Bananas are available all year round - green tips indicate the fruit is unripe; it is fully ripe once brown flecks appear on the otherwise yellow skin. Storing in the fridge will turn the skin black although the fruit inside will be fine. Fresh and dried bananas can be used as a straightforward snack, in savoury dishes like risottos and with chicken and fish, or in desserts and cakes. *AU*

Beans

The edible seeds of the legume family. Until the discovery of the New World only the broad bean (fava) and its few relatives were known. This bean was valued as a highly nutritious food and widely eaten - raw in salads, cooked as a soup or pounded into a paste or cake. They were also dried for the winter and made into flour for bread and cakes.

After Columbus discovered the Americas, many more beans, all varieties of haricot, were introduced to Europe. Some of these beans became special favourites of particular countries and began to feature as the star ingredient in a variety of dishes. The borlotti bean, for example, became particularly popular in Italy, the flageolet in France.

Dried beans (pulses) are richer in protein and the B vitamins thiamin and nicotinic acid than other vegetables and contain more carbohydrate and energy. *CS*

Beer

The ancient Greeks' word for a fermented barley drink was brutum (thought to come from the natural cry of children when they wanted drink), and it is from this that 'brew' and 'beer' derive.

In 1514 William IV of Bavaria promulgated the Consumer Protection Law ensuring beer purity. Since then most German beer has been made from just four ingredients - hops, malt, yeast and water. Arguments that Germans' health would be damaged by importing other EC beers because of the additives used were turned down in the European courts: first on the grounds that the alcohol was far more damaging than any additives and second because it was counterclaimed that exported German beers often contained the very same additives as in those they were trying to prohibit. You can now buy many EC beers in Germany but the German producers still have to play by the old rules. Beer is naturally rich in B vitamins and is an effective laxative. Of particular concern is the very high levels of chemical caramel in some dark beers, especially stouts. *MH*

Beta-carotene

Named after the natural colouring in carrots, beta-carotene is the most researched of the carotenoids, the yellow and red pigments found in many vegetables, fruits and meat products.

Also known as pro-vitamin A, it can be converted in the body to make vitamin A. Beta-carotene is very safe and an important antioxidant nutrient (see A.C.E.), linked to a 30 - 50 per cent decrease in lung and oral cancer risks.

High intake of beta-carotene, above 30 mg a day, can make the skin slightly yellow. Most of us, however, do not eat enough portions of fruit and vegetables for the 15 mg a day thought about right for good health. At least five portions daily are recommended. *MH*

Biscuits

The British eat more biscuits and chocolate confectionery than any other nation on earth, and the interests of the industry are effectively represented by the Biscuit, Cake, Chocolate and Confectionery Alliance, whose products make up one-eighth of all the calories consumed in Britain. (See Chocolate.) In any supermarket, the array of shelves stocking biscuits is awesome.

When the tax on imported sugar from the colonies was lifted in the 1870s, Britain was inundated with sugar. Enterprising businessmen found all sorts of ways of making sugar a major ingredient of cheap and cheerful foods for the working classes. Hence the booming British jam, cake, fizz and biscuit industries, whose products continue to rot teeth, clog guts and swell bellies.

Most sweet biscuits manufactured in Britain are a confection of sugar and unhealthy hard saturated fats, salt, and white flour, often tarted up and made more palatable by a sophisticated use of cosmetic food additives. Recently, manufacturers have promoted digestives and other biscuits made with wholegrain flour, but any benefits of the added nourishment are swamped by fat and sugar.

Sweet biscuits are fine once in a while; but that means maybe one twice a week, not three twice a day. Eat fresh fruit instead. *GC*

Blood pressure

Blood pressure is expressed in two numbers, as in 130/90, the first of which indicates the maximum, systolic pressure as the blood enters the arteries and the second the minimum, diastolic as the blood leaves the arteries and goes into the capillaries. 140/85 is normal; 145/95 indicates mild hypertension; 160/105 moderate; 175/115 severe.

There is much argument as to the effectiveness of reducing blood pressure that is not severe, especially by means of drug treatment. The side-effects may be as problematical as the condition, which is brought about by a combination of heredity, age, race (dark-skinned people are more liable), excess weight and perhaps salt and alcohol consumption. Meditation, yoga and fitness training have also been shown to be helpful in lowering blood pressure.

Heavy meals, fatty foods and high salt intake should be controlled. Vegetables and fruits that are high in potassium are protective. Polyunsaturated fats can reduce pressure, as can a high-fibre diet and elimination of more than two or three cups of coffee a day.

High blood pressure is a contributory factor in several health problems. If you are in a risk group it is better to alter your lifestyle before high blood pressure hits you rather than attempt to rebuild your life after a warning heart attack. *MH*

Blood sugar

Good health involves balance. It is unhealthy to be very fat, or very thin. Both a high and a low body temperature are signs of illness; likewise, high and low blood pressure. The same is true of the level of sugar in the blood. Blood-sugar levels of healthy people fluctuate, but only within certain limits. A healthy, relatively high level of blood sugar makes you feel alert and energetic for a day's work. A relatively low level creates a sense of drowsiness, just what you need at bedtime.

All types of carbohydrate are converted into sugar in the body and blood, as human fuel. Starchy foods such as wholegrain bread and cereal products, and legumes, raise blood-sugar levels relatively slowly. Sugary foods act faster, and manufactured foods and drinks containing a lot of refined sugar, such as sweet biscuits, cakes, candies and chocolate confectionery, colas and other soft drinks, are converted into blood sugar artificially fast. Indeed, some such products are advertised effectively as offering a 'quick hit'.

However, the body is not designed to be assaulted in this way. If it is, the blood-sugar level soars, too high. In reaction, the pancreas shoots insulin into the blood, pushing sugar levels down too low. In medical language this exaggerated downward fluctuation is known as 'rebound hypoglycaemia'. It causes a sense of elation followed by a sense of exhaustion. Sounds familiar?

Usually caused by refined sugar and sugary foods and drinks, this process is a type of addiction. The affected person has a danish pastry or a soft drink, gets high, sinks low, and so then craves another danish pastry or soft drink. Alcoholic drinks can have a similar effect. The ill-effects include mood swings, difficulty in concentrating, and weight gain. Some scientists believe that as a result of incessant over-use the pancreas may pack up, the result being adult-onset diabetes. Other scientists believe that diabetes has nothing to do with sugary food - a view shared by the sugar industry. (See Diabetes; Sugar.) *GC*

Body image

It is hardly a new phenomenon for both men and women to be concerned about their body image. The fashion industry has been in business for centuries, shaping trends for hairstyles, clothes and body shapes. Women have always gone to various lengths to attain the 'look' of the time, but what is new today is the scale of dissatisfaction with personal images, the ages of those affected, the effects on individuals, families and society, and finally, the lengths people will now go to alter various physical attributes in an attempt to improve their self-image and status.

Where is all this dissatisfaction coming from? Blame has partly to be laid at the door of the media. Images of bodily perfection are being constantly brought to us through magazines, newspapers, advertising bill-boards and television and radio. Anyone not fitting into the ideal is at risk of feeling inadequate. Poor self-perceptions soon follow.

People go about trying to improve their body image in different ways. If you have enough time and money you may go for the quick-fix option of surgery: noses can be honed, wrinkles removed, busts made larger or smaller, fat on thighs sucked out and fat in lips put in. Others, much more sensibly, look to themselves for the 'answer'.

Trying to lose weight is one of our national female obsessions. Many believe that their body image will improve if only they can slim down to the shape of the day. This is where the slimming industry must take its share of blame. Constant brain-washing with the idea that thinness equals happiness and desirability is a multi-million pound business involving dieting clubs, formula drinks, biscuits, meals, dedicated slimming magazines and so on. Unfortunately the desire to be thin often ends in misery compounding low self-esteem. Dieters either find themselves on the merry-go-round of losing and gaining weight or get totally obsessive and develop eating disorders. In the case of those wanting to assume current 'super-waif model' thinness in which hip-bones protrude and the overall look is skeletal, starvation seems to be the route adopted. Girls wishing to emulate top models are at increasing risk of developing the so-called 'slimmers' disease', anorexia nervosa. Those affected seem to be getting younger and younger. Girls of seven presenting with anorexia nervosa are now not uncommon. Older women trying in vain to change naturally rounded hips into those of long, lean ectomorphs like Twiggy are more at risk from the bingeing and purging eating disease, bulimia nervosa. (See Eating disorders.)

Men are not immune to media and peer pressure either. Recent research has shown growing male dissatisfaction with the shape and size of their bodies and the number of eating disorders among men is increasing. Many succumb to clever marketing of body-building products, spending hours in the gym; others may turn to drugs.

Poor or distorted body image not only leads to personal dissatisfaction and health risks, but often affects relationships with family and friends. Solutions are tricky to find, but rarely lie in diet alone. Emotional and psychological aspects are probably more important. *AU*

Boiling

To cook food immersed in water which is bubbling, that is, just over boiling point - 212°F (100°C). Sometimes terms like 'rolling boil' are used; this merely means a fierce bubbling. The term 'poaching' is sometimes used to describe a 'slow boil', meaning that the food is put into a liquid wine or stock which is gently heated and bubbles quietly. *CS*

Bowel diseases

Diseases of the bowel, otherwise known as the large intestine or colon, are not attractive topics of conversation, but disagreeable, disabling and even deadly gut disorders and diseases are very common in industrialized countries. As with other vital organs, the main single cause of at least some bowel diseases is the typical industrialized diet.

In Britain over 10 million people are estimated to suffer from chronic bowel problems. Of these the most common is severe constipation, whose chief cause is a refined, processed diet stripped of the fibre naturally present in wholegrain cereals, legumes, vegetables and fruit. Diverticular disease is probably a complication of constipation.

The most common deadly bowel disease is colon cancer, which in Britain is the second biggest cancer killer of men (after lung cancer) and of women (after breast cancer). Researchers in the field are now confident that colon cancer, like heart disease, is largely preventable by means of a life-long healthy diet. Best nourishment for the gut is a diet rich in fresh vegetables and fruit and wholegrain cereals, containing only small amounts of meat and fat.

Other common bowel diseases remain a mystery to modern medical science. These include irritable bowel syndrome, Crohn's Disease, and ulcerative colitis. The chronic malaise and pain caused by irritable bowel syndrome in particular are often provoked or made worse by eating certain foods. Such allergic-type reactions (also known as food intolerance) are a symptom of bowel injury, more serious in cases of Crohn's Disease and ulcerative colitis. The human body is designed to digest a lot of fibre, and it may be that the same sort of diet that causes constipation, diverticular disease and colon cancer is also a cause of other bowel diseases. In addition, antibiotics are known to be a common cause of gut inflammation and can cause serious bowel diseases. (See Diet; Food intolerance; Intestinal bacteria.) *GC*

Breads

We consume far less bread than we used to and far less than our European neighbours. Bread is a starchy carboydrate food which contrary to much popular opinion is not fattening, being low in fat. It is nutritious, a good source of protein, B vitamins and minerals such as calcium and iron. Wholemeal bread contains more fibre than white, but white bread is not the nutritional villain it's sometimes painted. By law it must contain added vitamins, calcium and iron.

While white bread still retains its popularity in Britain, accounting for 70 per cent of all bread sold, there has been growing interest in different kinds of bread. Wrapped sliced white may offer a cheap loaf, but by being adventurous, looking around and only sometimes paying a bit more, it is possible to enjoy a whole variety of tasty breads. Greek pitta pockets, Italian ciabatta (made with olive oil), pumpernickel, rye and flat Indian naan, are just a few examples. *SD*

Breakfast

Breakfast is an important meal, yet a surprisingly large number of people, including children, skip it altogether. A survey last year for Channel Four's Eat Up series found that a quarter of older girls were skipping breakfast regularly, compared generally to one in ten children. And many of them were filling up instead on the way to school with sweets, crisps, fizzy drinks and other fatty, sugary junk foods.

Some schools are now so concerned about this problem that they are extending their meals' service to provide breakfast as well as dinner. They know that children who do not eat a proper breakfast find it harder to concentrate and may be more disruptive. (See IQ and supplementation.)

Young girls and women who are slimming often miss breakfast. However, it is far better to eat a bowl of low-fat unsweetened cereal or toast with fresh fruit or juice than to skip eating altogether. You are less likely to snack later in the morning, and many people find they feel better when eating more regularly. Not skipping meals can help avoid migraine attacks and pre-menstrual syndrome (PMS). *SD*

Breakfast cereals

Breakfast cereals are heavily promoted as a healthy way to start the day. However, the refining process actually destroys many of the vitamins - which led to the old joke that there was more good nutrition to be had from the cardboard box than from the cereal itself. Manufacturers, however, fortify their cereals with added vitamins and minerals to make up for the loss of nutrients caused by refining. (See Fortification.)

Many brands of cereal are aimed specifically at children, yet the majority of these contain as much as 5 level teaspoons of sugar in a serving - and that's before any sugar is added at the table.

Interest in healthier eating has led to an explosion of high-fibre cereals and muesli-type mixes. In its original form, muesli was a mixture of wholegrain cereal, fresh fruit and nuts. But the modern food industry has turned it into a concoction of sugar, dried fruit, cereals (some wholegrain perhaps), more sugar, dried milk powder, extra bran, nuts, salt, still more sugar. In fact the sugar levels of some cereals advertised as 'healthy' muesli-type mixes can be as high as those of many regular 'sweetened' cereals. *SD*

Breast/bottle feeding

There are real health benefits to breast-feeding, yet surprisingly, only 63 per cent of women try it, and one-third give up by six weeks.

Breast-milk contains the perfect balance of nutrients for babies, it is naturally hygienic and less likely to cause colic or diarrhoea. It also contains antibodies that help guard your baby against infection in the first few months of life. There is also some evidence that breast-fed babies are less likely to develop allergies. It is convenient, free and can be a real pleasure. Breast-feeding for at least three months has been found to lessen women's risk of developing breast cancer.

However, many women find the idea of breast-feeding off-putting, particularly if their family and friends are not supportive. Many women believe that they are not given the help with breast-feeding that they need at the beginning if difficulties such as sore nipples arise, or if they are concerned as to whether their babies are getting enough to eat. There have also been concerns that the way baby milk companies promote their products can undermine breast-feeding. The choice of whether to bottle, or breast-feed is a personal one, and if you decide to bottle-feed there is no reason to feel guilty or inadequate. *SD*

BSE

The first case of Bovine Spongiform Encephalopathy, popularly known as 'mad cow disease', was confirmed in 1985. It is not known what the BSE agent is or exactly how it spreads. It is thought that cows were infected from the feed which contained processed sheep's brains infected with 'scrapie'. Animal protein on the labels of livestock feeds could mean rendered-down and processed remnants of sick and injured animals. The BSE agent attacks the spinal cord and brain of the animal, turning the nervous tissue into something resembling a sponge.

CJD (Creutzfeldt-Jacob Disease) is the human equivalent, and though still very rare, deaths from CJD in Britain have recently begun to rise. The Government has said repeatedly that consuming beef is perfectly safe, but it did not ban the consumption of brain and offal products from infected cows until 1988. These were processed into mechanically recovered meat (see MRM), which goes into meat products like cheaper pies, sausages and convenience foods, and as BSE and CJD have a long incubation period, there is no guarantee that the government prognosis is correct. Thousands of cows are continuing to be slaughtered that might very well be incubating the disease because they are killed before the symptoms are visible.

The truth is that we know very little about these diseases. For example, five out of eight antelope born at London Zoo since 1987, have developed BSE. Scientists do not know how they were infected. To date, over 100,000 cows have been slaughtered because of the disease. The Government told us three years ago that there would now be a decline in the number of cases, but in the first quarter of 1993 BSE cases were up by 42 per cent. It also told us that stopping cattle consuming the infected feed would eradicate the disease. But around 2,900 cases of BSE in cows have been confirmed since the feed was changed. *CS*

Bulimia

Bulimia is a serious eating disorder in which the sufferer is trapped in a starving/bingeing/vomiting cycle. Eating patterns are very erratic and perception of body image is often distorted. (See Eating disorders.) It is sometimes referred to as bulimia nervosa and may alternate with anorexia nervosa. (See Anorexia nervosa.) *AU*

Burgers

If all the burgers that are eaten world-wide in one year were lined up and to end, they would stretch around the world more than twenty-five times. The burger started out as a simple meat-ball rolled out flat in order to cook quickly. Then it was put inside a bread bun, so that people could eat it without getting their fingers greasy. The name is an abbreviation of the Hamburger Steak, named after the German city of Hamburg, and was introduced into the USA by German immigrants.

Now the big burger chains can be found in virtually every country of the globe. There have been concerns that too much rainforest, particularly in Central and South America, has been cut down to clear land for cattle ranching to supply beef for the world's burger market. Even when companies do not source their beef from these areas it is quite possible that the animals have been fed on soya grown on cleared forest land.

It is not always easy to tell what kind of quality meat you are getting in your burger. Legally 'meat' can include a hefty proportion of fat, and a label saying 'beefburger' does not mean that all the meat need be beef. The regulations allow 20 per cent of other meats, such as pork or poultry. Economy beefburgers can be 40 per cent other meats. It is very important that burgers are properly cooked. One dangerous strain of food poisoning bacteria, E. Coli 0157, has been associated with undercooked burgers. (See Food poisoning; Fast food.) *SD*

Butter

The trouble with butter, as with other tasty, relatively natural foods of animal origin, is that most people eat far too much of it, either as table fat or in processed foods. Basically butter is composed of highly saturated fat and water. Fresh farm butter is one of life's delights, eaten as an occasional luxurious treat on wholegrain toast or scones, say, or with a baked potato. But it is best to give mass-produced butter and other even cheaper table fats a miss. (See Margarine.)

People from other countries are intrigued by the British enthusiasm for table fats. Generally speaking any country where dairy farming is particularly profitable will produce a glut of butter and milk. In such circumstances governments and amenable scientists will promote dairy products as nourishing consumed in abundance. In Britain, the standard white loaf is so disgusting by itself that it needs to be perked up and made palatable by the addition of table fats and jams. On the other hand, freshly made breads such as the French baguette or German wholegrain loaves are delicious eaten by themselves as snacks or with meals.

And for cooking? Nothing beats a simple mushroom omelette made with butter, and there is no real substitute for it in other more elaborate, special occasion dishes. There is no need to ban butter altogether from your cooking: savour it occasionally. Happily, the British obsession with pseudo-haute cuisine food in which natural flavours are swamped with fats and sugars has almost become a thing of the past. The delicious and healthy Mediterranean diet, of which olive oil is an integral part, is now popular, as are cuisines from other parts of the world whose ingredients retain their own flavour, unadulterated by fat. *GC*

C

Caffeine and decaff

There are as many medical papers saying that coffee consumption is safe as that it is not, but a prudent view would be that more than six cups a day could give rise to high blood pressure and kidney problems. Caffeine is definitely addictive, and migraine-like withdrawal symptoms are not uncommon.

Caffeine and related substances such as theobromines from chocolate are found in coffee, tea, cocoa and cola. That is why these drinks give you a lift. They are rapidly absorbed, suppress fatigue and make you feel brighter. All these substances are diuretic, which means that for long-distance driving, for example, stimulant drinks are of limited benefit.

The decaffeination process is traditionally effected by steaming the green coffee beans with chemical solvents such as methylene chloride and then washing away and recycling the solvent. My own preference would be to avoid solvents which are carcinogenic at high doses and choose products from which the caffeine is extracted by water or steam. *MH*

Calcium

The most abundant mineral in our body, each of us has more than a kilo. Calcium forms almost all of our bone structure and teeth. Just as with our skin and cells, bones are biologically active with a continual movement of substances from the surface. If we do not consume enough calcium in our food to keep up the blood levels then bones will allow some of their own calcium to dissolve to keep the balance right. This is clearly bad news and so it is important from the earliest ages to have enough calcium, with vitamin D which enables it to be utilized, to make sure that we have and retain bones in a good state. Young girls are particularly at risk, often avoiding the fatty part of milk which contains vitamin D, or not drinking milk at all. Yet a mixture of exercise and calcium is the only way to lay down strong and lasting bones, which will help to protect against osteoporosis in later life.

You need to go for at least 500 mg of calcium a day. This takes the best part of a pint of skimmed or full milk, or a large portion of green leafy vegetables, or take a calcium supplement. (See Minerals.) *MH*

Calories

Just as petrol, the energy source for cars, is measured in gallons and litres, the energy from food and drink to fuel our bodies is traditionally measured in calories. Anyone who has tried losing weight, or has been in the company of someone battling with the bulge, will very likely be sick to death of the word. The energy provided by food and drink is ultimately converted into heat, and the calorie is a quantitative way of measuring a unit of heat. It is defined as the amount of energy needed to raise the temperature of water 1°, from 14.5°C to 15.5°C. In fact, the calorie is a rather old-fashioned measurement and nowadays scientists use the unit called a joule. You'll find that in a huge range of foods the energy it provides is given in both kilojoules and kilocalories. One kcal is equal to 4.184 kj.

As a basic guide we know that, per gram, fat provides the most calories: 1 g of fat gives 9 kcal. Any food which is rich in fat will therefore be reasonably high in total calories. Carbohydrates provide about 4 kcal per gram, as do proteins. A gram of alcohol contains 7 kcal. *AU*

Cancers

One in three people in Britain suffer cancer at some time in their lives, and cancer kills over one in five British people. While different cancers have different causes, there is a lot you can do to reduce the risk of cancer. Well-known good advice is: don't smoke (lung cancer); avoid sunburn (skin cancer); don't live near nuclear plants (leukaemia). Less well-known advice is to eat a healthy diet. Scientists who study the incidence of diseases (epidemiologists) reckon that maybe two-thirds or more of all cancers are avoidable by not smoking and by eating healthy food.

The World Health Organization, the Europe Against Cancer campaign, the American Cancer Society and other authoritative organizations emphasise that fresh vegetables and fruit provide vital protection against major killers such as stomach and colon cancer and also protect against lung cancer. People who drink little or no alcohol are less likely to suffer cancers of the mouth, throat and liver.

Some types of food processing and preparation are carcinogenic: these include salting, smoking and any cooking that burns food. A vegetable-based diet, with little if any fatty meat, protects against a number of common cancers. In Britain the best source of dietary advice is the World Cancer Research Fund (see list of Useful Addresses).

Key positive dietary advice to reduce cancer risk is to eat at least five servings of fresh vegetables and fruit every day, and plenty of wholegrain cereals too. This is consistent with advice designed to reduce the risk of heart attacks and other diseases. (See Bowel diseases; Heart disease; Hypertension.) *GC*

Candida

Candida is a type of fungus which is widespread in nature. Candida albicans is naturally present in the mouth, throat, vagina, gut and skin. Candidiasis is caused either by an overgrowth of candida, or individuals being hypersensitive to otherwise normal levels. In these cases it can cause thrush, vulvovaginitis and pulmonary diseases. Some claim it also causes irritable bowel syndrome, PMS and even mental disturbances. These outbreaks of infection can be triggered by use of wide-spectrum antibiotics, steroids, the contraceptive pill and immuno-suppressing drugs.

It can also take hold during pregnancy and can be secondary to diabetes. In addition to these causes, poor oral hygiene, including decayed teeth and poorly-fitting dentures, can also be a factor.

The main line of treatment of candida is with antifungal Nystatin tablets. Dietary modifications to accompany this treatment are also recommended by some doctors and include sugar-free, yeast- and mould-free diets. These should only be undertaken with the supervision and advice of a dietitian. *AU*

Canning

Canned and bottled food is often a good choice. Keep it as a standby for the winter, and for quick snacks and meals. Canned fish, tomatoes, beans and legumes are all very good value for money. The main problem with canning is that manufacturers add salt (to soup and vegetables) and sugar (to fruit) to pep up the flavour.

Canned products tarted up with sophisticated cocktails of cosmetic food additives are now less common, thanks to effective media campaigns drawing consumers' attention to long lists of E numbers on labels. (See Additives; Processing.) *GC*

Carbohydrates

The body is perfectly equipped to use carbohydrates to provide energy. They can be stored as glycogen or broken down to glucose and burnt - that is, oxidized - to provide the main type of energy needed by the nervous system and brain. Together with fatty acids, which are used when we are short of glucose, carbohydrates are one of only two energy sources for the muscles (see Exercise and nutrition).

Weight for weight, carbohydrates provide the same amount of energy as proteins, but less than half that provided by fat. Simple carbohydrates are mostly sweet and water-soluble, and can be quickly digested. There are two types:

1. Monosaccharides, which have just a single sugar unit with, like most carbohydrates, twice as much hydrogen as oxygen. The chief ones are galactose, fructose or fruit sugar and glucose, the basic energy provider.

2. Disaccharides are a combination of two monosaccharides and include sucrose or ordinary sugar, which is glucose with fructose; lactose or milk sugar, which is glucose with galactose; and maltose, which is two glucose molecules. The complex carbohydrates or polysaccharides can contain thousands of simple sugars in a molecular chain. They are the starchy carbohydrates found in cereals and beans which sometimes need cooking before they can be digested, and fibre, which cannot be digested by our enzymes.

There is substantial evidence that a diet high in the complex carbohydrates, featuring plenty of pasta and whole cereals for example, is very healthy and helps keep our blood sugar levels relatively constant.

There is a huge variation in carbohydrate intake amongst different groups of people: Eskimos, at the bottom of the list, obtain only a tenth of their energy from that source, whereas in Africa 80-90 per cent is often the norm.

In Britain, 44.5 per cent of our energy comes from cargbohydrates, 13.6 per cent from protein and 41.9 per cent from fat. We would be better off increasing carbohydrate intake to 60 per cent, at the expense of the fat. *MH*

Carrots

The crisp orange carrot we enjoy today is a great improvement on its tough, pale ancestor, thought to originate in Afghanistan. From the fourteenth century, Europeans gradually improved the wild carrot's texture and flavour - the Flemish brought the current version to Britain during Elizabeth I's reign.

The carrot's bright orange colour is due to its high content of beta-carotene, which is one of a large group of yellow and orange pigments found in plants. Beta-carotene is needed for healthy eyes, which is why it is said that carrots help you to see in the dark. It is also an important antioxidant. (See Beta-carotene.)

Carrots are low in calories, providing 25 per 100 g (4 oz). As well as being a delicious vegetable raw or cooked, their sweetness has for centuries made them a popular ingredient in cakes and steamed puddings. *AU*

Cellulite

Cellulite is one of those controversial subjects about which the medical world and the beauty industry seem to have polarized views. On the one hand many doctors will tell you that there is no such thing as cellulite, that it is just fat, and you should go on a diet and take more exercise. If you show it to a beautician, on the other hand, you'll probably get lots of sympathy and empathy, and find you've booked yourself a week of sessions on the toning tables and parted with lots of cash on creams, lotions and bobbly mittens to help rub it away.

A good healthy diet and plenty of exercise are probably the only answer for reducing the accumulation of dimply fat which we call cellulite. Avoid detoxification diets and other eating plans which claim to dissolve it: they don't. It is much safer to start eating sensibly and gradually build regular walking and swimming into your routine. *AU*

Cereals

(See Breakfast cereals; Grains and cereals.)

Cheese

Cheese is made by solidifying or coagulating the protein in milk, creating what is called the curd, and leaving a watery whey. If milk is left at room temperature for several days, this reaction occurs naturally, stimulated by the acid content of the milk; it can also be accelerated by adding rennet, an enzyme found in calves' stomachs. The first cheese was probably made quite by accident as wandering nomads discovered that the milk they carried in leather pouches formed lumps after several days' travelling. They soon found that it kept better if they pressed the lumpy curd to remove the moisture, then salted it and dried it in the sun. This method of cheese-making is still used in the Middle East.

Cheeses can be divided into five main types:

- *Curd cheese*, which coagulates due to the acids naturally present in the milk.
- *Cream-based cheeses*, which coagulate due to the addition of acids or rennet.
- *Soft cheeses*, made from milk coagulated by adding rennet.
- *Semi-hard cheeses*, which are lightly pressed to remove some water.
- *Hard cheeses*, which are fully pressed.

The nutritional profile of a cheese obviously depends on the category it falls into. Hard cheeses such as cheddar and parmesan have the highest fat content and so provide the most energy: 412 and 452 calories per 100 g (4 oz) respectively. Both are high in protein and calcium too. A curd cheese like cottage cheese or quark, on the other hand, has 98 calories for the same amount, because it contains more water and about half the protein.

Much packaged cheese can be disappointingly tasteless, but recently there has been a revival of real English cheeses. They are worth searching for in specialist cheese shops and good food stores. *AU*

Chicken

We are eating more chicken than ever before. Last year we each got through about ten small birds, 4 kg (8 lb) up on the 1980 figure. The trend towards less red meat, combined with an increase in availability of processed chicken dishes, and portions like thighs, breasts, drumsticks, wings and quarters probably account for chicken's growing popularity. Chicken meat is an excellent source of protein, containing all eight essential amino-acids (see Protein). Compared to many other meats, chicken is low in fat: a 100 g (4 oz) portion of roast chicken gives 142 calories, but most of these are in the skin. It also provides useful supplies of B vitamins like thiamin, riboflavin and nicotinic acid. If chicken is stored, prepared and cooked according to instructions, there is little risk of salmonella (see Food poisoning; Kitchen hygiene). *AU*

Children's food

It seems that the healthy-eating message has yet to make a huge impact on many children's diets. Surveys have shown that they are too high in fat and sugar and that many children do not get enough vitamins and minerals, particularly iron and calcium. Crisps, savoury snacks, chips, biscuits, cakes, soft drinks and sweets are all popular choices with children, but fruit and vegetables are far less so. A survey last year for Food File's sister series, Eat Up, found that a staggering 60 per cent of children ate no fruit and over half ate no vegetables on the day of the survey.

Nutritionists are concerned that many children may not only suffer from health problems such as dental decay or anaemia as a result of poor nutrition, but are setting up bad habits and eating patterns that can lead to ill-health in years to come. Diet in childhood lays the foundation for good eating patterns in later life. Experts now think that some diseases, such as heart disease and even some forms of cancer, can start in childhood. *SD*

Chillies

The hot variety of sweet pepper (*Capsicum frutescens*) was first discovered in the New World. Second to salt, it is the most popular seasoning in the world. From the moment of its discovery, it took a mere fifty years to colonize the globe. There are dozens of different chillies, in shapes varying from small bells to thin, curved pencils, in colours from green to vivid scarlet.

Neither the colour nor the shape denotes the scale of fieriness. The small habanero, commonly known as the Scotch bonnet, is by far the hottest. The heat is due to a substance called capsaicin, which is in the pith, not the seeds, though those are a little hotter than the skin. Red chillies are no hotter than green ones: the colour red just means the chilli is ripe and therefore has a higher sugar content.

Capsaicin triggers the release of endorphins, the body's natural painkillers, thus creating a sense of well-being. Capsaicin also has a beneficial effect on our digestive system, stimulating the saliva, gastric juices and the peristaltic movements in the gut. Chillies are also suprisingly high in vitamins A and C. Chillies can be bought fresh or dried; in dried form, they will keep in an airtight jar for years. On the whole, fresh chillies give dishes better flavour, though ultimately this depends on the recipe. *CS*

Chocolate

If you enjoy chocolate as an occasional drink before bedtime, go ahead. Treat yourself to real chocolate, though, not the cheap stuff made from hydrogenated vegetable fats and sugar by British manufacturers, and make it with skimmed milk and no extra added sugar.

Solid chocolate, whose quality comes from a high cocoa butter content is exquisitely delicious; if you enjoy it, become a connoisseur and relish the different textures and flavours of fine chocolate. Experiment with the different varieties of cooking chocolate.

Any food you love to eat is fine, once in a while. There is no need to become a food puritan in order to protect your health. The problem with chocolate and other sweet fat foods such as cakes, biscuits and confectionery that are stuffed with calories, is that most people in Britain overeat them. The very last thing that sedentary people who want to keep slim should eat is calorie-dense food.

Chocolate can be a special problem, particularly for women. It is heavily advertised as a comfort food and, like other sweetened products, can be addictive, hence the term 'chocoholic'. Chocolates and other candies with sugary centres are packaged and promoted to be especially tempting. Chocolate bars are also advertised as quick sources of energy. However, it is always better to snack on whole food, such as bananas. (See Blood sugar.) *GC*

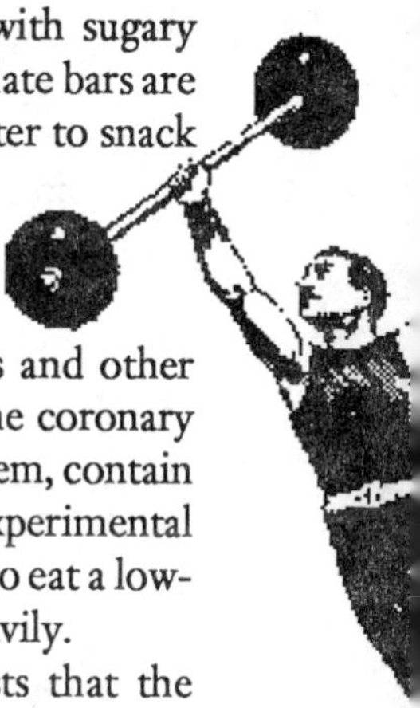

Cholesterol

Cholesterol is a hard, waxy substance found notably in meat, eggs and other foods of animal origin. The fatty deposits that gradually clog up the coronary and other arteries of people who suffer diseases of the circulation system, contain a lot of cholesterol. Based on this and on epidemiological and experimental evidence, scientists have concluded that for heart health it is sensible to eat a low-cholesterol diet. In America low-cholesterol foods are promoted heavily.

No problem for vegetarians. Recent evidence, however, suggests that the main dietary cause of heart disease is not so much dietary cholesterol as saturated fat. For practical purposes this does not make a lot of difference: meat and other foods of animal origin that contain a lot of cholesterol are almost always also heavy in saturated fat. However, early advice more or less to avoid eggs was probably too strict: up to four a week (the average in Britain) is probably fine. Shellfish such as prawns and shrimps are high in cholesterol yet low in saturated fats: enjoy them occasionally. (See Diet; Heart disease; Saturated fat.) *GC*

Coffee and tea

Coffee and tea are powerful drugs: legal of course, available in every supermarket and corner shop, enjoyed in almost all households, but drugs nonetheless. In moderation they are useful stimulants, but both can be fairly addictive and are harmful in excess. Withdrawal symptoms, especially from coffee, can be painful.

The potent elements in coffee and tea are complex chemical cocktails, of which caffeine and tannin are perhaps the best known. The Arabs identified coffee and the Chinese identified tea as having medicinal qualities, many hundreds of years before either was introduced to the West. Significantly, Arabs drink coffee, and Chinese (and Japanese) drink tea, without the addition of milk, and usually only at special times of day, with some ceremony.

By contrast, most people in America and Europe drink a lot of coffee and/or tea casually, and most of it is inferior stuff, drunk more for the 'hit' than the flavour. Moderate consumption of up to three or four cups of good-quality fresh coffee or leaf tea a day is one of life's pleasures; it is almost certainly harmless, and may have some positive health benefits, as well as perking you up. Heavy consumption, of six or more cups a day, is liable to make you jittery; and heavy coffee consumption is a common cause of sleeplessness and a pounding heart (palpitations).

Some scientists believe that heavy coffee and tea consumption may increase the risk of heart disease or cancer. On the whole this is probably not true, although it is a bad idea regularly to drink reheated coffee, which seems to raise blood cholesterol, which in turn increases the risk of a heart attack.

Tisanes (herbal teas) are commonly drunk in Germany and elsewhere in Europe. They are a pleasant, mild alternative to tea. Just as a thoughtful host will now offer guests fruit juices and water as an alternative to alcohol, it is good to have a stock of herbal teas at home to serve instead of conventional tea or coffee, and to enjoy them yourself as well. *GC*

Colds

Most colds are caused by viruses, which cannot be destroyed by antibiotics. Prescribing them to treat colds is not only a waste of money, but may create allergies.

Many people find, but trials have failed to confirm, that colds can be aborted by taking 1 g vitamin C every two or three hours, up to 5 g per day, as soon as the first signs are observed. You will know within a couple of days whether it has worked. Zinc lozenges can also be helpful.

To prevent colds and most other infections you need to build up a strong immune system. (See A.C.E.) A varied diet containing a wide selection of raw or lightly cooked fruit or vegetables, whole grains, and oily fish is your best protection. Some people like to take vitamin and mineral supplements as a kind of insurance policy against colds and 'flu.

Have you noticed that very busy people who have no time to be ill seem to have fewer infections than the norm? Mental and spiritual resistance may be important to keep 'fighting fit'. *MH*

Colouring in food

The senses of smell, taste and sight are so intertwined that colour is an essential part of the enjoyment of food. The question is to what extent those colours must be totally consistent throughout the year, regardless of the raw materials being used. If we insist, for example, that blackcurrant syrup must always be exactly the same shade, then it is quite hard to achieve this by natural means and artificial colouring may be the answer. If, on the other hand, we accept that variations have their charm, then far less colour can be used and much of that natural.

The azo dyes are those which cause more adverse reactions than any other colours (see Additives). Some natural colours would appear not to be all that safe,

the chief concern being caramel, which is fine in the form of burnt sugar used for its lovely flavour, but when produced by caustic or acid processes and used in large quantities (see Beer), an acceptable daily intake can easily be exceeded. The EC colouring proposals point out that the term 'caramel' relates to products of a brown colour intended for colouring and does not correspond to the aromatic product obtained from heating sugar. The azo dyes are:
E102 Tartrazine
E107 Yellow 2G
E110 Sunset yellow FCF
E122 Carmoisine
E123 Amaranth
E124 Ponceau 4R
E128 Red 2G
E154 Brown FK
E155 Chocolate brown HT
E151 Black PN
E180 Pigment rubine

The coal tar dyes are:
E104 Quinoline yellow
E127 Erythrosine
E131 Patent blue V
E132 Indigo carmine
E133 Brilliant blue FCF

I do not consciously buy foods containing any of these colours, even though I do not believe I react against them physically. *MH*

COMA

COMA stands for the Committee on Medical Aspects of Food Policy. This is a permanent official scientific body set up by the Department of Health, reporting to the Chief Medical Officer. Government policy on food, nutrition and public health depends on recommendations made in reports of specialist COMA panels appointed for the purpose. These are always chaired by a member of the main COMA committee.

Throughout the 1980s critics pointed out that members of the COMA committee and its panels were obliged to sign the Official Secrets Act; that some scientists appointed to COMA evidently thought there was nothing much wrong with the British diet; and that COMA recommendations not in line with general government policy to promote 'value-added' highly processed food were liable to be squashed, or redrafted by civil servants.

Perhaps partly as a result of constant media stories to this effect, the recommendations of recent COMA panel reports have become more in line with the general scientific consensus on food, diet and public health in America and elsewhere in Europe. The 1991 COMA report on Dietary Reference Values, setting standards for healthy intakes of fat, sugar, salt, vitamins and minerals, is generally admired and is the foundation for the progressive nutritional recommendations made in the government's white paper, The Health of the Nation.

In 1993 a COMA panel on diet and cancer was set up, and is due to produce a report and recommendations perhaps in 1996 or 1997. (See Department of Health; Health of the Nation; Ministry of Agriculture.) *GC*

Constipation

Constipation is a fibre deficiency disease. Most people in Britain are more or less constipated. This is because the average diet contains too much fat and sugar and refined foods stripped of fibre, or roughage. Constipation, which is to say straining to produce small, infrequent stools, also indicates increased risk of more serious bowel diseases, including diverticular disease and colon cancer. (See Bowel diseases; Stools.) *GC*

Consumers

As a shopper you have a great deal of influence in shaping the future of our food. You have 'purse power' - if you don't like a product or a supermarket, you can shop elsewhere. And you have the power to complain: food companies and supermarkets have become increasingly sensitive to public opinion.

It was consumer pressure, for example, which led to the apple Spary Alar being withdrawn, which has kept irradiated food off our supermarket shelves and cut the use of many food additives, particularly in foods for children.

Consumers and consumer organizations also play an important role in helping to shape the decisions that are made about our food, by the government and increasingly by the EC. The food industry, both farmers and large food companies, are very powerful and well-funded lobby groups with a great deal of influence. By joining and supporting consumer and public health organizations you will be making sure that your voice cannot be ignored. So next time you're worried or angry, turn it into action: contact one of the organizations working in the consumer interest (see Address section) and find out how your action can make a difference. Or start your own campaign. *SD*

Convenience foods

Many people do not want to spend a great deal of time shopping, preparing and cooking food, and not all convenience foods have to be unhealthy, although they are likely to be more expensive than when you cook your own.

- Frozen vegetables contain just as many vitamins as fresh.
- Baked beans - particularly the low-sugar/salt varieties - are a good source of protein and fibre.

- Canned pulses and beans, and fish such as tuna or sardines, are healthy choices.
- Pasta can be extremely useful for quick main meals.

It is best to cut down on the kinds of convenience foods that are high in fat, salt, preservatives and colourings: these include pies, burgers, sausages and canned meat. *SD*

Cookbooks

A collection of recipes which contain a list of ingredients and the method to combine and cook them. The term is recent, first coming into vogue some fifteen years ago. Before then the grammatically correct term 'cookery books' was used, meaning a manual on How to Cook. These manuals certainly go back as far as Ancient Greece; although the actual books are lost we have remnants of them and many references to recipes and books of cookery by other authors. We do have a volume from Ancient Rome by Apicius who lived in the first century. Le Viandier (1375) was the first French cookery book, compiled by Taillevent, chef to Charles VI of France, while the first English cookery book that we know of is Forme of Cury, which was compiled by Richard II's chef, Master Cokes, around 1390.

Throughout the last decade, hundreds of cookery books have been published every year, growing more and more specialized. These cater for particular markets, such as ethnic groups, students or diets, or compile recipes on variations of one dish alone, such as soup or cakes. Whether these books are used to cook from or are merely read as a leisure activity is debatable. Certainly as the cultivation and manufacture of food grows further away from the desires and interests of the consumer, there is a growing need for more information on what exactly goes into food, which is not always fulfilled by the cookery book. *CS*

Cook-chill foods

Britain has led the world in developing cook-chill technology for ready meals. The food is initially cooked to ensure that food-poisoning bacteria are killed. Then the food is quickly chilled, and kept cold enough to stop these bacteria from growing. The problems start if the temperature rises during transport or storage. In the late 1980s there was much concern when listeria was found in some ready-made meals and microwave ovens were found to be not heating foods thoroughly. Now new food hygiene regulations demand that cook-chill foods be kept at low temperatures. And microwave oven users have been advised to ensure that meals are thoroughly cooked. (See Microwaving; Food poisoning.)

Cook-chill foods are expensive. Many people are now rediscovering their cooking skills and finding that they can produce meals, using fresh ingredients, more cheaply and just as quickly as heating up a ready-prepared dinner in an oven. *SD*

Cooking

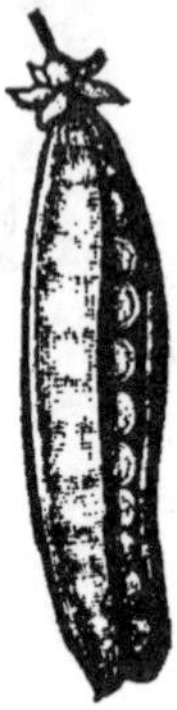

Most of the food we eat is cooked or processed in some way. How you cook food can make a key difference not only to its taste but also to its nutritional quality. As a general rule, the less food is cooked, the better it is for your health. The main exceptions to this rule are meat, poultry and other foods of animal origin that come from factory farms, or that may have been stored unhygienically. Such foods has to be cooked thoroughly, to kill off bacteria that otherwise could cause acute infectious diseases.

Vegetables and fruit are best eaten raw or lightly cooked. Eat salads with main meals. Prefer fruit to 'sweets' when you eat out.

Water-soluble B vitamins and vitamin C are lost when vegetables are boiled. When you do cook vegetables, it's best to steam them, or else to boil them gently in a pan with a tightly fitting-lid, using a small amount of water. Never throw vegetable water away: drink it, or use it as the basis of sauces, or instead of fat to make mashed potatoes juicy.

Green vegetables are best 'undercooked' so they remain crisp. This isn't just a pernickety point. There is fairly good evidence that one reason that spina bifida and other neural tube defects have been very common in Wales, is not only because women of child-bearing age there (and elsewhere in Britain) consume pitiably small amounts of vegetables, but also because the habit in Wales has been to destroy folic acid and other B vitamins in greens by over-boiling them 'to death'. (See Deficiency diseases; Vitamins.)

Any method of cooking that uses intense heat creates carcinogenic compounds, notably in meat. This is why guidelines issued by scientific bodies, designed to reduce the risk of cancers, usually recommend that you eat char-grilled or barbecued food only once in a while. Certainly, don't eat charred food such as burned sausages, bacon, or toast.

A good general anti-cancer tip is don't get burned. Protect yourself against intense sun; don't smoke; and don't habitually consume food or drink that is very hot (in either sense), or that feels abrasive in the throat (such as raw spirits), or that is itself burned.

As a general rule it's probably best to prefer the slower and gentler methods of cooking such as boiling and baking. If you enjoy a roast on Sundays, try methods that cook the meat or poultry more slowly at a lower heat. (See Baking; Boiling; Frying; Grilling; Roasting.) *GC*

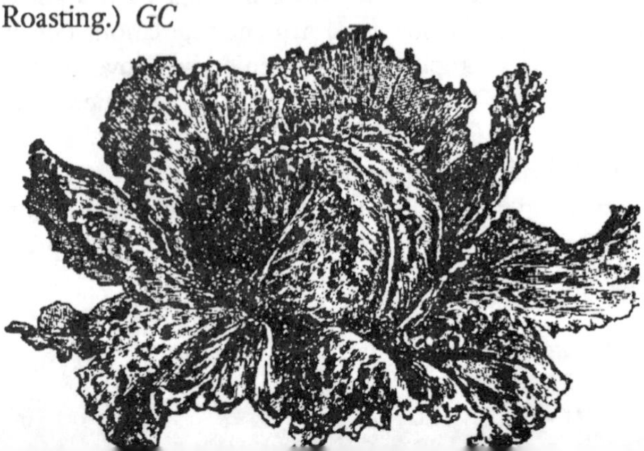

Crisps

Despite fierce competition from constant new inventions, potato crisps are still the most popular snack food in the Western world. An American-Indian, George Crumb, is the man usually credited with their invention. As a chef in Saratoga Springs he found himself faced with a fussy guest who kept sending back chips he thought were too thick. Crumb finally cut some potatoes as thin as paper, fried them and sent them out to the demanding guest. The story goes that the patron loved them and the potato crisp was born.

With current concern over salt and fat intakes, crisps have earned themselves an unhealthy image. Yet the salt content is no higher than that found in a couple of slices of wholemeal bread; it's because the salt is on the surface of the crisp that it is perceived by our taste-buds as being very salty. But crisps are certainly high in fat. Over 45 per cent of the total calories come from fat. If fried in vegetable oils, much of this is unsaturated, so the odd packet won't do any harm. Potatoes are a reasonable source of vitamin C, and since crisps are cooked quickly in oil, much of this is preserved in the final product. They also add some fibre to the diet. *AU*

Culture

All over the world and throughout history, the food that people eat has been and is profoundly influenced by climate, culture and terrain, which in turn largely determine traditional agriculture systems. In southern Europe, the Mediterranean cuisine varies in different countries and has evolved over thousands of years, but has always depended on olive oil, produced from trees that need hot sun and thrive on rugged land. And the best olive oil has been celebrated and treasured since the days of Greek and Roman antiquity.

Similarly, the small family farms of France have preserved the craft of cheese-making down the generations; and the savour of hundreds of varieties of cheese is part of the experience of being in France. Indeed, all authentic cuisines indicate a traditional, local, national or regional culture that has been valued and protected.

In Britain, most authentic, traditional agriculture and food has been destroyed, first by the industrial revolution of the eighteenth and early nineteenth centuries and its consequences, and more recently by agribusiness and mass food manufacture. An integral part of British culture has thus been wrecked. Three-quarters of the British food supply is now processed, and much of this is highly processed, made by giant multinational firms turning over billions of pounds and products every year.

What fragments of authentic local cuisine remain are often marketed as quaint relics in National Trust centres and duty free shops, or as cynical backdrops to television advertisements. Poets and novelists may write of pot noodles and instant whip, but only as ironical indications of the degradation of British culture. What's left? Haggis, black pudding, and fish'n'chips. Alas. *GC*

d

Dairy products

This term covers all those products that derive from the dairy herd (cows) or from sheep and goats: milk, butter, cheese, yogurt, buttermilk and cream. In today's diet, more than ever before, they represent the bulk of the saturated fat that we consume.

These products are produced, advertised and marketed to us with dogged persistence as healthy foods, a claim which is debatable (see Milk). *CS*

Deficiency diseases

Micronutrients, including vitamins and many minerals (some of which are also known as trace elements), are essential in small amounts, for health and for life itself. In the early years of this century, researchers observing or experimenting on animals, children, prisoners, soldiers, sailors, explorers, foreigners and other unfortunates identified a number of serious and sometimes potentially deadly diseases as being caused by diets devoid of or deficient in specific micronutrients. The classic deficiency diseases include:

Name	*Damage done to*	*End state*	*Deficiency in*
Xerophthalmia	Eyes	Blindness	vitamin A
Beri-beri	Nervous system	Death	vitamin B1
Pellagra	Skin, brain	Madness,	death vitamin B3
Scurvy	Connective tissue	Death	vitamin C
Rickets	Bones	Lameness	vitamin D
Goitre	Thyroid	Cretinism	iodine
Anaemia	Blood	Weakness	iron, B vitamins

All of these and other deficiency diseases are or have been common in different parts of the world. All are now uncommon in any severe or 'florid' state in Britain and other wealthy countries. Mild forms of scurvy and beri-beri are quite often evident in old age or in severely malnourished people (alcoholics, for example); and mild iron-deficiency anaemia is very common in young and teenage girls and pregnant women.

It is now generally accepted that neural tube defects including spina bifida are malformations caused by deficiency of folic acid in the diet of mothers around the time of conception. Some physicians and biochemists believe that anorexia nervosa is fundamentally not a psychological disorder, and is caused at least in part by deficiency of zinc. In both cases prudent advice is to eat a healthy diet throughout life. (See Diet; Essential fatty acids; Healthy food; Minerals; Trace elements; Vitamins; Zinc.) *GC*

Dehydration

Water accounts for 80 per cent of our body weight. The body's responses are so finely tuned that if you lose only 5 per cent of this water you can experience increased pulse rate, dizziness and heat exhaustion.

A 10 per cent loss leads to fatal heat stroke which is why in under-developed countries either rice water or a mixture of sugar and salt has to be used as a rehydrating solution to maintain both the body's salts and fluid levels, especially after diarrhoea or starvation.

A loss in water volume produces a concentration of sodium in the blood which triggers a receptor in the brain which tells you that you are thirsty. This is accompanied by a dry feeling in the mouth and more concentrated urine. At the same time, you have to pass at least 450 ml (3/4 pint) of water a day to remove the toxic wastes.

That is why you can survive for some weeks without food but need in excess of a litre (2 pints) of water a day. But beware of over-indulging: a huge consumption of water over a short period of time can lead to water intoxication which causes convulsions, unconsciousness and ultimately death.

Athletes and heavy manual workers need to make sure that they take in extra fluids to compensate for the loss which can take place before the body has had time to signal its response. (See Exercise; Nutrition.) *MH*

Department of Health

This is the department of the British government responsible for the nation's health, a responsibility which it reconciles with sponsorship of the British drug industry. Advised by many expert bodies, including the Committee on Medical Aspects of Food Policy (COMA), it devises nutrition policies in partnership with the Ministry of Agriculture. In 1992 the DOH published *The Health of the Nation*, a White Paper committing government to a new policy of prevention of disease in part by means of good food. (See COMA panels; the Health of the Nation; Ministry of Agriculture; WHO.) *GC*

Diabetes

Diabetes is on the increase because whereas sixty years ago sufferers did not live long, increasing knowledge and better methods of control have meant that a normal life span can be anticipated provided you take care. There is a hereditary factor involved, and one result of this improved life expectancy is that more diabetics now have children and so pass on the tendency.

The word diabetes covers a number of conditions in which there is a failure to metabolize glucose, or blood sugar. In young people this can be caused by the failure of the Islets of Langerhans in the pancreas to produce insulin, the hormone we all need to maintain a stable blood- sugar level. Older people can have a non-insulin-dependent diabetes, when the body produces insulin but cannot make use of it properly. There are also certain other temporary forms. Adult-onset diabetes is often also related to being overweight (see Obesity).

It used to be thought that diabetics had to cut out all carbohydrates and follow a fundamentally rather unhealthy diet. The situation has now changed; a suitable intake of insulin can allow the consumption of complex carbohydrates. It is very important to prevent the blood-sugar level from rising after a meal, which is why frequent small meals are beneficial in keeping levels stable.

Poorly controlled diabetes can lead to circulatory disorders, blindness and problems with nerve function, hence diabetics have every incentive to look after themselves well. A careful study of diet can produce very beneficial results. *MH*

Diet

What is a healthy diet? The good news is that the best diet for good health, the best diet for protection against many diseases, and the best diet to stay slim, is the same sort of diet the whole world over. This effectively is the positive message of the recent authoritative expert report issued by the World Health Organisation (WHO), 'Diet, Nutrition and the Prevention of Chronic Diseases'. This itself builds on and confirms the findings of many other expert reports on food, nutrition and health published all over the world since the 1960s and 1970s.

All types of food can usefully be divided into three healthy groups. First, vegetables and fruit are good for you. Scientific research practically always confirms this common sense. What is news, is just how vital these foods are for all-round health. The WHO report recommends that everyone would do well to eat around a pound of fruit, salads and vegetables every day. This excludes potatoes, but includes pulses, nuts and seeds.

Second, starchy foods like bread, potatoes and cereals are traditionally staple foods all over the world, and for good reason. Like vegetables and fruit, they are all good sources of fibre, vitamins (especially B vitamins) and minerals. Some people still believe that starchy foods (also known as complex carbohydrates) are fattening. This is not true: it's the fatty or sugary spreads used with them that cause the problem. Almost everybody in industrialized countries like Britain would do well to double consumption of starchy foods, and to prefer wholegrain bread and cereals.

Third, meat, poultry, seafood, dairy products and other foods of animal origin can all be part of a healthy diet if you choose them carefully. Eat all types of fish and seafood as often as you eat meat. Omnivores should eat meat, not fat: enjoy lean meat like game, cut away and discard fat from other meats and poultry; and switch to low-fat dairy products, including skimmed, fat-free milk. Table fats, whether 'spreads', margarines or butter, are all best avoided as everyday food. Similarly, enjoy good-quality cheese just once in a while.

Many disagreeable, disabling or deadly diseases are certainly or probably caused at least in part by the 'industrialized' diet, as typically eaten in Britain. Of these, the most serious are cardiovascular diseases, notably coronary heart disease and stroke, and common cancers including those of the breast and colon. Why?

Over the last 150 years or so the nature of the diet eaten by almost everybody in Britain has changed very dramatically. The typical industrialized diet is harmful to health because it is very fatty, very sugary, and correspondingly short of nourishing foods, especially vegetables, legumes, salads, fruits, bread, cereals, potatoes, and good-quality foods of animal origin. Put another way, the typical British diet now is calorie-dense, whereas a healthy diet is nutrient-dense. Also, the typical diet is mostly made up of foods of animal origin, whereas a healthy diet is mainly made up of foods of vegetable origin.

Summed up as 'seven steps to healthy eating', the message of the World Health Organisation is:

1. Abundance. Eat at least five portions of fruit and vegetables every day.
2. Satisfaction. Include bread, potatoes or cereal foods with every meal.
3. Quality. Choose lean meat and low-fat dairy products and all types of fish.
4. Value. Make healthy foods into good-value, delicious meals and snacks.
5. Nourishment. Keep consumption of fat, sugar and salt to a minimum.
6. Pleasure. Enjoy the variety of healthy food from all over the world.
7. Choice. Insist on healthy food, as a consumer and as a citizen. *GC*

Dietary Guidelines

Recommendations issued by governments or scientific bodies designed to encourage healthy diets usually on a population basis. May take the form of quantified goals or targets for foods or nutrients (see Diet).

Guidelines may be accompanied by guides to healthy eating aimed at the consumer. In Britain a good example is 'Eat Well...Live Well!', designed to put WHO guidelines into plain language: this is available, price £1.95 including postage and packing, from the Coronary Prevention Group, Plantation House (Suites 5/4 D&M), 31-35 Fenchurch Street, London EC3M 3NN. *GC*

Dieting

Dieting is the word commonly used to describe the process of trying to lose weight through altering eating habits. (See Slimming; Body image.)

Dietitians

Dietitians are trained to put the theory of nutrition into practice. Based in both hospitals and community centres, they work with people who are ill and need therapeutic diets, such as diabetics, those with kidney and liver problems and those who need to avoid certain foods, like coeliacs. Dietitians also work to prevent illness, educating individuals and groups of people about healthy eating through talks, the media and one-to-one counselling.

In this country, to practise as a dietitian in the National Health Service, you must be State Registered. This can be achieved by several means. You can either study for a four year degree in nutrition and dietetics or take a science degree such as nutrition, physiology or biochemistry, followed by a postgraduate course in dietetics. The British Dietetic Association is the professional body for State Registered Dietitians. You can be referred to an SRD by your GP or a hospital doctor. *AU*

Digestion

It takes between twenty-four and forty-eight hours for a meal to pass through the body, and this happens faster in men then in women.

As you chew your way through a meal, you produce no less than 600 ml (1 pint) of saliva, which begins to liquidize the food during the first stage of the digestive process. When you swallow, the food and drink descend into your stomach via the oesophagus, and are moved along by a muscular squeezing action called peristalsis, the length of the digestive tract.

In the stomach, juices (mainly hydrochloric acid) start to act on the food. The semi-liquified food is then fed in controlled amounts into the first part of the small intestine, the duodenum, where it meets secretions from the pancreas and the liver (bile). The entire small intestine (duodenum, jejunum and ileum) is about 3 metres (10 feet) long, and the walls of the ileum are covered in millions of little 'fingers' (villi), which create a surface area about the size of a tennis court through which the nutrients are absorbed into the bloodstream.

At this point, a dinner of steak and chips will have been liquidized into about 600 ml (1 pint) of fluid and mixed with another 3.2 litres (6 pints) of fluid made up of saliva as well as the gastric and pancreatic juices and bile, that flow into the gut during digestion.

In the bloodstream, nutrients are either used straight away or retained in the system. Meanwhile, indigestible foodstuffs such as fibre and some starches pass from the small intestine into the large bowel (colon) where water is taken into the bloodstream and the remaining material ferments. Less than 10 per cent of what we eat is eventually evacuated, but eating more dietary fibre such as that in fruit and vegetables produces looser and bigger stools (see Stools). *SD*

Diuretics

A diuretic is any agent which has the effect of increasing the flow of urine. Diuretics are used in medicine to help treat excess accumulation of water and salt, which leads to swelling known as oedema. Oedema can occur as the result of heart failure, liver, kidney and lung problems and through starvation. Oedema is also common in normal pregnancy and is sometimes a symptom of PMS. Diuretics should only be taken under medical supervision. At one time they were a popular method of treating obesity. This is strongly discouraged now since they are potentially dangerous and are of no value in burning fat. Sports people such as jockeys and boxers who needed to drop a few pounds before competitions have been known to use diuretics to help achieve the required weight. Again, this is dangerous and not advised. *AU*

Diverticular disease

(See Bowel diseases.)

Drying

A traditional food process which preserves the nourishment in food by natural means.

Drying food is one of the oldest methods of preservation and is particularly reliable for fruits, vegetables, meat and fish. When the water evaporates, no bacteria or mould can form.

Dried fruits are highly nourishing. Being high in fruit sugar, fructose, they are very often much sweeter than in their fresh form. Various kinds of grapes are dried as raisins, sultanas and currents. Apricots, figs, dates, bananas, apples, peaches and pears also dry particularly successfully. They contain a lot of energy, so should be eaten in moderation in a calorie-controlled diet. Unlike fresh fruits, they do not contain vitamin C, but they are rich in potassium, iron and other minerals and vitamins A and B. Sun-drying is the traditional method for drying fruit and vegetables such as tomatoes and mushrooms but nowadays sulphur dioxide, heat drying or freeze-drying is often used. Pulses are the dried seeds of pod vegetables, peas and beans, and are available in great variety. They are an important source of dietary fibre. Meat and fish can all be successfully dried - jerky is a popular dried beef snack in America. Dried foods can be stored for long periods in airtight containers - it is essential they do not get damp. *SD*

Drug-nutrient interactions

Some drugs, such as penicillin, can have a reduced absorption when taken with food; others, such as aspirin, can irritate the gut if taken on an empty stomach. The effect of vitamin C is increased when taken with food and drink, but iron supplements are best taken separately. Most antibiotics should be taken at least an hour before meals as should laxatives.

Most good pharmacists ensure that appropriate information on these interactions is given on the label of prescribed drugs but if in doubt, always ask. These interactions can be a special problem for the elderly. *MH*

e

Eating disorders

The two most widespread eating disorders in Britain are anorexia nervosa and bulimia nervosa. Anorexia nervosa sufferers are usually young females, although the problem is spreading to older women and is becoming more common in men too. The main characteristics of anorexia nervosa are an obsessional aim to lose more and more weight, even once the original target is met, an obsession with body size and fear of fatness along with a distorted body image. There is often a lack of awareness, or refusal to admit, that there is a problem. Many anorexia nervosa sufferers wear loose, bulky clothes to disguise thinness and commonly find it hard to sleep at night and difficult to concentrate during the day. Work may start to suffer. Menstruation in women frequently stops, and depression, high blood pressure and heart problems may develop.

Treatment is a long haul and not always successful. It requires input from psychiatrists, nurses and dietitians as well as family cooperation. Unlike anorexics, bulimics are often slightly overweight and are slightly older. The problem revolves around being trapped in a binge/vomit cycle. Eating patterns are erratic and vomiting and use of laxatives are common. The large amounts of food, drugs and possibly also alcohol which are consumed can often lead to financial problems. Treatment aims to reverse all these problems and help restore normal body weight. This can often be done on an outpatient basis with a dietitian and doctor working together. (See Body image.) *AU*

Eating out

Eating out in Britain can be a disappointing experience. Critics say our restaurants are too expensive, too unfriendly - particularly to children - and the food all too often is badly served and boring. However, much has changed in recent years, and while we may still have a long way to go, we are becoming more interested in our food, more adventurous in our tastes and more willing to complain.

We like to think that behind the restaurant door there are a whole army of chefs preparing our meal from fresh ingredients. Sadly, many caterers, particularly at the middle and lower end of the market, increasingly rely on pre-packed, pre-prepared food and ingredients.

While a meal out with family or friends should be an enjoyable occasion, sometimes it is not. Always check your bill and don't be afraid to question it. If you have a complaint ask politely to speak to the manager. (Don't shout at the waiter - it's usually not his/her fault). It may help if you complain in front of other customers. If the restaurant is part of a franchise, write to the regional manager of the company concerned.

If this fails, and you think that the food is unfit to eat, or the premises are unclean, contact the Environmental Health Department at your local town hall. Hygiene is especially important in catering, because so many people can be affected if one batch of contaminated food is served. (See Fast food; Food poisoning.) *SD*

EC food policies

There is only one underlying and basic policy which sets the course for all EC legislation and that is the creation of a Single European Market without any barriers to trade.

At the same time, political pressures mean that farmers need to be supported, and this is normally done regardless of any nutritional consequence. For example, Italian farmers in Calabria are being subsidized to root up ancient olive groves to obtain an EC subsidy. Even the basic aims of a so-called level playing-field are nowhere near being accomplished. Britain is rigorous in its enforcement policies, whereas many countries pass draconian laws which are then ignored. Products such as vitamins which are freely sold in Britain under our food law with adequate controls and no complaints are the subject of confiscation and heavy fines in Greece.

Britain can no longer inspect foods from other EC countries at the port of entry and yet we know that standards of production, especially for meat products and with respect to the sprays being used on fruit and vegetables, give cause for serious concern. Britain is by no means alone in wanting the high standards that are perhaps not so common in the Southern European countries, but we have signally failed to get together and demand rights for our producers and safeguards for our consumers. MH

Eggs

The image of the egg as a healthy, nutritious food, previously known as an 'oval square meal', took a blow in 1989 when the salmonella scare blew up. Since then we have gradually accepted eggs back into our diets with the understanding that if handled, stored and cooked properly, they still make a valuable contribution to a mixed diet.

The poultry industry provides around 15 million eggs a year in the UK, and must maintain strict controls over quality and size, as well as packaging, warehousing, transportation, presentation and marketing of eggs. Some eggs are now date-stamped for freshness.

As the natural function of eggs is to feed developing chicks, it is not surprising that they contain a full range of nutrients to support the process. Both the yolk and the white provide an excellent source of protein. Eggs are also rich in calcium and phosphorous needed for building and maintaining strong bones and teeth, and in iron, all of which are found in the yolk. Eggs have their fair share of vitamins, too, with fat-soluble A and D in the yolk and B12 and riboflavin in the white.

Eggs do contain cholesterol and some saturated fat but since dietary cholesterol has little influence on circulating levels of blood cholesterol in healthy people, it does no harm to eat three or so a week.

Eggs have versatile properties in cooking: the whites have the ability to trap air in the making of meringues, souffles and sponges, the yolks have binding and emulsifying properties. (See Food poisoning; Pregnancy and diet.) *AU*

Elderly

Whilst sound nutritional principles are needed for all age groups, it is important not to get over-zealous about foisting healthy eating guidelines on to elderly people. In this age group there is usually far more of a problem with deficiencies than excesses, so restricting and excluding certain types of food and drink may do more harm than good.

Energy needs tend to fall as people get older but requirements for all the other nutrients remain the same. This means the food eaten has to be full of goodness. The best way to ensure this is to have a good varied diet. Try to eat one main meal and two snack meals each day, including items from all the following groups:

1. 300 - 600 ml (½ - 1 pint) milk or equivalent as yogurts, cheese and milk puddings
2. Meat, fish, poultry, offal, cheese, pulses, eggs
3. Bread, potatoes, pasta, rice, pitta, chapatti, yam, cereals. One serving with each meal
4. 2 - 3 servings of vegetables a day
5. Fruit and fruit juices (2 a day)
6. Butter or other spreads in small amounts
7. Tea, water, coffee, soups, juices (8 cups a day)

Some nutrients need special attention. Vitamin D is needed for our bodies to absorb calcium. Most of our vitamin D requirement results from the sun shining on our skin. If elderly people are housebound they must rely on diet instead for vitamin D. Only oily fish, eggs, butter and fortified breakfast cereals are reasonable sources. If few of these foods are eaten regularly, a supplement may be necessary. Vitamin C is also vital. A lack of fruit and vegetables could lead to low intakes of this vitamin which can result in poor wound-healing and a lowered immune response. A poor fruit and veg. intake can lead to low potassium levels which may cause confusion and depression. Bananas are a good source of potassium. Fibre from wholegrain foods and fruit and vegetables, along with a good fluid intake of 6 - 8 cups a day, will help reduce problems of constipation. This liquid will also help prevent dehydration which can cause headaches and irritability. As for alcoholic drinks: A little of what you fancy . . . *AU*

Energy

A healthy, varied diet should provide plenty of energy to enjoy life. Energy comes from food which derives directly from plants, or from animals which have themselves eaten plants. The energy is bound in molecules of carbohydrate, fat, protein and alcohol. The energy we consume fuels physical activity, maintains the tissues of the body and supports growth. Energy is measured in calories and joules. (See Calories.) *AU*

E numbers

(See Additives.)

Essential fatty acids

Essential fats are certain types of polyunsaturated fat so-called because, like vitamins, they are essential for health and for life itself. Only some polyunsaturated fats are essential. Some nutritional scientists, following the late Dr Hugh Sinclair, believe that the dietary cause of cardiovascular diseases is not so much excess of saturated fats and fats generally, as deficiency of essential fats, and new evidence supports this view. Prevalence of heart disease is strongly correlated with levels of essential fats in the blood, and while most people consume moderate amounts of essential fat in their diet, its metabolism may be blocked by antagonistic trans-fatty acids (see Trans-fatty acids).

In nature foods are comparatively rich in essential fats. Good sources include the germ of wheat and other grains (best eaten in wholegrain bread); a great range of fresh and lightly cooked vegetables; and wild or free-range meat, poultry and seafood, such as game animals and birds, and oily fish from seas and rivers.

Because they are perishable and also because they are useful in animal feed, essential fats tend to be refined or otherwise stripped out of food manufactured for human consumption. (See Fats; Polyunsaturated fats; Saturated fats.) *GC*

Evening Primrose Oil

(See Omega 3 and Omega 6 fatty acids.)

Exclusion diets

Exclusion diets involve removing one or more food types or substances from the diet. The food or substance is then re-introduced so that the effect can be observed.

Exclusion diets are often used in the diagnosis and treatment of food intolerances. They should be carried out under medical and dietetic supervision and only when a good reason for doing so has been established. Self-styled exclusion diets can be dangerous. (See Food intolerance.) *AU*

Exercise and nutrition

The important role diet plays in sports people's lives, whether top-class athletes, professional footballers or serious keep-fitters, is becoming increasingly recognized in this country. Obviously nutritional advice differs with the wide variety of sporting activities undertaken, but there are two specific points which need to be taken into consideration by us all: first, that we have enough dietary carbohydrate to maintain reserves of muscle energy during training and competition; second, that the intake of fluids before, during and after exercise is sufficient to maintain our bodies' cooling system. A problem with either of these will lead to decreased performance with potentially serious side-effects.

One of the main sources of energy to a working muscle is the carbohydrate store of glycogen. Without adequate reserves the ability to train and compete will be reduced. It is vital, therefore, that at least 60 per cent of energy in the diet comes from carbohydrate foods (these include bread, pasta, rice, breakfast cereals, chapattis, naan, bananas and fruit juices). The typical British diet, however, currently has only around 35 per cent of its energy coming from carbohydrate.

The glycogen supplies which are used during exercise must be replaced as soon as possible to allow the next exercise session to be supported. If this does not occur, glycogen stores get gradually depleted and eventually exercise and training just will not be possible. To increase carbohydrate in the diet, make sure all meals and snacks are based around the foods mentioned above.

Fluid intake is crucial, too. During exercise, as energy is burnt up to fuel the muscles, we produce heat. This heat is lost through sweating which, as we all know, involves loss of water. Sweating is a very effective way of losing heat, but it is vital that the process is not interfered with by our bodies becoming dehydrated. The only way to prevent this happening is to drink plenty of fluids before, during and immediately after exercise. Waiting until you're thirsty is too late, as thirst is our body's way of telling us we are already dehydrated. Isotonic drinks available on the market are a good way of replacing fluids as quickly as possible, but water is fine too.

As far as other nutrients are concerned, there is no need to worry about loading up with extra protein. Most British diets contain sufficient to cope with the small additional requirements created by training. There is little evidence that eating large protein supplements increases muscle size or strength, indeed consuming large amounts of protein could be a problem since this may reduce the room for carbohydrates. Nor is there research to support the idea that vitamin and mineral supplementation improves the performance of anyone whose diet is otherwise well balanced. *AU*

f

Factory farming

The term is used to describe modern farming methods that are based upon several factors: a large amount of livestock reared inside housing units; a reliance on antibiotics to keep the animals free of disease in their short life-span; a rich protein diet so that the animals put on the maximum amount of weight in the shortest amount of time.

Factory farming began in the 1950s when governments wanted to build up protein supplies after the war. At the same time research into new drugs induced pharmaceutical companies to finance farming, while new technology allowed computerization of feeds and the construction of highly sophisticated buildings. This led to a huge loss in employment for farm labourers (one stockman can oversee several sheds containing thousands of animals) and a rise in animal disease and affliction which was not always noticed in time. The rise in disease was countered with a corresponding rise in the use of antibiotics, some of which remain as residues in the carcasses. Hormones which act upon the animal's metabolism to make it put on lean meat in a shorter time have also been used on certain species, and there is concern about the effects of residues (see Growth hormones). Public anxiety and outrage over some of these practices, committed in the name of profit, go some way to keep them contained.

Factory farming flies in the face of all the humane tenets contained in the Animal Welfare mandates, which explains why these have not become law (see Animal welfare). There can also be no doubt that many of the practices are both horrific and cruel. Egg-laying hens are de-beaked and crammed into small cages with three or four others, living in tiers for one or even two years until slaughter for stock cubes and soups must seem a happy release. Sows can be chained up for life in small concrete stalls where they are barely able to move or lie down. Broiler chickens are kept in windowless sheds on urine-soaked and excreta-splattered wood chips, so selectively bred that they suffer from legs which break easily and often lie injured until they die unnoticed. The dairy herd is so overworked and exploited to give us our daily pinta that it is slaughtered long before its natural life-span. Calves only a few days old are exported from the UK to live in small wooden crates where they are kept on a liquid diet deficient in iron so that people can eat white veal. (See Veal.)

Although the public is now far more aware of these brutal conditions, there is little sign that the worst excesses of factory farming are being moderated, or will be unless public opinion becomes a force for change. (See Animal welfare; Abattoirs; Farm animals; Game. *CS*

Farm animals

Animals which have been domesticated since around 10,000 BC to give people not only their meat on slaughter but their wool, milk and hair while alive. The first animals to be domesticated were all mammals: cattle, sheep, goats, pigs and dogs. The first three were particularly useful to the early farmer because they eat unpromising foods such as dry grass, leaves, straw, twigs and green fodder when available: all are high in cellulose that human beings cannot digest. They are also immensely valuable as sources of hide, horn, hair and wool.

Fowl - hens, ducks, geese and turkeys (the last only discovered in the New World) - became domesticated later. In the west the dog proved its worth in hunting and as a guard on the early homestead.

Cows, pigs and hens are now most widely factory farmed, but other animals are also being intensively farmed, like deer, ostrich and kangaroo. Game birds: quail, pheasant and partridge, are also being farmed in housing units. Intensification radically alters the flavour of the meat, so that the game birds become bland and fatty. However, traditional farms that rear their animals humanely according to Animal Welfare rules are now making a come-back. (See Growth hormones.) *CS*

Fast food

The rise of fast-food culture has been one of the major changes in the way we eat. Much fast food is generally considered unhealthy, yet there is no reason why it should be. It really depends on what you choose, how often you eat take-aways, and what you eat in the rest of your diet. A burger, for example, contains protein and some iron, there is some starchy carbohydrate in the bun and a bit of vitamin C in the salad garnish But if you add loads of fries, mayonnaise, sauces and cheese and top up with a milkshake, the calorie and fat levels really start to shoot up.

Pizza, baked potatoes and shish kebab with lots of salad and pitta bread are healthier fast-food choices. Fried chicken, Chinese and Indian take-aways are often fatty, but it can be hard to tell as take-away food does not come with information labels. This makes it more difficult to choose lower-fat foods, to avoid additives or certain ingredients if, for example, you are a vegetarian or have a food allergy.

For healthier fast-food eating choose thicker chips rather than thinner ones as they contain less fat, try a salad with your burger instead of fries, go easy on the sauces, and choose orange juice instead of shakes. *SD*

Fat

Just over two-fifths of the calories contained in the British food supply and thus the British diet are in the form of fat. Put another way, 40 per cent or more of the calories an average person consumes are in the form of fat, of which up to half, or 20 percent, is hard or hardened saturated fat, the main dietary cause of heart disease.

Fat is also very high in calories and is therefore liable to make you fat. In the amounts typically consumed in Britain, fat is almost certainly an important cause of a number of common cancers, as well as diseases of the circulation and other systems of the body. The more fatty (and sugary) any diet is, the less nourishment it contains, and any largely sedentary population needs nutrient-dense food.

After 10 years and more of campaigning by health professionals and others committed to the improvement of public health, the British government has eventually agreed that the national diet is unhealthy and that everybody would do well to eat less fat and saturated fat, if only to reduce the risk of heart attacks.

British government-backed guidelines now recommend relatively modest reductions in consumption of total and saturated fat, readily achieved by switching to lean meat and low-fat milk and other dairy products, from highly saturated table and cooking fats to high-polyunsaturated margarines, and by grossing out on grease-burgers and pastries only once in a while.

Whether or not it is followed, such timorous advice is not likely to make a radical difference to the incidence of heart attacks, nor to premature suffering and death from cancer. Based on studies of populations round the world and on laboratory evidence, the World Health Organisation recommends that only 15 - 30 per cent of total calories is in the form of fats, and only 0 - 10 per cent saturated fats.

This means that a healthy diet is mainly made up of foods of plant origin, especially vegetables, legumes, fruit and starchy staples, includes substantial amounts of meat only occasionally, and cuts highly processed fatty and/or sugary products right out. In effect, the less fat and saturated fat you eat, the better. (See Monounsaturated fats; Polyunsaturated fats; Saturated fats.) *GC*

F(e)asting

All over the world and throughout history, people have marked great communal days, including those of birth, marriage, achievement and death, with feasting, burning off the extra calories by energetic dancing. Conversely, a common theme of traditional cultures and great religions is also fasting, often for periods of a week or more, as a means of contemplation, inspiration or remembrance.

Both feasting and fasting are or should be memorable special occasions. Unfortunately, we now tend to consume feast food and drink, such as meat, cakes and alcohol, every day, so we can lose a sense of occasion on special days. Sitting round eating and drinking vastly more than our sedentary bodies can handle, and then dozing off, is all too common at Christmas and on other feast days, with resulting disappointment, dyspepsia and fear of weighing machines.

Fasting is now usually seen just as the most extreme way of losing fat: 'the ultimate diet', to quote one book. For sedentary people, continual low-calorie dieting typically creates the condition it is supposed to cure; weight rebounds after the diet is stopped, lean tissue is gradually replaced by adipose tissue, and in this sense, dieting makes you fat.

But occasionally fasting as a self-disciplined holiday from food and a means to enhance good health is an excellent idea. Any healthy person can readily fast for up to five days, drinking plenty of spring or mineral water, perhaps vegetable or fruit juices, and multivitamin and mineral pills if desired. After two or three days, hunger fades and is often replaced by a sense of light well-being. And when you break the fast, the flavours of fresh food are almost explosively delicious. Try it, after consulting your doctor. *GC*

Fibre

Also known as roughage, this is the indigestible part of plant foods, including the bran of cereals, the casing of pulses and legumes, and the skin and core of vegetables and fruit. There are different types of fibre, including cellulose, gums, pectin and lignin.

Until a generation ago, fibre was thought to be better discarded and irrelevant to human health except as relief for constipation. Food is refined in factory manufacture and home preparation by means of stripping fibre away. Thus we have sugar, extracted from cane or beet; white bread and flour, without bran; mashed potatoes, without peel; fruit juice, without pith. Not surprisingly therefore, the British diet is short of fibre. Constipation is a fibre deficiency disease. Lack of fibre in the diet is probably also a cause of diverticular disease and more serious gut diseases, including colon cancer. Gummy fibre such as that found in oatmeal may protect against heart attacks.

The World Health Organisation recommends that for good gut health we should eat twice as much fibre as we do now, most readily from wholegrain bread and cereals, fresh or lightly cooked vegetables, pulses and legumes, and whole or dried fruit. Wholegrain unsweetened and unsalted muesli, porridge and breakfast cereals are also good healthy sources of fibre. (See Bowel diseases). *GC*

Fish

Fish, especially oily fish, provide us with a delicious and plentiful source of food which we now know is extremely good for us. Fish can be divided into freshwater and seawater types. Of the freshwater variety some, like pike, spend their whole life-cycle in lakes and rivers, and others, like salmon, live as adults at sea, returning to spawn in the river.

Seafish can be round, like cod, mackerel, herring, whitebait and tuna, or flat like plaice, halibut and sole. Shellfish include crab, lobster, mussels and oysters. Shellfish are rich in protein and fairly low in calories. Some are particularly good sources of micronutrients. Oysters, for example, are the richest known source of zinc, needed for a healthy immune system, activation of enzymes, and taste.

All fish are excellent sources of protein and certain minerals like iodine, selenium, fluoride and zinc. The B vitamins riboflavin, thiamin and B12 are also in good supply . Fish eaten with the bones, like tinned salmon and pilchards, are full of calcium. White fish like cod, coley and plaice have very little fat in their flesh, storing it instead in their livers. Oily fish like mackerel, tuna and salmon store their fat throughout their flesh.

Eating plenty of these oily fish may help reduce the risk of heart disease. The oil is rich in so-called omega-3 fatty acids, in particular EPA and DHA. These fatty acids are converted to hormone-like compounds called prostaglandins which seem to reduce the risk of blood-clotting as well as possibly helping to improve the immune system and reducing inflammation in rheumatoid arthritis. Try to eat a portion of fish several times a week. (See Omega 3 and Omega 6 fatty acids.) *AU*

Fish and chips

Eaten as a staple, cheap take-away by working people for 100 years and more, fish and chips tend to be despised as just another type of greasy fast food. In fact, both fish and chips can be good for you and your children. It all depends on the fish, the chips, and what's cooking in the deep-fryer.

Any fresh fish by itself is healthy food, as are potatoes. If your chippie takes care to select good-quality fish, that's a good start, and better still if he uses a small amount of good batter. The first key test of any chippie is the fish itself. Is it flaky, fresh, dry and delicious eaten without the batter? Good. Is it limp? Bad. The second test is the chip. Is it big and fat and crisp outside yet floury inside? Good. Is it thin and crisped all through, or else soggy? Bad: in these cases it will be saturated with fat.

The third key test is what's in the deep-fryer. Ask your chippie what oil he uses to fry the fish and chips, and how often he changes it. If he doesn't give you a clear answer, and especially if his shop smells like a garage, full of fumes from constantly heated grease, take a walk. Healthy fish and chips are fried in sizzling-hot unsaturated oil that is constantly changed. Be prepared to pay more for the best: it's worth it. (See Fast food.) *GC*

Flatulence

I once gave Jerusalem Artichoke soup to the Chaplain of King's College, Cambridge. Next day in chapel the resonant acoustics confirmed that there are few foods better able to feed gastric bacteria in the system generating copious quantities of mixed gases, the normal composition of which is half nitrogen, one-third carbon dioxide, methane, hydrogen, ammonia, and the remarkably smelly hydrogen sulphide, indoles and skatoles. The proportion of these can vary quite widely, as you have probably noticed.

The normal adult produces about half a litre of gas a day. The war made the

study of the subject a necessity because in an unpressurized aeroplane flying at 37,000 feet the gas volume expands to five and a half times the volume at sea level, causing the pilots to lose concentration. Astronauts posed another problem: because of the toxic nature of the smelly gas, special diets and cleansing systems had to be devised to prevent them coming under risk from their and their partners' flatulence.

Never break wind near an open flame because it can be very inflammable. The hole in the ozone layer above New Zealand, for example, is caused by the methane expelled by 60 million sheep.

There are a number of substances in legumes (peas and beans) which are specially potent feeders of gastric bacteria. These oligosaccharides are linked complex sugar molecules which cause wind because we cannot digest them. Along with the lectins and protease inhibitors also common in legumes, they are largely destroyed by heat. The lima bean also contains substances which can turn into cyanide. It is essential that legumes are rapidly boiled in copious quantities of water in an open-topped pan for at least 10 minutes, then cooked until tender. Sprouted beans are safe to eat uncooked because the substances that harm us are there to protect the mature seed from being eaten and are reduced on germination. *MH*

Food chains

'From plough to plate'; a food chain, or agriculture and food system, begins with the cultivation of land, and ends with meals as eaten at home. Each part of the system, from farming to food manufacture and sale, distribution, catering and cooking, is linked and interdependent; hence the metaphor of links in a chain.

In Britain the government department responsible for the food chain is the Ministry of Agriculture, Fisheries and Food (MAFF); in the USA, it is the Department of Agriculture (USDA). In industrialized countries the food and drink processing industries taken together are a vast resource of capital and labour, and government policy is invariably to favour the development of ever-more economically 'value-added' highly processed food, with chemical aids. It is sometimes supposed that the food chain is consumer-led. In fact it is producer and manufacturer-led, and unresponsive to consumer demand. For example, there is currently no sign that production and therefore consumption of fat and sugar in Britain is decreasing. (See MAFF.) *GC*

Food intolerance

As long ago as the fifth century BC, Hippocrates was aware that a significant number of people reacted adversely to certain foods which they needed to be instructed to avoid. Few people are allergic to only one substance and fortunately, as they grow older, most affected people grow out of their sensitivities which, in any case, can change from time to time.

Food intolerance is a highly individual response to foods or additives which are toxic only to certain people. They include sensitivity to gluten (the protein part of flour) or intolerance to lactose (milk sugar) which is the genetic condition of possibly half the people on earth and usually occurs after the age of weaning. From the sufferer's point of view the symptoms can be similar to an allergy either because the food can trigger your own mast cells to release histamine, as in the case of shellfish, cheeses and chocolate, or it can contain histamines that some people cannot cope with, such as those found in eggs, sausage, fish and tomatoes. Quite frequently people who are sensitive to aspirins, including 5 - 10 per cent of asthmatics, are also sensitive to some of the foods which contain salicylates, such as almonds, apples, apricots, peaches, prunes, oranges, tomatoes, tangerines, cucumbers, most soft fruits, cherries, grapes and raisins. Allergies are a specific and identifiable response to proteins to which the individual is sensitive, the commonest example of which is probably the protein in pollens, which cause hay fever.

The allergic reaction occurs in people who have antibodies specific to the protein they are eating. Thus those who have a reaction after eating peanuts, for example, already have an antibody which can unite with the protein and cause histamines to be released. The first time the offending substance is consumed the union takes place with no observable effect, but subsequently, when the food is eaten again, the release of histamine or other chemicals can create symptoms which are often on the skin, because the mast cells are most numerous there, including rashes, redness, itching and swelling. Other symptoms may be a runny nose, blurred vision, nausea and vomiting. Recently a number of cases of deaths from eating peanuts have illustrated the most violent effect of a food allergy, which is called an anaphylactic reaction. This can create a complete collapse of the respiratory system and blood vessels. Those at risk often carry inhalers or filled injectable preparations of adrenaline given under the skin at a dose of about 1 ml as a 1 in 1000 solution. This may have to be repeated every ten minutes until blood pressure returns to normal. Regrettably some food manufacturers are incorporating peanuts in food in ways that are not at all obvious, bringing potential death to consumers.

The key difference between an allergy and an intolerance is that an allergy can be identified by the presence of the antigens and the intolerance cannot. A problem is that some reactions could be a bit of one and a bit of the other, E102 tartrazine being a case in point.

Migraines can also be triggered by certain foods including mature cheeses, chicken livers, raw beans and some alcoholic drinks. The process of elimination (see Exclusion diets), often helps to reduce the frequency of attacks.

Asthmatics. One in twenty asthmatics are very sensitive to the sulphites used to preserve foods (E220 - E227). It is scandalous that producers are not yet obliged to declare the presence of artificial ingredients in alcoholic drinks. Every year many asthmatics die from the consumption of highly sulphited cheap wines which carry no warnings.

Eczema, multiple sclerosis and rheumatoid arthritis are all capable of being aggravated by eating certain foods or additives.

Hyperactivity is not to be confused with the normal abundant activity of childhood. Most hyperactive children are excitable and impulsive, very fidgety, have a short attention span, are compulsively aggressive, can hurt themselves and are sometimes very antisocial in a way which is quite beyond their control, and they may also, during an attack, suffer poor co-ordination of the muscles. Simple operations such as writing, buckling shoes or tying bows, become impossible. There may be a genetic basis for certain cases because blue-eyed boys seem to suffer more than other children.

Treatment begins with trying to provide a stable family environment and by restricting the diet to exclude those foods and additives which provoke the attack. Artificial colours and preservatives are particularly implicated but it is important to ensure that the child is not isolated from friends through excessive restrictions. Therefore qualified advice is essential. Many hospitals have special departments who can be very helpful and Great Ormond Street Hospital for Sick Children has published a number of papers linking foods, additives and hyperactivity.

Although any food can provoke an adverse response in an individual, the most common are milk and milk products, eggs, foods containing wheat, maize (corn), peas, beans and peanuts, nuts and seeds, some fruits such as strawberries, alcohol, chocolate and coffee. This is a fairly daunting list; you may say that there is not much left but if you eliminate all these foods from your diet and get better you can then reintroduce them one at a time to work out your own diagnosis. This is a rigorous and time-consuming exercise and it is vital to discuss it with your doctor first. *MH*

Food poisoning

The number of reported cases of food poisoning has increased dramatically in the last ten years, with some experts estimating that the real incidence may exceed 2 million cases a year as only about one in 100 cases of food poisoning is ever reported, let alone traced back to a source. While the symptoms are often mild - an upset stomach or headache - food poisoning can sometimes be more serious, causing vomiting, diarrhoea, severe pain and fever. It can even prove fatal - babies, young children, elderly people and those whose immune systems are impaired are most at risk. If symptoms are severe it is important to consult a doctor.

It is a problem which exists throughout the food chain from the farm to the table. Contamination of animal feed, intense husbandry practices, products of new technology such as cook-chill foods and microwave ovens, increasing sales of convenience foods with long shelf-life and poor levels of training and hygiene in some food businesses have all added to the risks. And cross-contamination in the kitchen can cause problems. (See Kitchen safety.)

There are over 2000 strains of salmonella bacteria, most commonly found in chickens and eggs. For a time flocks of hens infected with salmonella were required to be slaughtered but this precaution has now been lifted. Numbers of food poisoning cases continue to rise, however, and the Department of Health still advises that all eggs should be cooked until the yolks are firm.

Cases of food poisoning caused by campylobacter have also increased, affecting more people than salmonella, though this is rarely fatal. One relatively new problem is listeria. It is particularly worrying because the bacteria can grow at temperatures as low as 3°C, and refrigeration, whilst reducing the risk of most food poisoning, may actually encourage listeriosis. If pregnant women contract listeriosis the effects can include miscarriage, still-birth or severe illness in the new-born child. Listeria have been found in soft cheeses, cook-chill foods, pâtés and salads. Whilst its incidence is still relatively low, pregnant women and those whose immune systems may be impaired should avoid soft cheeses, such as Brie and Camembert, and ensure that reheated foods are thoroughly cooked, particularly when using a microwave oven. All salads should be washed.

Another relative newcomer among bacteria is known as E. Coli 0157. This strain has been found in the meat of cattle, poultry and pigs and in unpasteurized milk, and a possible link may have been established with under-cooked beefburgers. Although cases of E. Coli 0157 poisoning are still relatively rare, their incidence has risen sharply since the 1980s and is now the most common cause in Britain of acute kidney failure in children - some cases have proved fatal. To guard against this type of poisoning the government's chief medical officer now advises caterers to ensure that burgers are cooked right through. When cooking burgers at home it is best to cook them over a low heat for around 18 minutes, to ensure that they are cooked on the inside but not burned on the outside. And if you are eating out, check that the centre of the burger is thoroughly cooked. If it is not, ask for it to be cooked longer. *SD*

Food supplements

It is frequently said that a well-balanced diet gives you everything you need for good health. The flaw of this argument is that it's often difficult to know whether your diet is well-balanced. So is there a case for supplementing your diet with extra nutrients, usually taken as pills or capsules?.

Unless our diet is determinedly Mediterranean, with at least five fruit and vegetable servings a day, we are unlikely to be getting enough beta-carotene, and vitamins C and E. These are the key antioxidant nutrients now known to neutralize the damaging effects of free radicals (see A.C.E.). There is also such a wide variation in the natural nutrient content of foods, which is further affected by storage and cooking, that a sensible insurance policy is to take a modest level of supplementation. Pregnant and nursing mothers, the elderly and children who eat poorly will all benefit from taking extra nutrients.

However, there is no point in taking vastly excessive quantities of nutrients which at best will give you very expensive urine! The upper levels I have listed (see A.C.E.) are safe, with most of the figures derived from the latest Scientific Committee for Food's report published by the EC. If you find that taking supplements upsets the tummy, try taking them with food. *MH*

Fortification

I met a man in Nashville who had weighed almost 400 lb and was determined to lose weight. He sought out the ideal food, which contained all the nutrients he would need, and consumed it, with nothing but water for the next four years. When I met him he was a normal weight. The miracle food? Corn flakes.

American corn flakes are a good example of fortification: nutrients are added to restore ingredients which have been refined away to their normal nutritional status and also to provide better-balanced nutrition.

Appropriate fortification can be valuable in a world where persuading people to eat good food is not that easy. There are also excellent arguments for increasing fortification with certain nutrients, such as folic acid and the antioxidants (see A.C.E.) which have a protective effect when consumed in quantities greater than that normally found in the diet. Labelling should make it clear whether the nutrients come from the food itself or additions. *MH*

Freezing

A method of preserving food where the water content crystallizes into ice, which halts all chemical activity. All frozen food should be well-wrapped to prevent freezer burn and drying out; the process of dry-freezing is now widely used in the commercial preparation of dried foods. (See Dried Fruits.) Freezing can damage the cell structure, water crystals puncture the cell membranes and so the product deteriorates more commonly in meat than in vegetables. Fish suffers most, for the ice crystals can destroy the collagen (the muscle wall) and the flesh becomes flabby and limp. There is also a loss of fluid when fish and meat are thawed, and as this fluid is rich in protein, vitamins and salts, the result is a drier, less nutritional product when cooked. Frozen fish, meat and poultry must never exceed recommended freezing times, and must be very thoroughly thawed before cooking. Another drawback of freezing is that it oxidizes fats, and the alteration of fat molecules leads to rancid flavours. None of this of course occurs in the freezing of vegetables, many of which freeze with great success. They must, however, be blanched before freezing, to inactivate the enzymic and chemical activity which will brown the vegetables and destroy vitamin content. Food that has been frozen and thawed must not be refrozen. *CS*

Fruit

The fruit supply available to us today has never been so varied. As transport and marketing have improved, so too has the range of fresh fruits for us to buy all the year round. On the one hand this gives an untold variety of fruits; on the other, it is argued, we lose all sense of seasonality and the mass importation of fruits from tropical countries may be considered environmentally unsound. Consumers are speaking with their pockets, however, and everything points to the majority enjoying this relatively new-found choice. The use of fresh fruit is increasing and fresh fruit juices are enjoying a huge rise in popularity.

Botanically speaking, fruits are closely related to vegetables, and some foods we commonly refer to as vegetables, such as tomatoes and aubergines, are really fruits.

Within the broad family described as fruits there exist a huge variety of textures, flavours and colours. Some provide significant amounts of nutrients and energy, others consist mostly of water and provide few nutrients. Fruit sugar, or fructose, is found in many fruits and is responsible for their sweet taste. With the exception of avocados, fruits contain very little fat. Many, such as citrus fruits and blackcurrants, are excellent sources of vitamin C and most provide fibre. Yellow, red and orange fruits usually contain fair amounts of the antioxidant pigment beta-carotene. (See Beta-carotene; A.C.E.) *AU*

Frying

There are three main types: shallow, stir and deep-frying. The first involves placing the food in enough hot fat just to film the base of the pan. The fat must be very hot, brown and sear the exterior and cook the interior sufficiently. Olive oil is the best fat to use for flavouring fried foods, though a mixture of olive oil and butter can also be used.

Stir-frying uses less fat: a tablespoon of oil or less in a wok or pan is heated and the food, cut into small pieces, is thrown into the pan then moved around very quickly while various flavours, spices and herbs are added. The food gets covered in oil and flavouring, loses a little of its moisture which is driven off in steam and should be still fairly crisp. This method ensures that most of the nutrients in the food remain intact. Sesame, soy, sunflower and peanut oils are the traditional fats used in stir-frying.

Deep-frying is rarely used nowadays as the amount of fat needed can be both uneconomical and unhealthy. As a technique it resembles boiling as the food is completely immersed in the hot fat. The best fat to use is one of the polyunsaturated oils like maize, sunflower or safflower. *CS*

Fungi

This is the term used to describe those plants that grow by myceliums, the white, thread-like filament often seen in soil beneath dead wood, and includes mushrooms (from the French 'mousseron', meaning certain umbrella-shaped fungi), toadstools and moulds. Edible fungi number over 3000 different kinds. From the earliest times, they were associated with magic, for they appeared overnight from nothing and many of them have been discovered to be hallucinogenic.

Lately fungi-hunting has become something of a foodie sport. It is best to arm yourself with two good guides, to double-check on any specimens that seem doubtful. Ideally, fungi should be collected in a group, conducted by a knowledgeable leader. In France, pharmacists will tell you whether fungi are poisonous or safe to eat. Otherwise, stick to the few fungi specimens experience has told you are worth gathering and cooking. There are a couple of dozen fungi of such gastronomic worth that it makes fungi hunting almost an autumnal duty as well as a pleasure. The top five are: field mushrooms, ceps, chanterelles, parasols and puffballs. The best method of cooking is to slice garlic and fry quickly with the mushrooms in olive oil. *CS*

g

Gall stones

As the name implies, solid deposits that may build up in the gall bladder, and have the appearance of small pebbles. These can cause intense pain and have to be removed by surgery. They are relatively common in industrialized countries and likely to be diet-related. There is some evidence that gall stones are in part caused by a fatty and/or sugary diet, likewise kidney stones. *GC*

Game

A term which refers to wild animals or birds killed for their meat. The term covers the live animal and its raw or cooked flesh. In the past many more animals and birds were hunted for the table than now; all but a very few have become extinct. Today, game refers to wild boar and venison (which both can be farmed) hare and rabbit (still wild), pheasant, partridge, grouse, mallard, snipe, pigeon and woodcock. Of these , pheasant and partridge can start off in hatcheries on a high-protein diet and be let out into their natural habitat after the first four months. These birds present a poor shot, for they are half tame and their flesh tends to be too fatty and tasteless because of their early diet. The advantage of real game is that the animal or bird has unending exercise in its hunt for food, so has virtually no fat at all (what little there is being polyunsaturated), while its flesh is muscular. To cook, roast the birds breast down so that they do not dry out. Turn right way up for the last 10 minutes in order to brown. *CS*

Garlic

Garlic (Allium sativam) is one of the most ancient of flavourings, a cousin to onions and leeks. Its pungent aroma upon the breath has earned it a connotation of vulgarity. From the earliest times it has been thought to have the most beneficial, medicinal qualities. Pliny includes sixty-one garlic remedies in his Natural History. This has now been proved to be true. Garlic is a powerful antibiotic (cooking destroys this anti-bacterial agent though it leaves other therapeutic qualities untouched) and also helps to retard heart disease, cancers and strokes. Cooked garlic can lower blood cholesterol and be a decongestant. Garlic contains minerals, calcium, phosphorus, iron and potassium, also thiamin, riboflavin, niacin and vitamin C. Some people are addicted to it. One raw clove of garlic crushed into olive oil for a green salad seems a reasonable daily intake. But a garlic soup made from 50 - 100 cloves is an enormous help when suffering from the common cold. *CS*

GATT

The initials GATT stand for General Agreement on Tariffs and Trade, a global agreement on trade terms. The general purpose of GATT, now applied to agriculture and food as well as other commodities, is to accelerate so-called market economies all over the world, by means of dismantling laws designed to protect local, national or regional interests.

It is generally believed that free trade as embodied in GATT will create wealth, make food cheaper, and is in the public interest. The key question is, however, 'free for whom?' The GATT talks have been dominated and driven by an alliance of rich nations and multinational companies. GATT will mean more intensive agriculture, and the erosion of traditional food and agriculture systems. *GC*

Gelatin

This is extracted from animal skin and bone. It comes from collagen which is the connective tissue connecting muscles to bones and skin. Culinary gelatin comes from pig skins and from fallen stock and slaughter casualties deemed unsuitable for human consumption. Gelatin has no nutritional value. It is used for setting cold dishes, either sweet, like fruit jellies, or savoury, like aspic. It was in great vogue in the nineteenth century when no Victorian banquet was complete without a great joint of cold meat decorated and covered in aspic jelly. Today, if used in catering, it can be a snare for food poisoning. *CS*

Genetic engineering

Scientists now know how to alter the genetic make-up of many plants and animals. In the UK, foods made from genetically modified organisms are already on sale, though you won't find anything on the label to tell you this. Cheese, including that labelled as 'vegetarian', can now be made by using a genetically modified enzyme (chymosin) instead of rennet. One large retail chain has just announced that it will label its vegetarian cheese as using gene technology. Also approved for use is a genetically engineered yeast for bread-making. And there are many more developments in the pipeline - crops that are more resistant to pests and produce higher yields, enzymes which speed up food processing or foods which have a longer shelf-life. Scientists say there will be more choice and improved products for consumers, yet this new technology is already causing controversy.

Many consumer groups want to see better procedures to regulate the development and safety of genetically modified organisms and are calling for all food products produced by this technology to be labelled. There are also ethical concerns about taking genetic material from one species and introducing it into another, which can go far beyond what can be achieved by conventional breeding. Muslims and Jews for example, are likely to object to genetic material from pigs being used in other foods and vegetarians are certain to be unhappy about vegetables containing genes from animals. *SD*

Get Cooking

These days we are eating more and more ready-prepared convenience foods and are losing our ability to prepare basic, cheap, nutritious meals. Learning how to cook is a skill for life, but sadly, while 93 per cent of children know how to play computer games, only half this number know how to boil an egg. Changes in the national curriculum have added to the problem, with much less emphasis on practical cooking skills.

In an attempt to remedy the situation, a new project was launched last year with the backing of the Department of Health. Called 'Get Cooking', it aims to give every young person the chance to develop the skills and confidence to be able to cook (see Addresses). 'Get Cooking' is encouraging parents, youth organizations and schools to set up food clubs where children can learn to cook in a way that is fun as well as educational. Food File has supported this campaign, and our book, *Cook It*, is a great introduction to the fun of cooking. *SD*

Ginger

Ginger (Zingiber officinale) is a tropical rhizome native to South East Asia which has been renowned for its medicinal value as much as its unique and sensational flavour since pre-history. It has been valued as an aid to digestion, to alleviate nausea (good for travel sickness), to combat colds and stimulate appetite. It is also good for the circulation. The Chinese think of it as an inner fire, which awakens the internal organs, so they also use it for all rheumatic pains.

Before buying, weigh the ginger root in your hand. The heaviest will be the freshest, containing the most moisture; it becomes more fibrous with age. For cooking, peel the root and grate it or slice in matchstick lengths. Use as a flavouring in stir-frying at the beginning of cooking, with sesame oil and garlic. Make ginger tea by grating a tablespoon of the root and leaving it to infuse in boiling water for five minutes. Excellent for colds. *CS*

Glucose

Glucose is a carbohydrate and carbohydrates provide most of the energy in many diets around the world. Green plants make carbohydrates from water and carbon dioxide under the influence of sunlight. Carbohydrates can be broadly divided into simple sugars, double sugars and complex carbohydrates. Glucose is a simple sugar. It rarely occurs alone in foods and is often found linked with other simple sugars. Sucrose - what we know as table sugar, for example - is glucose linked with another simple carbohydrate called fructose. Lactose or milk sugar is glucose plus galactose. If lots of glucose molecules are linked together, a complex carbohydrate is formed which we know as starch. *AU*

Gluten

(See Food intolerance.)

Gout

Gout is a recurrent attack of joint inflammation caused by deposits of uric acid crystals in the joints affecting especially the big toe but also the elbow, knee, hand, foot, ankle, arm or shoulder. There is a genetic predispositon to the condition and it is also a side-effect of some of the more powerful diuretic (water-eliminating) drugs. Twenty times more common in men than women, gout usually begins between the ages of forty and fifty, although women are protected until after the menopause. Drugs are now effective in controlling attacks which are frequently triggered by foods high in purines and also by excess alcohol. Sufferers should avoid organ foods such as liver, kidneys and brains; smoked or pickled meat or fish; anchovies, sardines and mackerel; meat extracts; dried fruits; salt and salted sauces; dried beans, peas and asparagus. *MH*

Grains and cereals

Grains and cereals, such as wheat (used to make bread and pasta), rice, millet, sorghum, maize, rye, oats and barley have been used as cheap food staples by communities all over the world for thousands of years. They are all starchy complex carbohydrate foods which we are advised should form the bulk of our diet. Contrary to popular belief carbohydrates are not fattening in themselves - it's the spreads and sauces they are served with that top up the calories.

Wholegrains are generally highly nutritious foods. However, refining, to produce white rice and flour, removes the outer husks from the grain. Thus refined cereals tend to be lower in fibre, in the form of bran, and contain less vitamins and minerals.

Many grains are cheap to buy, fun to cook and nutritious to eat. Try bulgar or cracked wheat, couscous, millet flakes, or semolina. *SD*

Grilling

This means to cook food quickly without fat under an intense heat. The grill is an interior barbecue (the oldest cooking method known to humankind). It is popular today because its no-fat cooking technique is good for the health. Switch the grill on for a minute before cooking to ensure maximum heat. Place the food under it and watch carefully to prevent burning. Portions of meat and fish grill successfully as do some vegetables, for example tomatoes, sweet peppers, fennel and aubergines, if lightly oiled. *CS*

Growth hormones

Getting farm animals to grow faster and larger is one way for farmers to boost profits. Growth-boosting steroid hormones for beef production have been illegal since an EC ban in 1989, but they are still permitted in other countries, such as the USA, where much of the meat for beefburgers comes from. One drug that is being illegally used by some European farmers is clenbuterol. Known as 'Angel Dust', the drug is used by vets to treat lung diseases in cattle and horses. But if added to animal feed at high doses it reduces body fat and encourages muscle growth and weight gain. Residues of the drug have been found in some meat and pâté.

Antibiotics which are regularly fed to farm animals can have the added bonus for farmers of helping to increase growth. But residues of one antibiotic, sulfadimidine, which is banned in the USA because of its cancer risk, have been found in over a quarter of pig-kidney samples tested by government.

The development of the milk-boosting hormone, BST (bovine somatotropin) has caused much controversy. Consumers, retailers and Animal Welfare organizations in the UK united to oppose the use of a drug which they argued would cause suffering to cows at a time when milk production was already higher than needed. *SD*

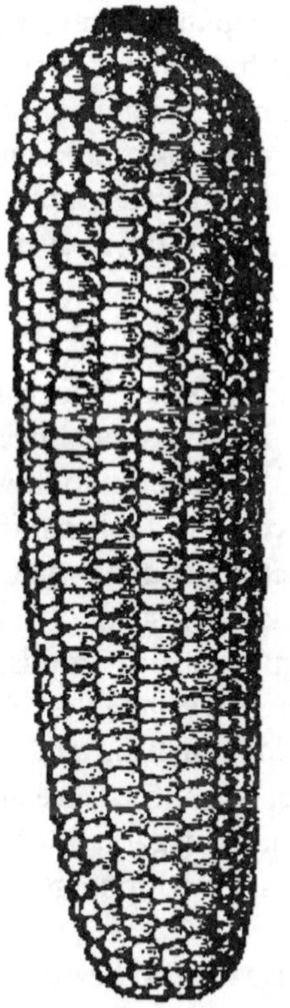

food file

h

Health of the Nation

This is the title of an official White Paper published in 1992 and updated in 1993. It commits the government to a policy of preventive medicine, in England only, designed to promote health and specifically to reduce coronary heart disease and obesity by means of an improved national diet.

The Paper includes dietary targets that specify somewhat less consumption of fat and saturated fat, with vaguer recommendations for more vegetables, fruit and starchy foods. At the end of 1992, the government set up a national Nutrition Task Force with representatives from government and industry, health/medical organisations, and consumer/public interest groups, charged to find ways and means to achieve the Health of Nation targets. At the end of 1993 it was noted that overweight and obesity in Britain continues to increase. In 1994 Task Force work was progressing by means of advisory project teams without powers or funds. By comparison, the industry advertising spend, mostly on processed fatty and/or sugary foods and drinks, is over £500 million a year. *GC*

Healthy food

Manufacturers of fatty and/or sugary foods have a little slogan: 'There is no such thing as healthy or unhealthy food. There are only healthy or unhealthy diets.' In the sense that only contaminated or infected food will make you acutely ill, this is obviously true. And you will come to no harm if once a month you eat a pork pie (unless it is infested with salmonella) or a chocolate confectionery bar (unless it sticks in your throat or makes you sick).

Healthy diets are largely made up of healthy foods; that is, whole, fresh or lightly processed perishable foods such as vegetables, legumes, fruit, wholegrain bread and cereals, lean meat, all kinds of fish, and unsaturated oils used for cooking and salads. Unhealthy foods, by contrast, are high in calories and low in nourishment; they tend to be fatty and/or sugary, often salty too, and are usually highly processed with long shelf-lives. Good food goes bad; the trick is to eat it when it's fresh.

Curiously, healthy food is not the same as 'health food'. Health food shops may stock some healthy food, but make most of their money selling vitamin and mineral pills and other concoctions. Better news is that the big supermarket chains have now got the message, in response to national healthy food campaigns and consumer demand. Economies of scale, vigorous competition and tough deals with suppliers, mean that well-stocked supermarkets now supply a great range of well-priced healthy foods. (See Diet; Processing; Whole foods.) *GC*

Heart disease

Every year around a quarter of a million British people die from heart attacks and other diseases of the circulatory system. The rates of premature suffering and death from heart attacks in Britain and in Northern Ireland are higher than in any other countries in the European Union. This is a national disgrace, because it is now well known that the key underlying cause of heart disease is the typical highly processed fatty, sugary, salty British diet, together with cigarette smoking.

The British government is committed to a policy of prevention of heart disease by means of a healthy diet. This now goes beyond advice to individuals. A national Nutrition Task Force set up by government in 1992 is finding ways and means to achieve a national diet containing less fat, especially saturated fat, as recommended in the official White Paper, *The Health of the Nation*.

Agreed targets now include a policy to encourage the production and consumption of healthy foods, notably fresh vegetables and fruit, cereal foods, and fish. Industry is also being asked to reformulate processed food so that it is lower in fat. Some attention is also being paid to the fact that millions of impoverished British people, including the long-term unemployed, are at high risk of heart attacks and other killer diseases simply because they cannot afford or obtain fresh food.

Standard dietary advice to reduce the risk of heart disease is reliable. The more fresh and lightly processed food such as vegetables and fruit, and wholegrain bread and cereal products you eat, the better. The more highly processed fatty, sugary, salty food you eat, the worse for your health. New scientific evidence strongly suggests that some highly processed products with long shelf-lives, including table fats, biscuits and other baked goods, that include substantial amounts of trans-fatty acids, should be cut right out. (See Diet; Fat; Health of the Nation; Trans-fatty acids.) *GC*

Herbs

Several herbs are now available fresh in supermarkets and some will grow on a sunny window-sill. Traditionally herbs are used dried when the fresh plant is not available: in fact they taste better if chopped and freeze-dried or frozen either in containers or in little blocks of ice from the ice cube tray.

Basil A large aromatic leaf which is the perfect partner for tomato salads and most Italian food. Gives an interesting flavour to cooked apples.
Bay leaves Crumble to release the flavours from the tough leaves, essential in

slow-cooking savoury dishes.

Borage Use the flowers and stems for flavouring wine cups such as Pimms. The young leaves are good in salads and the bright blue flowers look sensational as decoration for cakes and desserts.

Bouquet garni This is a small sprig each of thyme and parsley and a bay leaf which are tied together and used to flavour stews, poached fish and soups. It is normally removed before serving. For a more exotic effect also include basil, chervil, burnet, tarragon and rosemary.

Burnet The young leaves have a flavour reminiscent of cucumbers which goes well with soups, salads and drinks.

Chervil Like parsley with a hint of aniseed and good as a salad garnish and for flavouring soups, especially potato soup. Chervil sauce goes well with fish and poultry.

Chives Can be grown in a pot and sprinkled over soups and yogurts, stirred into cream cheese, scrambled eggs or jacket potato fillings. A mild onion flavour.

Coriander Introduced into Britain by the Romans, the berries are used as a spice and the leaves for flavouring soups or Middle Eastern dishes.

Dill An essential component of gravlax (marinated salmon) and good with fish generally.

Fennel The seeds have a pronounced aniseed flavour - brilliant with fish on a barbecue.

Herbes Fines A mixture of a number of chopped herbs such as tarragon, burnet, chervil, thyme, marjoram, chives and parsley. Specially good in omelettes and sauces.

Herbes de Provence Typically a mixture of dried rosemary, savoury thyme, oregano and marjoram. A convenient mixture, but to obtain a Provençal flavour you need to add plenty of tomato and garlic.

Lemon grass A citrus-flavoured staple of Thai cuisine with the disadvantage that it is usually so tough as to be inedible but is rarely removed before serving.

Lovage A celery-flavoured, parsley-like herb which makes a splendid addition to salads, stews and sauces but is so strong that a touch too much can spoil a dish completely.

Marjoram A delicate form of oregano which works well in salads, meat cheese or egg dishes.

Mint Probably the best way of destroying the subtle flavour of young lamb, mint is nevertheless delicious in many fish dishes and cold soups. Try some of the uncommon varieties such as orange, lemon and pineapple.

Oregano A form of marjoram. Italian and Greek dishes taste bland without a good sprinkling of this aromatic herb.

Parsley Rich in vitamin C, parsley is principally used with fish, in sauces for vegetables, and as a garnish.

Rosemary Marvellous with lamb, poultry and other meats and also with fruit drinks.

Sage An over-rated herb which can predominate, destroying the balance of a

dish. Used with subtlety it can add an attractively bitter note.
Sorrel Can be used either as a vegetable or a herb and has an acid taste from the oxalate present.
Tarragon Best for use in tarragon vinegar which you can make by stuffing some stalks into a bottle of cider or wine vinegar and leaving it for a month. You can then prepare the most delightful sauces and salad dressings.
Thyme A whole range of subtly different herbs under the same name, thyme was traditionally used to cure nightmares. Good with chicken, fish and Greek food. Also try Greek thyme honey. *MH*

HIV/AIDS and nutrition

The debilitating effect of the virus HIV (Human Immunodeficiency Virus) and the illness AIDS (Acquired Immunodeficiency Syndrome) has serious implications for diet. Many people who are HIV positive or who have AIDS, experience weight loss, and their diet must be adjusted accordingly to try to regain this weight. However, high sugar and high carbohydrate diets - which can assist with weight gain - can cause further symptoms such as candida.

Some of the most obvious symptoms - nausea, vomiting and diarrhoea - can inhibit the absorption of food and nutrients so even if you are eating a good, high energy diet, weight loss can continue. When this happens, your diet must be adjusted to allow for the greatest absorption of nutrients. But these symptoms can also be the result of side-effects from the drugs prescribed to treat the illness; if this is the case the effects can be minimized by consuming small, low-fat meals before taking the medication.

A good diet is essential to your health and, whilst its composition is still being debated, there is evidence that if your diet is carefully selected and monitored right from the start, it is possible that the effects of the illness can be reduced. *AU*

Honey

Cave paintings show that honey has been collected by humans for at least 10,000 years. Bees certainly deserve their busy reputation - for one to produce 450 g (1 lb) of honey it would require a flight equivalent to three times round the globe. The use of honey as a sweetening agent in food went hand in hand with its undoubted effectiveness as a wound healer; especially for burns and as a preservative (honey prevented the body of Alexander the Great from decaying).

When sugar became more widely available at the beginning of the sixteenth century, two honey-based drinks, mead and hydromel were still enjoyed, although the use of honey had declined.

Honey is about 76 per cent carbohydrate, divided fairly equally between fructose and glucose, and 23 per cent water. It contains small quantities of minerals, especially potassium and zinc, and traces of some B vitamins. If you wish to make solid honey clear, maintain it for a few days in a warm place at around 86°C, having started off the warming process in a pan of hot water. To turn clear honey crystalline, 'seed' it by stirring in a little honey of the crystal type that you wish to produce. For example, Canadian clover is very fine whereas Mexican is rather granular. *MH*

Hospital food

For several reasons, most food served to people in hospital, or brought in by relatives and friends, is inappropriate and may impede their recovery or even actually make them ill. Hospital caterers are given almost impossible budgets and are practically forced to produce dull, cheap, fatty, sugary meals; much hospital food is now 'cook-chill', that is prepared off-site and reheated at mealtimes, and thus unappetising and occasionally infected with bacteria.

Hospital dietitians and caterers are given little guidance in preparing healthy food, and many still believe that patients need 'feeding up' with fat and sugar. In fact, small amounts of freshly prepared, very nourishing food are what most ill people need and enjoy.

If you are looking after somebody in hospital, don't let them depend on hospital food. Ask them what they want to eat, and trust their judgement. Ensure a daily supply of tempting wholegrain breads, home-cooked fresh vegetable soups, plain live yogurts, and a variety of fruit (not just grapes!). Dips like hummus and guacamole are excellent for hungry patients.

Consult the ward sister for courtesy's sake, or if your relative or friend has been prescribed a special diet. And if anybody in authority objects? Be politely insistent. Patients are people, not objects: they are entitled to good food that is most likely to make them better. *GC*

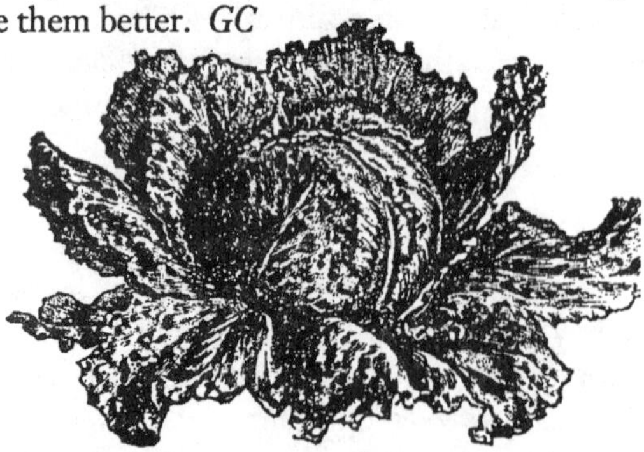

Hydrogenation

Look at the label of any manufactured food containing fat, and you will probably see that the ingredients list refers to 'hydrogenated' fat or oil, of vegetable or animal origin. This is a warning sign. The more hydrogenated fat or oil is contained in any diet, the worse it is for your health. Eating such products occasionally, say twice a week, is unlikely to do you any harm. And relatively trivial amounts of hydrogenated fat or oil, indicated by the item appearing towards the end of the ingredients list, are also unlikely to be a problem.

That said, though, hydrogenation may well turn out to be the most malign food process ever developed, and to have contributed to the premature deaths of countless millions of people from heart disease. What is it?

We all know now that saturated fats, eaten in the quantity typical in industrialized countries like Britain, are a major cause of heart disease; and that unsaturated fats, eaten in modest amounts, are relatively healthy. From the chemical point of view, 'saturation' refers to the amount of hydrogen attached to any fat molecule.

Hydrogenation is an industrial process whereby fats and oils are rendered more saturated by manipulation of their molecules, so that more hydrogen is introduced. The process was invented early this century, and enables manufacturers to turn the cheapest oils and fats on the world market into uniform products. Like sugar and salt, saturated fat is a useful commodity. Unsaturated fats and oils are unstable and go rancid: saturated fats travel and store well. The hydrogenation process has enabled grocers everywhere to stock a range of packaged branded fatty products with long shelf-lives; it is very good for business, but not for health. Happily, mass availability of industrial and domestic refrigeration is now encouraging consumers in rich countries to prefer nourishing, perishable foods.

At the same time the food industry is beginning to find ways and means to reduce the amounts of hydrogenated fats and oils in processed foods. This change for the better will be speeded up if you make a habit of telling your supermarket manager that you prefer not to buy products that include hydrogenated fats and oils. (See Processing; Saturated fats; Trans-fatty acids.) *GC*

Hyperactivity

(See Food intolerance.)

Hypertension

High blood pressure (hypertension) is epidemic in countries whose food supply contains a lot of salt; these include industrialized countries like Britain, and countries whose diet traditionally includes a lot of salted food, such as Japan and Portugal. High blood pressure is a symptom of diseased blood vessels, and commonly leads to stroke. The earlier in life you protect your health by avoiding salted foods and using little if any salt in cooking and at table, the better. For savour, use herbs instead. (See Blood pressure; Salt; Stroke.) *GC*

Hypoglycaemia

The term usually refers to unhealthy or even dangerously low blood-sugar levels literally, low ('hypo'), glucose ('glyc'), blood ('aemia'). The condition can be caused by consuming sugared foods and drinks. (See Blood sugar; Diabetes.) *GC*

Ice cream

Traditionally ice cream is made of milk, cream, sugar and eggs and you can still find specialist quality ice creams made to this traditional recipe. But the vast majority of ice cream eaten in the UK is made of air and water whipped up with fat, sugar and milk powder, with additives such as emulsifiers and stabilizers to make it look like the real thing. Colours and flavourings are often used to disguise the lack of real ingredients. Ice cream is rich in fat and sugar and loaded with calories. You may prefer to indulge only occasionally and pay the extra to enjoy the real thing. *SD*

Immunity

(See Colds; HIV.)

Intestinal bacteria

Our first line of defence against bacterial infection is our own bacteria, one-cell organisms that have evolved with us and live in vast profusion on our skin, within all the openings of our bodies (notably the mouth and nose, the ears, the vagina and the back passage), and in greatest numbers of all within the colon or bowel. We are brought up to believe that bacteria are bad, and that a clean, healthy body is bug-free. But in fact, almost all the bacteria on and in us are harmless or positively useful. The bacteria or 'flora' in our colon amount to a vital organ of the body; they are intrinsic to digestion, produce nutrients, and protect the integrity of the gut wall.

Our good health depends on nourishing not only ourselves but also our friendly flora. The best kind of diet for gut health is high in fibre, and low in meat and sugar. There is some evidence that fermented foods rich in benign bacterial species are generally beneficial to health; live sugar-free yogurt either eaten or applied to the affected place, may help to replace species of friendly flora devastated by antibiotics. (See Bowel diseases; Diet.) *GC*

Iodine

Iodine, mostly found in the surface soil and the sea, is essential for the production of thyroxine and try-iodothyronine which are necessary for optimal cellular metabolism, normal growth and development. Iodine deficiency can cause goitre, a swelling which used to be called Derbyshire Neck and is widespread in other parts of the world. Kelp is a valuable supplementary source of iodine. Following the identification of large fluctuations in the content, manufacturers are controlling the iodine levels so that the daily dose does not exceed 0.5 mg iodine. The World Health Organization (WHO) suggests a daily intake of up to 0.2 mg to eradicate iodine deficiency. The average British diet provides 0.25 mg. *MH*

IQ and diet

Recent studies on the effects of vitamin and mineral supplementation in increasing IQ are divided in their results and research is still in progress. It seems to me likely that children on a good diet do not need to take supplements but that children with poor diets could well benefit in a general sense from vitamin and mineral supplements appropriate to their age.

The educational benefits of a nutritious diet were confirmed in a major study in 803 schools in New York City State, carried out by Dr Liz Cagan in the early eighties. In spite of having excellent teachers, many of the school children had been ill behaved and on the widely used annual CAT test, had a very low level of educational attainment. Over a four-year period and with well organised inter-reaction with the pupils, the nutritionists and catering staff aimed to provide meals that were enjoyable and from which they progressively eliminated artificial colours, flavours and the preservatives BHA and BHT (E320 - E321). The sugar content of foods was also reduced so that the maximum contribution was about 11 per cent of calories.

The results were astounding. There was a 15.7 per cent increase in mean academic ranking over and above the rest of the nation's schools using the same tests. Before the changes the variations had been less than 1 per cent. Behaviour improved and Dr Cagan, on a visit, was given an ovation by the pupils at what had been the roughest school in New York. What is more the new meals system, which began with breakfast, cost no more than before. (See School meals.) *MH*

Iron

Iron is necessary to form haemoglobin in red blood cells, which is responsible for the transfer of oxygen from the lungs, myoglobin in muscles and also as part of some enzymes. There are two sorts of iron in the diet: haem in meat and meat products, of which about 25 per cent is absorbed by the body, and non-haem from bread, cereal products, vegetables and fruits, which represents about 90 per cent of our dietary iron intake. Non-haem absorption depends on the rest of the diet, being improved by the presence of vitamin C, fish and meat and reduced by phytate (found in wholemeal flour) and calcium. Especially good food sources of iron, apart from meat, are pulses, whole grains, nuts, dark green leafy vegetables and dried fruits.

Only about 15 per cent of the total iron eaten is ultimately absorbed. This can rise to 17 per cent for massive meat eaters and reduce to 5 per cent with vegetarian diets low in vitamin C. Recommended daily iron intake for men is 10 mg and for women 12 mg. Women of child-bearing age lose some 26 mg iron per month during menstruation and need 5 - 6 mg extra daily during the last three months of pregnancy to prevent anaemia.

Iron is a powerful oxidizer, thus excess intake can neutralize the effectiveness of antioxidant nutrients in destroying excess free radicals. (See A.C.E.) *MH*

Irradiation

To many scientists, food irradiation seemed to offer great possibilities when they discovered that bombarding fresh foods with ionizing radiation made them last longer. But this new technology caused a huge controversy during the 1980s when the government wanted to lift the ban on irradiating food. Consumers soon realized that irradiated food would look fresh but would actually be old, stale and contain fewer vitamins. And despite promises that irradiated food would be labelled, this quick-fix technology has not gained the support and confidence of the public or supermarkets.

Despite this opposition, the government did lift the ban in 1991, although so far the technology has only been used to irradiate herbs and spices. But with no accepted test for irradiation, it is hard to know whether other foods, irradiated abroad, are being imported and sold without proper labelling in the UK. *SD*

Irritable Bowel Syndrome

(See Bowel disease.)

j

Juices

Fruit juices can be an enjoyable and easy way of eating fruit. But you do lose out on valuable nutrients - juice contains 30 - 50 per cent less vitamin C and virtually none of the fibre of fruit. The processing also destroys the cell structure so that the fruit sugars in fruit juices are just as damaging to teeth as other sweet drinks; they should always be well diluted for babies and young children.

Real fruit juice is available in concentrated form. Fresh fruit juice has a short shelf-life, even in the refrigerator, and will ferment after a relatively short while. Fruit drinks are often sold to look like pure juices but contain only a small amount of real fruit juice. Instead they are made up with lots of added water, and often with added sugar as well as colouring agents, stabilizers and artificial sweeteners.

Government tests have also revealed problems with the composition of some juices. In one set of tests some pure orange juices were found to contain added sugar above the legal limit. And in other tests some apple juices were found to contain small amounts of a toxin, patulin. This caused a storm of protest from consumer groups as the Ministry refused to name which brands were affected and tried to keep the test results secret. Alar, a chemical sprayed on fruit trees, was withdrawn when it was found that residues remained in apple juice, but only after parents and consumer groups led a fight to get it banned. *SD*

Junk Food

The term junk food was coined to describe foods considered to be intrinsically bad for you: burgers and chips, crisps, sweets and chocolate are commonly condemned with this title. It's a misleading classification because there is no such thing as a bad food, only a bad diet. Eaten in moderation and as part of a mixed and balanced plan, these foods can prove a valuable source of nutrients. Of course, if you or your children's diet is made up solely or mainly from these foods, then it will be unbalanced and need adjusting. *AU*

k

Kilojoules

Kilojoules are the metric measurement for calculating energy and will eventually take the place of the calorie. (See Calories.) *AU*

Kitchen hygiene and safety

It is important to remember a few basic hygiene rules in the kitchen to ensure that you and your family eat safely.

1. Keep all working surfaces scrupulously clean.
2. Wash all utensils and chopping boards after they have come into contact with raw meat, poultry or eggs, to prevent cross-contamination with foods that will not be cooked.
3. Wash your hands before preparing food.
4. Wash all food thoroughly, including salads and raw fruit and vegetables.
5. Wash dishcloths and tea-towels regularly. Leaving washing up to drain or using a dishwasher is more hygienic than using a tea-towel.
6. Don't leave food standing around in the kitchen.
7. Cool cooked food as quickly as possible, then refrigerate.
8. Keep waste-bins covered and away from food. Clean them regularly with disinfectant.
9. Keep pets off work surfaces and away from food.

Your fridge should be kept between 0° and 5°C to prevent the growth of food-poisoning bacteria. Place a fridge thermometer near the centre and regularly check the temperature, after the door has been closed for some time, such as first thing in the morning. Remember to defrost your fridge regularly; don't overload it or leave the door open for too long. It is important that cooked and raw foods are kept separate. Covering foods will prevent cross-contamination and stop food from drying out or making the fridge smell. Most importantly, follow 'use-by' instructions. (See Food poisoning; Microwaving.) *SD*

l

Labelling

When so much of our food comes processed and packaged, we rely on labelling to tell us what it is we are actually buying. But these days, it can sometimes seem as if you need a degree in chemistry to understand all the small-print. Learning some basic ways to read food labels can help you make more informed choices.

By law, food labels must give information such as the weight of the product, the name of the manufacturer and a 'best before' or 'eat by' date. Most foods, with certain exceptions, must also include a list of ingredients. Ingredients must be listed in descending order by weight: thus the first ingredient is the largest. So you can, to some extent, judge the quality of products by seeing how the amount of added water or sugar compares with the weight of other, more nutritious ingredients. The ingredients list also includes additives, indicated by an 'E' number. A long list of E numbers, including colourings, flavourings and thickeners, probably means there is very little 'real' food in the product.

The 'minimum meat content' some meat products are obliged to declare is supposed to indicate how much meat you can expect to find. But what the law allows manufacturers to mean by the word 'meat' and what a customer means, are not the same. Legally 'meat' can include a hefty proportion of fat, and lean meat can include heart, kidney, tongue, tail and head meat, and even brains, feet, intestines, udder and testicles in some canned meats and soups.

But for other foods it can be impossible to tell how much of the main ingredient a product contains, for example, the amount of fish in a fish finger or the amount of juice in a fruit drink. The EC wants to see food giving a 'quantitative ingredient declaration' or 'QUID', as it has been termed. This would be good news for consumers, but British food manufacturers are not rushing to give us the information.

Even when there are definitions they can be confusing. For example, 'orange-flavoured' means that some real orange has been used, but food described as 'orange-flavour' won't have seen any hint of real orange.

It's wise to beware of bold claims on the front of packets. That low-fat claim may hide the fact that the product is crammed with salt and sugar. And the more a packaged product claims to be 'traditional' or 'farmhouse' with pictures of idyllic rural scenes, you can bet it's never been anywhere nearer the countryside than the M25.

Although consumers say they want more information about a food's nutritional value, manufacturers are not obliged to provide any. And even when some basic information on the amount of energy, protein, carbohydrate and total fat is given, it isn't really too much help. We're advised to cut back on our saturated fat, sugar and salt and increase dietary fibre, yet far too few labels actually give any information about these nutrients.

However hard you look you won't find much information about some of the processes the food has been through. Nothing will be said about the fertilizers, pesticides, storage methods, fumigants, processing methods, solvents, lubricants or packaging used to bring the product to you. It's difficult not to assume that many manufacturers don't always want their customers to know exactly what they are eating. *SD*

Lactose and lactose intolerance

Lactose is milk sugar to which a significant proportion of people in the USA and UK are to some extent intolerant. Symptoms of lactose intolerance are a lot of wind, diarrhoea and cramps following eating milky products. The only remedy is to avoid them. When milk becomes yogurt it undergoes changes which make it suitable for most lactose-intolerant people, who can only take small quantities of milk or ice cream. The art is to test your threshold of tolerance. *MH*

Laxatives

Pregnant women and the elderly are frequently constipated but those eating mostly refined foods can also be in trouble. Laxatives work to prevent constipation either by increasing the bulk of stools, as with bran, or by making the gut work faster, as with senna.

Laxatives are sometimes sold to help weight loss but, like diuretics, any benefit is temporary and excessive use can be damaging.

The use of laxatives can usually be avoided by increasing dietary fibre in the diet by eating more wholemeal bread, brown rice, beans, live yogurt and fruits, especially grapes, dates, prunes and figs. Beer can have a laxative effect. If all else fails use a gentle laxative from time to time such as one based on a little senna leaf, or concentrated fibre and fruit. Exercise the abdomen as well. *MH*

Legumes

Derived from the Latin word for pod, the term describes all plants which carry their seeds in pods. Peas and lentils as well as beans are legumes. They are sometimes referred to as farinaceous plants, meaning that a flour can be made from the dried seeds. (See Pulses.) *CS*

Lifespan

The Bible seems to have been not so far out when it referred to 'three score years and ten' as being the natural healthy human lifespan, after which decline and decay set in. In rich countries relatively free from pestilence, famine and war, average lifespans now are not greatly different, varying from early to mid-seventies for men, and middle to late seventies for women.

Does this mean that we are prisoners of our genes, mostly programmed to die in or around our seventies? Some leading scientists believe not, and claim that the average maximum human lifespan can be extended to 100 years and more. Backed by experiments on animals and plausible reasoning, such scientists recommend a diet low in calories and very high in nourishment. This means virtual elimination of saturated fats, sugars and alcohol, whose calories are empty of nourishment, and abundant consumption of fresh foods of vegetable origin, together with megadoses of anti-oxidant vitamins and other nutrients believed to protect genes against damage. Will this work? Time will tell.

Killer diseases such as heart attacks and cancers very often cause prolonged illness and misery for several or many years before death; and what many middle-aged people understandably fear is an old age ruined by pain, illness and disability. It certainly is true that a nourishing diet increases your chances of prolonged health - more life in your years, if not years in your life. (See A.C.E.; Diet; Healthy food.) *GC*

Low birth weights

Research has linked a low birth weight with the development in later life of health problems such as high blood pressure, which is a factor in the development of heart disease and stroke. And the diet you eat at the beginning of pregnancy is much more strongly associated with its outcome and the birth weight of the baby than what you eat later on in pregnancy.

While a number of factors, including smoking, are linked to small birth weight babies, women who make poor weight gain during pregnancy are two and a half times more likely to give birth to small babies. And women who are underweight at the time they conceive are about twice as likely to have small babies. In the UK every year, 54,000 babies are born underweight - that's 6.8 per cent of all births, which compares unfavourably with other countries in the west. In Scandinavia for example, only 2 per cent of births result in low-weight babies. (See Pregnancy; Diet.) *SD*

Low-fat foods

For all practical purposes, the less fat you eat, the better for your health. Do you want to stay slim, or lose weight? Eat less fat. Do you want to reduce your risk of a heart attack and of common cancers? Eat less fat.

Foods naturally low in fat are good for you. Fresh vegetables and fruits are full of nourishment and almost free of fat, with the odd exception like avocado pears. Wholegrain bread and cereals contain small amounts of fat, of the healthy unsaturated variety as contained in the germ of the grain. Eat all these abundantly.

However, ironically, many manufactured foods advertised as 'low-fat' are misleading. Watch out! It is fair enough for bread and breakfast cereal manufacturers to boast that their products are low-fat; and if cereal products are low in sugar and salt and preferably wholegrain, they are indeed good for you. Similarly, fully skimmed milk contains very little fat. But so-called 'low-fat' meat products are usually still very fatty; the 'low-fat' sausage is a contradiction in terms. Often what 'low-fat' really means is 'lower-fat'; reduction from extremely fatty to very fatty, or very fatty to fatty.

Also the so-called 'nutritional' lists on the labels of processed foods list their fat content as a percentage of the weight of the food. This is highly misleading; what you really need to know is the fat content as a percentage of total energy or calories. Take a sausage (or most meat products). The percentage of fat by weight will be around 25 per cent, which makes them seem a low-fat product, compared with the now well-known recommendation that we should all cut down our fat consumption to 30 - 35 per cent or lower. But this means percentage of total calories: and around 70 per cent or more of the calories of meat products are from fat.

Likewise, some prepared foods that have acquired a bit of a health image, such as quiches, are loaded with fat. If you can't tell by looking or tasting whether any manufactured food is fatty (and this shouldn't be difficult: if it makes your hands or mouth greasy, it's fatty), look at the ingredients' list on the label. If 'fat' or 'oil' is listed near the top of the list, it's fatty. *GC*

Low income: is it possible to eat healthily?

The cost of healthy eating continues to cause controversy. There has been a prevailing attitude, particularly from politicians, that healthy eating is cheaper than unhealthy eating and that the poor could eat healthily if only they chose more wisely.

In fact studies have shown that pound for pound, low- income consumers buy calories much more efficiently than higher-income shoppers. While families on low income spend about half the amount of money on fresh fruit and vegetables compared with more affluent families, this is understandable when it's far cheaper to fill up on cheap fatty, sugary foods such as biscuits than on fruit.

And it's not only money that makes shopping for a healthier diet difficult on a low income. Getting to a supermarket, where prices are cheaper than in local shops, can be difficult and expensive without a car. Lack of storage or cooking facilities can also make feeding the family more expensive.

As levels of poverty continue to increase in the UK there is growing evidence that poverty equals poor nutrition. *SD*

Nutritional tips: The clever way to maximize little money is to cook with basic raw ingredients. For example, a minestrone soup can contain different green vegetables, an assortment of beans, wholemeal pasta, carrots, onions and be accompanied with wholemeal bread, perhaps home-made. This deeply satisfying dish is nutritionally complete if sprinkled with grated cheese.

Potatoes baked in their jackets and filled with fish, spiced meat or cheese, accompanied by a salad, provides the complete spectrum of nutritional needs.

Eggs, dairy products, lean tough cuts of meat that take a long time to cook but taste wonderful, such as oxtail, flank and stewing steak are just as nutritious as their expensive counterparts and no less delicious.

At closing time at street markets, especially Saturday afternoons, fine foods of all sorts are available for very low prices.

Schools should be encouraged to teach the art of cheap healthy cookery and sensible choices from infancy. That will give parents a lot less trouble at home than when they have to compete with the fast-food outlets.

At all income levels it is bad psychology and poor nutrition to feed children separately. Try to make time for at least one coming-together daily, when the family can share a meal and talk through the problems and triumphs of the day. (Many of the one-pot dishes in the 'World in a Stew' section make economical meals.) *MH*

Lunch Boxes

For children who do not eat a school meal, a packed lunch is the most popular alternative. But surveys have shown that sandwiches, crisps, biscuits, fizzy drinks and chocolate top the list of favourite lunch-box foods. Fruit is far less popular. Children need the right balance of nutrients and vitamins for fitness and concentration. While encouraging youngsters into healthier eating habits is not always easy, here are a few suggestions to make their lunch-box more nutritious as well as enjoyable.

1. Try using different kinds of bread and don't get into a rut with fillings. Remember variety is the spice of life.
2. Slices of delicious home-made pizza can be stored in the freezer for lunch-boxes.
3. For something sweet, give children a small pot of low-fat yogurt or fromage frais but avoid the ones with lots of added sugar.
4. Fresh fruit such as apples, pears, seedless grapes, bananas, oranges or satsumas are very refreshing and nutritious. For younger children peel the fruit and cut it into small pieces so they'll be able to enjoy it more easily.
5. Dried fruit such as dates, figs or apricots are yummy and small packs of nuts and raisins will provide a healthier alternative to crisps.
6. Cartons of pure fruit juices will provide a vitamin- packed thirst-quencher.

SD

m

Macrobiotic diet

Also known as the Zen Macrobiotic diet. This is a sort of naturopathic diet, influenced by the traditional Japanese diet; as such uses wholegrain (brown) rice and tofu (soya curds) as staples. Extreme versions in which rice makes up almost all the diet can be dangerous. It also proposes that any exotic food (natural to foreign climates) should be avoided. In other respects it is rational and very healthy.

Zen macrobiotics is a way of life as well as a diet, to the point of being a modern quasi-religion. In this it is similar to Rastafarianism; Rastas also eat a highly-nourishing largely wholefood diet. Enthusiasts say that the macrobiotic diet can be a successful treatment for serious diseases, including cancer.

People who follow the macrobiotic way of life emphasize the value of awareness, family and community, and see cooking, dancing, meditation, massage and other personal and social skills as means to enlightenment and mutual support. They are therefore sometimes dismissed as freaks. (See Naturopathy; Zen macrobiotics.) *GC*

Mail order foods

We are seeing an increase in mail order foods and a wide variety such as smoked salmon, clotted cream and smoked meats can now be bought by mail order. But according to the Consumers' Association too many mail order companies are not taking enough care with hygiene. Of the 100 products tested by the Consumers' Association in 1993, half were judged to be of good microbiological quality; a third fell into a 'could be better' category; seventeen samples had worryingly high bacterial counts and were rated as 'dubious'. These wouldn't necessarily give you food poisoning provided the foods were kept in a fridge and eaten within a couple of days, but the high number of bacteria indicated poor standards of hygiene, poor temperature control, over-long storage, or a combination of all of these.

Many of the foods tested would, if sold in shops, by law need to be kept in chill cabinets at low temperatures. Mail order foods are exempt from these regulations.

If buying by mail, use companies that can deliver in 24 hours or which

guarantee chilled delivery. Don't eat the food if the inner packaging is swollen or if you are unsure about the smell or appearance. Ask the supplier for a replacement.
SD

Margarine

The first version of margarine was invented in France in the 1870s as a cheap substitute for butter. Then early this century, the hydrogenation process was developed, and margarine became mass-manufactured in a big way. Very hard block margarines made out of the cheapest oils on the world market, turned into solid fat with a long shelf-life by the hydrogenation process, undersold butter and became a staple food for the working classes.

Hard margarines should be phased out of the human food supply, everywhere in the world. They taste awful. Their fat is intensely saturated and also contains substantial amounts of trans-fatty acids, which may well prove to be more noxious than saturates. Recently, manufacturers have promoted softer margarines as healthy products. These are relatively high in polyunsaturated fats, while still containing substantial though variable amounts of saturated and trans-fats. More impudent manufacturers have made health claims for spreads that are margarine or mixtures of butter and margarine, diluted with water or air, both of which are even cheaper than fat.

The story that some types of margarine are positively good for you, is one of the great advertising and marketing campaign successes of the late twentieth century, and has been backed by a large number of reputable scientists. It may very well may turn out to be incorrect. Margarines and other table spreads are artificial products; you don't need them and are probably better off without them. (See Hydrogenation; Trans-fatty acids.) *GC*

Meat

The butchered carcasses of dead animals prepared for cooking. The eating of meat came late in the evolutionary scale. Primates are herbivores, the small amounts of insects they eat have not changed their dentistry, nor has the group killing of tiny mammals which is both arbitrary and opportunistic. Hominid fossils dating back three million years ago were also herbivores. Hunting started around one and a half million years ago, but before then it is believed that early humans became scavengers of the kill left by the great cats, eating the brains and bone marrow. It has also been estimated that once hunting began, meat would only have occupied about one-tenth of the diet - berries, fruits, pods, seeds, grasses, roots and leaves made up the rest. As fire was not discovered until 150,000 years ago there were one million, three hundred and fifty thousand years of raw meat chewing and it seems likely drying and salting of meat must have been discovered, probably by accident, in that long span of time. The herding of flocks began around 30,000 years ago with the killing of the young

males (leaving one prime stud) as the main source of meat. Domestication began 10,000 years ago. (See Farm animals.)

In early societies the number of livestock kept by a farmer represented wealth and power. Livestock was only killed on special occasions, festivities and ritual celebrations. Throughout history the ruling class ate the most meat because they represented the dominating power in the society. However, that amount of meat would still not be anything like the quantity that society now consumes and which has been growing for the last fifty years. Fifteen billion livestock are now slaughtered each year worldwide.

The meat that is reared today is very different from what was eaten in the past. Because of modern feeding methods animals now carry a great deal more saturated fat upon them. Wild beasts have a minuscule amount of fat and what there is tends to be polyunsaturated. Therefore meat eating today has become a major health problem, as well as raising major problems for the environment.

Today, meat is sold everywhere, you do not have to visit the butcher's. And although there has been a noticeable move away from the eating of meat, especially red meat, in the last fifteen years in both the UK and the USA, a very small percentage of people are truly vegetarian. (See Vegetarian.) *CS*

Nutritional note: Lean meat is a good source of high-quality protein. A 100 g (4 oz) portion of beef, for example, provides 20 g or ¾ oz of protein which is a third of the recommended daily intake for women and men.

Other notable nutrients in meat include the minerals iron and zinc. Both are particularly well absorbed when eaten in meat rather than from plants. The B vitamins are also well represented, especially B_{12} which comes mainly from animal products.

Lean cuts of meat are more expensive than their fatty counterparts. However, in real terms you are getting more nutrients for your money with lean cuts, although it sometimes doesn't look that way. You can make good-quality meat go further by extending it with other ingredients, for example adding red kidney beans to lean mince to make chilli con carne. *AU*

Mechanically Recovered Meat

Mechanically recovered meat (MRM) can appear in chicken and turkey burgers, sausages, meatballs, ravioli, faggots, salami and other convenience foods. MRM is a slurry made from all the tiny scraps of meat, flesh, sinew and cartilage still clinging to the bones, plus all the seemingly inedible scraps from the carcass. There is no legislation which says that a food manufacturer must indicate MRM on the food label. *CS*

Mediterranean diet

The term 'Mediterranean diet' has been adopted to describe the kind of diet traditionally eaten by people in southern Mediterranean countries, in particular southern Italy. The mainstay of their diet is starchy carbohydrates like pasta and bread. They eat plenty of fresh vegetables and fruits which are rich in antioxidant nutrients (see Antioxidants), have lots of fish and seafood and eat relatively small amounts of meat and dairy products. Fat in the diet comes almost exclusively from olive oil which is rich in unsaturated fats and low in saturated fats.

Over the past ten years or so, convincing evidence has begun to emerge that eating along these nutritional lines may protect against heart disease and some kinds of cancers. It has therefore become a popular way of describing the perfect kind of healthy diet. Whilst we can never hope to bring the sunshine and all of the glorious local foods of the Mediterranean to our tables in this country, we can adapt our diets to a similar style. We may prefer potatoes to pasta as a main source of starchy carbohydrate and some vegetables may be frozen instead of fresh. It's the balance of different food groups that counts.

The Mediterranean style of eating is exactly what is being suggested in the government's *Health of the Nation* document and by all the bodies working with them, including the British Dietetic Association, the Health Education Authority, the Ministry of Agriculture, Fisheries and Food and the Department of Health. *AU*

Metabolism

Our food supplies the chemicals for anabolic growth, renewal and repair, balancing the catabolic activities that cause cells to decay. The amount and quality of the food we eat profoundly influences the metabolic outcome. Too little and you grow thin, the wrong balance and you become unhealthy. Consume too much and you grow fat. The body's storage system was designed to survive the famines that are still so common in the Third World though rare in ours.

We all have different basal metabolic rates (BMRs) which indicate the minimum amount of energy required to sustain the processes of life. That is why some people with high BMRs can eat like a horse and stay thin and others with low BMRs eat much less and grow fat. *AU*

Microwaving

The majority of families now own a microwave and find that for defrosting and reheating food and for cooking vegetables and fish quickly and efficiently they can be extremely useful.

But microwave ovens may be less efficient than conventional ovens at destroying the bacteria that cause food poisoning. Sometimes they can fail to heat food evenly, leaving so-called cold spots where temperatures may not be high enough to kill potentially harmful bacteria. Therefore it's important to follow microwave cooking instructions carefully and ensure foods are properly cooked to at least 70°C for at least two minutes. Don't ignore standing times and if possible stir and turn foods, particularly if your microwave does not have a turntable. (See Food poisoning.)

The government asked food manufacturers to improve microwave cooking instructions to specify cooking times for different power-rated ovens. While information is now generally clearer, the Consumers' Association has found that some problems of uneven heating still remain. If ready-meals do not feature microwave cooking instructions, assume that they are unsuitable for reheating in a microwave oven.

Contrary to some people's fears, microwaves are unable to leak out from ovens. It is important, though, to remember to keep the oven, particularly the door and hinge areas, clean and free from food deposits. If you find any signs of corrosion or if the oven has been damaged in some way, arrange for the machine to be serviced. *SD*

Migraine

(See Food intolerance.)

Milk

Secretion from female mammals to feed their offspring, between the time of birth and the end of infancy. The milk of each species of mammal is nutritiously tailored to benefit their particular needs. Cow's milk is designed to build a strong bone structure in the calf. Human milk is intended to build up the nervous system and varies in composition during the first few weeks according to the baby's needs. The milk of each species transfers immunity to its offspring.

Homo sapiens has used the milk of sheep, goats, cattle and mares as a food since pre-history. But as raw milk quickly becomes sour it was used largely to make yogurt, sour milk drinks, cheeses and butter, while the whey only was drunk.

A great amount of cow's milk is drunk today. There is a myth that this is a healthy food for adults because it contains quantities of essential nutrients like protein and calcium. Unfortunately, the protein of cow's milk contains an insoluble substance, caseinogen, which is difficult to digest; this helps to form mucous and clogs the system. Eighty per cent of the world's adults are also lactose-intolerant and cannot digest milk at all. These peoples need not be deficient in calcium, however, sunflower seeds contain as much calcium as milk, kale leaves more than twice as much, sesame seeds about eleven times as much and sea vegetables over thirteen times as much.

Milk and its products are the main source of saturated fats in our diet. The over-consumption of milk leads to storage of excess fats in the circulatory system, the joints and the organs. Hard physical labour or living in a cold climate help to burn off this excess fat. Many people now prefer to drink skimmed or semi-skimmed milk which is lower in fat. But the fat skimmed from the milk goes into yogurts, frozen desserts and ice cream, and the sales of these products are rising, so the total fat from milk consumed in the diet remains unchanged. *CS*

Minerals

Minerals are non-carbon based nutrients which make up substantial parts of our body structure and like vitamins are frequently necessary in bodily processes (see Table). There are about 20 key minerals found in the human body with an average adult having a total of 3 kilos, most of which is in the bones. The trace elements are simply minerals found in small quantities in the body. (See Calcium.) *MH*

Minerals and trace elements

Mineral	*RDA*	*Upper Safe Level*	*Mineral*
Calcium	800mg	none	Necessary for bones and teeth in conjunction with excercise and vitamin D.
Phosphorus	800mg	1.5mg	Necessary for healthy bones, energy transfer and storage processes.
Fluoride	none	1mg	Commonly used for promoting dental health and cutting down decay. An excess mottles the tooth enamel and occurs when water supplies contain more than 1mg of fluoride per litre. It is dangerous in large doses.
Selenium	Proposed EC RDA 55µg	450µg	Helps protect against oxidation and free radical damage. Between 50–100mg a day is a safe supplementary level.
Copper	Proposed EC RDA 1.1mg	2mg	Essential for cellular energy and the production of connective tissue. High doses above 10mg per day can cause nausea and 2mg is a reasonable upper limit for supplementation.
Manganese	An acceptable range of intakes would seem to be between 1 and 10mg		Necessary for growth and for many cellular functions.
Molybdenum	none	3mg	An essential trace element which takes part in a number of cellular processes.
Potassium	Proposed EC RDA 3100mg	5000mg	Used for the electrochemical physiology of nerves and muscles. The large quantities in fruit and vegetables could help keep blood pressure stable.
Magnesium	An acceptable daily intake would seem to lie between 150–500mg		Used in the regulation of cellular metabolism in the synthesis of proteins. An excess can cause diarrhoea.

Ministry of Agriculture

The Ministry of Agriculture, Fisheries and Food (MAFF) is responsible for the nation's food, along with sponsorship of the British food manufacturing industry. Nutrition policies are devised in partnership with the Department of Health. MAFF is formally committed to the goals for prevention of disease by means of good food set out in the government white paper, the Health of the Nation. (See COMA panels; Department of Health; the Health of the Nation.) *GC*

Modified atmosphere packaging

New packaging techniques have been developed to extend the shelf-life of fresh foods such as meat, fruit and vegetables, fish, ready-meals and pasta. Modified atmosphere packaging replaces most of the oxygen in food packaging with carbon dioxide and nitrogen. This slows the growth of some spoilage organisms to such an extent that food looks, tastes and smells fresh for weeks instead of days. Vacuum packaging keeps foods in anaerobic (no-oxygen) conditions and thus prolongs shelf-life.

However, if bacteria are not killed or if the food is contaminated during processing, the extended shelf-life can give dangerous bacteria the opportunity to reach high levels before the food is eaten. Botulism is of particular concern as the bacteria responsible grows in the absence of oxygen. So it is vitally important that foods produced in this way meet high standards of manufacturing practices; strict hygiene, adequate refrigeration (during transport and in the supermarket cabinet) and thorough cooking. Unlike France, the UK has no legislation to cover these technologies but the industry has developed it own code of practice and to date there have been no major problems with the safety of these products. The EC is proposing that all modified atmosphere packaged foods should be labelled as such. *SD*

Monosodium glutamate (MSG) E621

Since ancient times Japanese cooks used stock from the sea-weed *Laminaria japonica* to bring a delicious flavour called umami to savoury food. The active substance was purified in 1908 and found to be glutamic acid. MSG is the sodium salt of this amino-acid which makes up about 20 per cent of the protein in the average diet. MSG is usually made by the fermentation of cane or beet molasses and is widely used in Chinese cooking. A few people are adversely affected by MSG, an effect sometimes known as Chinese Restaurant Syndrome. Some take-aways and restaurants use far too much. I believe in using the tail rather than the bowl of the teaspoon as a measure and my guests have thrived. *MH*

Monounsaturated fats

These are good for you, if consumed sparingly. The best source is first-pressing 'extra-virgin' olive oil. Like any fat and oil these will make you fat if you eat too much. (See Polyunsaturated fats; Saturated fats.) *GC*

Mussels

A bivalve mollusc which clings to rocks and breakwaters. Easily gathered, it is one of the oldest foods of human kind. Mussels that are damaged or open should be thrown away, for it means that the mussel inside is dead.

Mussels should be washed in running water, the exterior shells scrubbed, then cooked in a saucepan with shallots and white wine as moules mariniere. All mussels that do not open after cooking must be thrown away. Once opened, mussels can have a paste of breadcrumbs, garlic, parsley and butter placed over them in each shell, then grilled. *CS*

Naturopathy

Naturopaths are doctors and therapists who avoid drugs and instead, prescribe or recommend nutrients in the form of food or pills to prevent or treat disease. They are generally regarded as cranks or quacks by the medical establishment, although quite a lot of physicians themselves use naturopathy at least as complementary therapy.

The older generation of naturopaths tend to follow Bircher-Benner (who devised the original muesli) and other pioneers, in recommending a diet mostly made up of raw food. In Britain their ideas have been popularized by Leslie Kenton in such books as Raw Energy.

Younger naturopaths tend to recommend nutrients more aggressively, in effect as drugs, in the form of pharmacological amounts or 'mega-doses' of vitamins, minerals and other micro-nutrients, in combinations devised to treat specific diseases. Medically qualified naturopaths are often members of the British Society for Nutritional Medicine.

Traditional Indian and Chinese medicine is in part naturopathic, as is herbalism. Many people have turned to naturopathy and have found it works for them, even after years of drugs and/or surgery. (See Macrobiotic diet.) *GC*

Night blindness

During the second world war the propaganda machine put it about that British pilots consumed vast quantities of carrots and thereby improved their night vision because of the beta-carotene content. The purpose of this ploy was to conceal the invention of radar. None the less, like most good stories it was based on truth.

Vitamin A is essential for good night vision and the safest way of taking it is in the form of beta-carotene which converts it into just the right amount to give the desired effect without any worries about safety. *MH*

Nitrates in food and water

The effect of nitrate consumption on human health has been a subject of controversy since the 1970s. High nitrate levels in drinking water pose a small risk to bottle-fed babies. Nitrate which is converted to nitrite has also been linked with human cancer, particularly stomach, oesophagus and bladder cancers.

In the last fifty years the amount of nitrate fertilizer that has been put onto intensively farmed agricultural land has led to pollution of some drinking water supplies, particularly in the east of England. In order to meet EC laws the government has attempted to restrict the use of fertilizers in the worst-affected areas. But many environmentalists say this does not go far enough to protect the environment and public health.

Excess nitrate levels have been found in some horticultural crops dosed with fertilizers. Nitrates and nitrites (E249 - 252) have also long been used as a preservative for cured meats such as bacon and other meat products. Cancer experts recommend limiting consumption of these foods. *SD*

Novel foods

Food technologists are constantly searching for new types of food. Margarine was originally invented as a cheaper alternative to butter. Now artificial sweeteners are used in many foods and drinks instead of sugar, and new ingredients to replace fat are in the pipeline. Soon, it seems, we will be able to eat foods that are made completely from non-food. It may sound like a dieter's dream to be able to eat cake that contains no calories, but is this really the kind of future food we want?

Quorn is one early product of this revolution in biotechnology. Derived from a fungus which is a distant relative of the mushroom, it is a low-fat source of protein. Though in itself rather tasteless, manufacturers have spiced it up with ready-made sauces.

Growing interest in health has also led to the development, particularly in Japan, of so-called 'functional foods' which are designed to help prevent ill-health. Products available in the UK include milk with added fibre, foods with added fish oils or vitamins, and bio-yogurts. However, the law does not allow manufacturers to claim that products can treat disease. *SD*

Nutritionists

Anyone can set up as a nutritionist. There's nothing stopping you reading a book on the subject and going off to start a practice advising people on what and what not to eat. To be registered as an Accredited Nutritionist by the Biological Society, however, it is necessary to have a science degree and to have specialized in nutrition, either animal or human. Courses giving a basic grounding in the subject are run by the British Nutrition Foundation. Degrees are run by several universities including London and Surrey. If you want to consult a qualified nutritionist who is also trained as a State Registered Dietitian, ask to be referred to one by your GP. *AU*

Nuts

The edible kernel or seed of fruits. There are hundreds of varieties, many of them unknown outside the area they grow in. (The macadamia nut, indigenous to the Queensland coast, was known only to the Aborigines until some time after the discovery of Australia. Nuts are rich in polyunsaturated fat (many nuts and seeds give us valuable oil), protein, carbohydrate, vitamins - particularly E - and minerals. Some can provide essential substances not always available in our general diet. One brazil nut per day, for example, contains our daily requirement of the mineral selenium. Latest research also informs us that nuts are not only an important source of dietary fibre but a valuable ally against high blood pressure and cholesterol. A study of 34,000 Americans found that those who ate a handful of nuts five times a week halved their risk of heart attacks compared with those who ate them once a week. One hypothesis is that the vitamin E prevents the oxidation of cholesterol.

Commercially the most important nuts are almonds (used for thickening in Ancient Rome and the medieval world), peanuts, hazel nuts, walnuts, chestnuts, coconuts and pistachio nuts. Nuts are used in confectionery and sweet desserts and also in savoury dishes. They are honoured as a central part of the vegan and vegetarian diet. It should be borne in mind that nuts are high in calories. *CS*

O

Oats

A cereal which, like rye, grows in northern climes, and has become a staple in the diet of northern Europe. It has certainly been cultivated since the Bronze Age. As oats do not contain gluten they cannot be used to make bread; instead, they became associated early on with porridge, made by sprinkling oats on hot water, or water and milk, stirring and then boiling, still stirring, for 20 minutes. Porridge can also be made very successfully in a microwave oven. Oats are a valuable food, one of the best sources of soluble fibre; research now shows that they are effective against cholesterol, and a daily portion will lower high blood pressure. Oatmeal is traditionally made by stone-grinding the grain, making fine, medium or coarse; fine is used for oatcakes; coarse for porridge. Rolled oats have had their husk rolled off and they are steam-softened and flattened, a process called 'pearling'. The heating destroys the enzymes which would react with the fat and make the meal go rancid. Oats are also the main ingredient in muesli, the breakfast dish that Dr Bircher-Benner found a Swiss shepherd eating at the beginning of the century and subsequently made fashionable as a health food. *CS*

Obesity

Although many of us believe that we are over-weight and may diet constantly, only a relatively small proportion of people really do need to lose weight. The figures in the UK for people suffering from clinical obesity are not vast, but on the other hand there is a steady increase in the problem. Whilst the causes for obesity are not fully established, a high-fat diet and an increasingly sedentary life-style can be held partly responsible.

Being seriously overweight carries an increased risk of several life-threatening diseases including heart disease, adult onset diabetes and certain forms of cancer. Less serious illnesses can include osteoarthritis and joint problems. As well as physical problems there is the increased psychological pressure placed on seriously overweight people as a result of social attitudes and discrimination.

Long-term changes in diet and life-style can result in weight loss which if carefully maintained and monitored can greatly improve health and well- being. (See Body image; Weight; Slimming.) *AU*

Oils

As a general rule, hard fats are bad for you; liquid oils used sparingly are good for you. Fats are relatively saturated; oils are relatively unsaturated. Exceptions to this rule are coconut and palm oil: both are highly saturated, although for reasons not yet fully understood, they may be not particularly harmful to health. Food manufacturing processes that turn oils into fats, notably by means of hydrogenation, therefore have an adverse effect on human health.

Just like fats, oils are energy-dense (9 calories per gram, in contrast with roughly 4 calories per gram for protein and carbohydrate), and fats, oils and any greasy foods are therefore liable to make you fat.

Margarine manufacturers have spent hundreds of millions of pounds in successful campaigns persuading consumers to switch from butter to margarine, and to use highly polyunsaturated oils made from corn, sunflower, safflower and other plant sources, for cooking and salad dressing. Many of these cheap oils and margarines are pretty disgusting, and a better choice is to eat fresh bread by itself, and to make really sparing use of good quality olive oil in food preparation, with butter for special treats. As a rule of thumb, any food that looks, smells and tastes nasty, is nasty. (See Fat; Hydrogenation; Olive oil.) *GC*

Olive oil

Olive oil is a Good Thing, right? Right. The Mediterranean diet, or rather diets, as they have evolved over thousands of years in southern Europe, depend on olive oil as the staple means to cook food and to make salads toothsome. Trade in wine and olive oil in ancient times is well documented and evident from the recovery of amphorae, massive earthenware storage containers, from the sea bed.

Nutritionally, olive oil is special; low in saturates and also low in polyunsaturates. Most of its fatty acids are monounsaturated and, in moderation, benign. Like any other oil or fat, olive oil will make you fat if you consume a lot of it: country people in southern Italy and Greece who use a lot of olive oil in older age after becoming inactive are liable to become obese, just as much as sedentary British people on a fatty diet.

Available in any well-stocked supermarket, olive oil is the best choice for cooking and salads, and most of all for Mediterranean-style meals. Always buy and use first-pressing 'extra virgin' oil. Inferior varieties called 'virgin' or just 'olive oil' are cheaper, but taste nasty and have lost much of the health-giving quality of the viscous, green oil first pressed without chemical solvents from whole olives. (See Mediterranean diet; Oils.) *GC*

Omega 3 and Omega 6 fatty acids

These acids act rather like biological keys, unlocking a wide range of our natural functions which have fallen into disuse through diet, drugs or life-style. They appear to improve well-being without any reported side-effects.

Omega 3: There are two main Omega 3 fatty acids, docosahexaenoic and eicosapentaenoic, found in oily fish, which includes salmon, mackerel and herring. Trials show that as little as 100 g (4 oz) per week of such fish will help protect against thrombosis. Blood pressure may be decreased and the immune system strengthened. There are many supplements on the market; look for standardized EHA and DHA contents.

Omega 6: Dr David Horrobin of Efamol has spent more than £20 million researching the effects of evening primrose oil and developing effective strains. It is licensed as a medicine for conditions including atopic eczema and tender breasts. Clinical trials have demonstrated usefulness in counteracting pre-menstrual tension and nearly all consumers report a greatly improved skin quality. The effective Omega 6 is likely to be GLA, but although borage and blackcurrant seed oils are valuable sources, they have not been researched as fully as evening primrose oil. *MH*

Onions

Onions (Allium cepa) have been cultivated for so long that their wild ancestor has disappeared. Any onions found in the wild are escapees from the garden. Onion is the most widely used flavouring in existence. There are dozens of varieties which grow all over the world; they are all pungent and can be eaten cooked or raw.

Since antiquity, onions have been reputed to be of great use medicinally. Modern research bears this out. Like garlic, the onion is packed with therapeutic compounds: vitamins B, C and E, carotene, calcium, iron and other minerals. Like garlic, too, they contain a natural antiseptic oil, allyl disulphate, and cycloallin, an anticoagulant which helps to dissolve clots which form on the walls of blood vessels. Cooking does not destroy the therapeutic qualities, while only a very little onion per day, about a tablespoon, has the result of lowering cholesterol. *CS*

Organic food

Organic foods are grown without the use of artificial fertilizers, pesticides, growth regulators, antibiotics or intensive livestock systems. Organic farming follows traditional methods of agriculture and animal husbandry, while drawing on knowledge of ecology and the soil.

Most major supermarkets now stock a range of organic produce. While prices may be higher you can be assured that you are investing in sustainable agriculture that does not damage the environment, pollute water or threaten wildlife. Some organic producers are now supplying their produce direct to the consumer - contact the Soil Association to find out if there is a scheme near you.

With concern about over-production and the introduction of EC set-aside schemes now is the perfect time to encourage farmers to convert to organic farming methods. But while conventional farmers receive large subsidies, it is still the case that too few resources are made available to encourage growers and farmers to climb off the agrochemical treadmill. As a result, much of the growing demand in the UK for organic produce is being met by imports.

There are now agreed standards for organic food production and food should be clearly labelled. Conservation grade products meet slightly less stringent standards but go some way towards meeting consumers' concerns about intensive production.

Regular consumers of organic food are convinced it tastes better, though this is something that continues to be the subject of argument. Certainly free-range meat scores well in taste tests though with vegetables the situation is less clear-cut. Organic producers tend to emphasize taste rather than appearance. *SD*

Osteoporosis

This is a condition of thinning and weakening of the bones. Osteomalacia, in which bones become porous, is a similar disease. Osteoporosis is most common in elderly people; in particular, sedentary women in their 70s and 80s are very vulnerable to fractures of the thighs and hips after a fall as a result of osteoporosis, and thus may be crippled and suffer pain and misery for the last years of their lives.

Because calcium is vital to bone integrity and strength in growing children, it is often thought that calcium supplementation in adult life will guard against osteoporosis. This view is heavily advertised by the milk industry. While milk is nourishing (as long as you drink it skimmed), it is probable that the only effective protection against weak, thin or porous bones in adult life is regular vigorous physical activity. The body is designed to be used, and osteoporosis is uncommon in populations where it is normal to stay active into old age.

Hormone replacement therapy (HRT) taken during and after the menopause may help prevent osteoporosis; however, there is some evidence that HRT may increase the risk of breast cancer. *GC*

Oysters

A bivalve mollusc, there are over 300 types of oyster distributed around the world's seas, only the polar seas being too cold for them. The native British oyster (*Ostrea edulis*) was cultivated by the Romans and many of our oyster-beds like the one at Colchester can be traced back as far. This variety retains its eggs within the shell until fertilization; the eggs are carried in the summer months (when there is no R in the month) and make the oyster taste unpleasant. However, the Pacific oyster (*Crassostrea gigas*) and others like the Portuguese oyster (*Crassostrea angulata*) and the American oyster (*Crassostrea virginica*) do not retain their eggs and thus can be eaten all the year round. Most of the old British beds have now gone over to cultivating the Pacific oyster (which came originally from the Orient). This is a shame as the Pacific has a soft, woolly texture and is not as pleasant eaten raw, though it cooks very well indeed. Most oysters are eaten raw,

Amanda and Mair ap Mervyn prepare the ingredients for Cawl, a favourite Welsh stew made with meat and vegetables.

Amanda, Graciella Sanchez and her family enjoy Mexico's traditional Sunday lunch: Mole Poblano, refried beans and rice with Mexico's favourite corn or wheat tortilla.

The ingredients for Mole Poblano: chocolate, chillies, nuts, chicken and spices.

Amanda enjoys Cawl eaten the traditional way in two courses. First the broth, then the meat and vegetables as a second course.

Left: Saeng Sun Tchige - 'tchige' means stew. This is a luxury Korean stew made with an abundance of seafood, beancurd and vegetables.

Below: Just some of the ingredients CJ Kim uses in his Saeng Sun Tchige.

Anna Hegarty prepares Jansson's Temptation, a favourite part of the Smorgasbord on Swedish feast days.

Amanda and Michel Guillon go shopping in Nice market for ingredients to make Ratatouille Niçoise.

Above: Amanda and Lali admire the wonderful Kabuli, a traditional dish from Hyderabad in Southern India.

Left: Kabuli is an unusual one-pot Indian meal. The garnish of almonds and caramelized onions makes it look as good as it tastes.

A party is not a party without a Doro Wat - Ethiopia's favourite chicken and egg stew.

Bethelhem Yohannes proudly presents Ethiopia's favourite meal of Doro Wat served on a bread called Enjera.

however - in fact they are alive until they are cut from their base shell. If you squeeze lemon on a live oyster you will see it visibly contract.

There is always a risk of food poisoning, as oysters, like all bivalves, feed on small organisms and other material that they filter out of the water and thus can easily pick up harmful bacteria. Oysters are cleaned commercially by placing them in tanks of clean sea-water under ultra-violet light for a day, which kills any dangerous organisms. The Japanese sell frozen oysters in cartons. The Chinese dry them and make a sauce out of them.

Oysters change sex according to their feeding conditions and the temperature of the water. They can live up to twenty or thirty years, but they are eaten in the third or fourth year. Oysters are males in cold water and become female in the summer when they give birth. It is a practice that homo sapiens might try, as the only way of acquiring true sex equality. *CS* however - in fact they are alive until they are cut from their base shell. If you squeeze lemon on a live oyster you will see it visibly contract.

There is always a risk of food poisoning, as oysters, like all bivalves, feed on small organisms and other material that they filter out of the water and thus can easily pick up harmful bacteria. Oysters are cleaned commercially by placing them in tanks of clean sea-water under ultra-violet light for a day, which kills any dangerous organisms. The Japanese sell frozen oysters in cartons. The Chinese dry them and make a sauce out of them.

Oysters change sex according to their feeding conditions and the temperature of the water. They can live up to twenty or thirty years, but they are eaten in the third or fourth year. Oysters are males in cold water and become female in the summer when they give birth. It is a practice that homo sapiens might try, as the only way of acquiring true sex equality. *CS*

Packaging

Packaging of food plays an important part in ensuring good hygiene during storage and transport. Traditional glass bottles and tins have now been joined on supermarket shelves by tetrapacks, modified atmosphere packaging and a range of plastics. And that makes for a lot of waste. The average family throws out around two black sackfuls a week of rubbish.

As food packaging can be a major contributor to household waste, it is worth finding out about recycling and cutting down on unnecessary packaging. Find out where your local bottle-bank, aluminium can and paper recycling collection points are - supermarkets often provide details. You can also make a difference by buying products made from recycled materials, taking your own shopping bags to the supermarket and choosing products that are not overpackaged. Complain if you thing the packaging is excessive.

In recent years there has been concern about the migration of small amounts of chemicals from some types of packaging into food. In most cases there is little to be worried about, but concerns over dioxins from bleached paper, tin and lead from metal cans and possible risks from plastic wraps have all prompted investigation. Cling-film should not be used to wrap fatty foods, nor should it be used in contact with food in a microwave oven. (See Canning; Modified atmosphere packaging.) *SD*

Parents

Parent power can be very influential where their children's food is concerned. One supermarket recently announced that it had removed sweets from the checkout because parents had complained. Other parents have got together to defend and improve school meals or have campaigned for healthy tuck shops.

Parents' own eating patterns are important role models for their children. Young children, particularly, learn to eat and enjoy the same kinds of foods as their parents. Girls can also pick up unhealthy slimming fads from their mothers. So if you want to encourage your children to eat healthily, make eating together a pleasure. *SD*

Pesticides

As with antibiotics, nobody knows for sure whether or not the minute traces of pesticides that contaminate industrially produced and processed food are a significant danger to human health. Because many pesticides and other chemicals intrinsic to modern intensive agriculture are intensely toxic, their use is carefully monitored in well-regulated countries. In all but freakish circumstances, human consumption of pesticide residues in Britain is way below officially determined safety limits.

However, pesticide limits are set and monitoring is overseen by international expert committees remote from any democratic process. These committees are influenced if not dominated by agrichemical manufacturers, and bidden to create conditions favourable to intensive farming and food manufacturing methods that depend on systematic use of pesticides and other contaminants. Moreover, in 1994 the British government is throwing out many regulations, some of which are designed to protect the consumer against unsafe food.

It is often supposed that only vegetables and fruit contain traces of pesticides. This is not so. Farm animals eat grass and other feed that itself is contaminated, and animal fat in meat and processed foods is therefore liable to contain minute but identifiable traces of pesticides. If this worries you, buy and eat food reared and produced by sustainable 'organic' methods to recognised standards, such as those of the Soil Association in Britain. (See Organic foods.) *GC*

Pet food

According to the statistics we now care as much about the food our moggies and mongrels eat as we do about our own diet. But is it doing them any good? Pets rely on their owners to understand their nutritional requirements. So are we getting it right? The 3 million obese cats and dogs in Britain suggest that we are not. But the blame does not lie solely with the owner. Labelling of pet food in Britain is complex, conflicting and confusing. The pet food industry, which spends £42 million a year on advertising, appears to be less generous when it comes to educating the public. *SD*

Pickling

An ancient method of preserving food by immersing it in brine or vinegar. Any food can be pickled: meat, fish, vegetables, fruits (though the latter would be pickled in a sugar syrup). It is the salt and ascetic acid in the pickling fluid that destroys the bacteria. Nowadays we tend to preserve meat and fish by freezing, but vegetables are still pickled for the special taste. One of the oldest recipes in existence in Central Europe is for sauerkraut, which goes back to the Dark Ages. Pickled cabbage was, and still is, an excellent way of preserving the vitamin C needed in the diet in the winter months when green-leaf vegetables were scarce.

In Britain we like to pickle gherkins, beetroot, walnuts and onions and are fond of a commercial mustard pickle which has mixed vegetables in it - piccalilli. Make your own at home if you like it because it is easy to prepare and the flavour is infinitely better. In the Middle East and North Africa, turnip is pickled and coloured pink with a piece of added beetroot. Malt vinegar is used in commercial pickles, but its flavour tends to be overpowering - wine or cider vinegar are more subtle alternatives. Oil can be used in pickling as it covers the food and excludes all the air from it, acting as a seal. Pickles made with oil are common in India and the Far East. *CS*

Poaching

Used mainly in connection with cooking eggs in simmering water, the term comes from the French for pocket and denotes the nest of white of egg which surrounds the yolk. The poaching technique can be extended to any food cooked by simmering at a temperature just below boiling in liquid - wine or stock as well as water. Poaching is especially suitable for fish. *CS*

Polyunsaturated fats

A Good Thing? Well, like any unsaturated fats, up to a point. All fats are energy-dense, which is to say, they contain 9 calories a gram, in contrast with protein and carbohydrate, which contain about 4 calories a gram. All fats are liable to make you fat.

Consumed sparingly, and usually in their natural form as part of wholegrain bread and cereals, raw and lightly cooked vegetables, meat from free-ranging animals, and fatty fish, polyunsaturated fats are good for you. Such whole food is rich in nourishment, including many minerals and trace elements; and the fats themselves come with fat-soluble vitamins.

Some polyunsaturated fats are essential; that is to say, we need them in small quantities for health and life itself. Scientific research has consistently shown that a relatively high level of polyunsaturated fats circulating in the blood (an indication of the amount consumed) reduces the risk of a heart attack. It is sometimes said that polyunsaturates may increase the risk of some cancers, but this alarming story is misleading. If you consume polyunsaturates in moderation and as part of whole food, they are altogether good for you and are not a cancer risk. (See Fat; Margarine; Monounsaturated fats; Saturated fats.) *GC*

Potatoes

The Potato (*Solanum tuberosum*) is a native of southern Chile. The earliest signs of its consumption can be dated back to 3000 BC and it became the Incas' staple food. Brought back to Europe after the discovery of the New World with other food plants - peppers, chillies, tomatoes - it was not greeted with much enthusiasm at first. It became the food of the poor, given to the Spanish armed forces and to prisoners; it was thought to be poisonous and a cause of leprosy. Perhaps someone had boiled the leaves, which are toxic, at any rate, potatoes were shunned for the next 200 years. The potato began to creep into the diet by the end of the eighteenth century, especially as people realized that it was a practical food crop in wartime. Potatoes could be left beneath the earth and would remain in cold storage ready to be dug up after the pillaging armies had continued on their way.

The potato became a staple of the Irish people's diet, and the potato famine in the nineteenth century was a terrible disaster, when the crops failed and millions of people died of starvation. Now the potato has become a universal major staple food, 90 per cent of the world's crop being grown in Europe. Though a potato consists of 80 per cent water it is high in vitamin C and potassium and has 2 per cent protein. The nutrients tend to be in the skin and just beneath it. The longer a potato is stored and the more it is processed, the less nutritious it will be. There are over 400 varieties of potato. They can roughly be divided up into floury types, good for mashing (King Edward, Wilja and Maris Piper); salad types, good for boiling and steaming (Jersey Royal, La Ratte, Pink Fir Apple, Charlotte, Kipfler); and baking (Cara, Pentland Squire, Romano, Golden Wonder). *CS*

Pregnancy and diet

The latest research has shown that diet and health can be critical even before conception. So if you are planning to have a child, it is never too early to start thinking about your diet.

The best advice is to eat a variety of foods and follow guidelines for healthy eating - plenty of starchy carbohydrate foods like bread, potatoes, rice and pasta, lots of fruit and vegetables, and cutting down on fats, sugars and salt. Your own appetite is the best indication of how much food you need to eat - there is no truth in the adage that you need to 'eat for two' when you are pregnant.

During pregnancy you do need extra amounts of some nutrients: calcium, vitamin D, iron and folate (folic acid). Generally, if you eat a varied diet containing plenty of fresh foods, you should not require vitamin and mineral supplements. However, the Chief Medical Officer has advised women to increase their folate intake to help prevent neural tube defects such as spina bifida. Folate is found particularly in potatoes, raw and lightly cooked green vegetables, pulses, fortified breakfast cereals and breads, fruit, nuts and yeast extract. All women who are planning a pregnancy are now advised to take a daily supplement of 400 µg (micrograms) of folate and also to include 300 µg of folate in their diet.

It is extremely important to avoid risk of infections such as listeria, salmonella and toxoplasmosis during pregnancy. Cut out raw and undercooked eggs, pâté and soft cheeses in particular. (See Food poisoning; Low birth weights.) *SD*

Processing

Almost all the food we eat in Britain is processed: most days, most people eat little if any raw food. This in itself is bad news. For good health we should eat vegetables and fruit at least five times a day, including plenty of raw fruit and vegetables as snacks, starters or to accompany a meal.

Processing is not intrinsically unhealthy. When you cook, you are processing food at home. Bread, for example, is processed and many forms of processing are benign such as drying, canning, bottling or freezing.

Other methods of processing and packaging are problematic, either because they degrade food, or may introduce microbiological hazards, or because they have the effect of increasing the amount of fats and/or sugars in the product. (See Cook-chill; Irradiation; Hydrogenation.; Processing) *GC*

Prostate

Dietary intervention for prevention and treatment of benign prostate disease is worth taking seriously. The prostate is a small gland in men which surrounds the urethra, the tube which carries urine from the bladder through the penis. Most men don't even know they've got one until it goes wrong! At around fifty years of age the prostrate starts benignly swelling and in 50 per cent of men the swelling is pronounced enough to pinch the urethra and interfere with peeing. Typical symptoms are dribbling and the need to urinate very frequently, including during the night, which disturbs sleep for both sufferer and partner.

There is increasing evidence that eating a diet which is rich in the minerals zinc and selenium, low in fat, especially saturated fats, and contains plenty of fruit and vegetables plus starchy carbohydrates may help counter the prostate's demise. Zinc, it seems, could inhibit the action of the enzyme which causes the swelling. Oysters are one of the richest sources of zinc; more practically bread and breakfast cereals, semi-skimmed or skimmed milk and milk products like yogurts are also good sources. Pumpkin, sesame and sunflower seeds contain reasonable amounts of zinc too. Some supplements may help: Evening primrose oil provides essential fatty acids which increase prostaglandin synthesis. These prostaglandins seem to reduce levels of the hormone causing swelling. An extract of rye called cernilton has undergone extensive testing and appears to reduce swelling too. (See Omega 3 and Omega 6 fatty acids.) *AU*

Protein

One fact you won't need to learn from a book like this, is that protein is good for you and therefore that foods high in protein like beef (steak preferably), eggs and bacon, cheese and milk are or should be staple foods to ensure growth and strength. Correct? Essentially, no. Nutritionists who have preached protein as the master-nutrient, and who are still busy persuading governments in Africa, Asia and Latin America to replace traditional agriculture with inappropriate meat and dairy farming, have done and are doing vast untold damage to human health.

It is of course true that protein (or more precisely about half of the amino acids of which protein is composed) is essential for growth and indeed life. We need protein. But this does not mean that the more protein we consume, the better. Nor does it meant that protein from foods of animal origin (like meat and dairy products) is in any way superior to protein from foods of vegetable origin (like bread, cereals, pulses and legumes). To the contrary. If anything the average British diet contains too much protein, and certainly far too much protein of animal origin.

Protein was identified as a vital nutrient in the first half of the nineteenth century in Germany, by Baron Justus von Liebig, whose other great discovery was artificial fertilizer for plants. What von Liebig and his followers found is that a diet high in protein (and fat) accelerates growth. Children fed a lot of protein in the form of meat, milk, eggs and such-like foods, grow big, become sexually mature early, and are taller adults. In the days of imperial expansion the notion of 'the bigger, the better' seemed self-evident. High-protein diets containing goodly amounts of vitamins and minerals did indeed do much to eliminate childhood stunting and deficiency diseases in Europe and America in the early twentieth century.

However, this high protein (and high fat) diet has turned out to increase the incidence of heart attacks, cancers, and a number of other common serious diseases in later life, and there is quite good evidence that animal protein (eaten in large amounts habitually) does itself increase the risk of some common cancers. Common sense suggests that a diet that pushes growth, making people bigger and taller, may well eventually be dangerous. After all, we all know that it's a bad idea continually to over-rev a car.

And so it has turned out. What distinguishes us from the animals is big brains and slow growth. It is too soon for boys and girls to become sexually mature aged 11 and 12; the natural time is four or five years later. Von Liebig can be said to have invented adolescence, those years of turmoil caused by a child's mind in an adult's body. As in other industrialized countries, we in Britain are von Liebig's monsters.

Vegetarians and vegans get all the protein they need from whole foods of vegetable origin. A healthy diet is plant-based. If you like meat and other foods of animal origin, fine; but for good health, avoid animal fat, and don't imagine you need lots of animal protein. (See Diet.) *GC*

q

Quail

This referred originally to the smallest game bird, the European quail, which migrated south in the winter. But the quail you will find in the supermarket will be the Japanese quail which can be bred in small cages. It starts laying at six weeks of age and lays one egg a day and it makes efficient use of very little food, so it has become an economically important bird reared for the table. Quails used to be wrapped in bacon and a vine leaf and roasted, they are now often split in half (spatchcocked) and grilled. Smoked quail can be eaten cold or the meat taken from the bones and stir-fried or used to make a risotto. Tiny speckled quail's eggs are a popular 'foodie' ingredient in salads and starters especially. They are most often served hardboiled or poached.

It was quails that killed great numbers of Israelites in the wilderness. The all-knowing Yahweh failed to warn His people and did not include them as unclean animals in Jewish dietary law. But the peoples of the northern Mediterranean knew that the birds migrating southwards reached their shores exhausted and were often toxic after eating the seeds of henbane and hellebore during their flight. The toxic residues could kill people eating the quail flesh. *CS*

r

Recipe

The original spelling was receipt, which meant a formula or prescription of the ingredients used and the method necessary for the making of a preparation in medicine or cookery. The term recipe is now only used in cooking, but the meaning remains the same.

Many people claim that they do not need to follow recipes but prefer to improvise. However, to find out how the recipe writer intended the dish to turn out, you need to follow the instructions at least once before making your own improvements. Writers and publishers do make mistakes in recipes - if you find one in this or any other book, let them know. *CS*

Refrigeration

A benign process for the preservation of food. If mass use of industrial and domestic refrigeration replaced hydrogenation and salting , the effect would be to reduce heart disease and stroke as epidemic killers. It is important to make the best use of a domestic refrigerator by cleaning and defrosting regularly, and by storing different foods in the right positions - the top of the fridge is not as cold as the lower section. The vegetable drawer on the floor of most fridges keeps salads and other vegetables crisp for several days. (See Freezing; Hydrogenation; Processing; Salt; Stroke.) *GC*

Religion and food

All the world religions have rules which cover the consumption of food. Many of them forbid the eating of a particular food (sometimes the same ones, for example, pork in both Judaism and Islam) or a group of foods, while other religions might eat the same foods quite happily. Hinduism is exclusively vegetarian, but really strict Hindus also avoid onions and garlic, for they are related to meat in that they flavour it. Buddhism is mostly vegetarian, too, though again there is a scale of belief and piety. A large number of Seventh Day Adventists (a Christian sect that believes in the Second Coming) are also vegetarian, as are many Quakers. For almost 2000 years Roman Catholics had Fast days when they could not eat meat; now the rules are far more relaxed, though many Catholics still keep Friday as a fish-only day.

Orthodox Jews are the most detailed in their taboos: not mixing meat with dairy products in the same meal is but one rule among many in the long list which God gave in Leviticus and Deuteronomy. (See The Heretic's Feast for a full exploration of the subject.)

It is important to remember that each food taboo has a theological rationale, however absurd it might strike the unbeliever. Anthropologists see such taboos as an attempt to individualize a social group so that it is distinguished from its neighbours and retains a striking identity of its own. This is seen vividly in the Middle East if you compare the highly spiced food of the Arab nations with the much milder and less adventurous food of Israel. *CS*

Retailing

In 1961, before the self-service revolution took off, there were more than 150,000 grocery shops in the UK. Now there are about 40,000 with just a handful of major food retailing companies controlling nearly three-quarters of all the food we buy.

Supermarkets have played an important role in the huge changes that have affected the choice of food now available and the way that we shop. They may offer us a larger than ever range of products but many people are now arguing that their growth has been to the detriment of real choice and that the number of super stores should be limited. Fewer people now have access to small specialist shops and for those without cars, stocking up at the supermarket can be difficult and expensive. Computer and interactive technology, is already revolutionizing the 'shopping experience' and one day going out to shop may become a thing of the past.

Major retailers are very powerful - they decide what is produced and to what standards. In the current economic climate, prices have become increasingly competitive. This has led to price wars and the opening of many 'low-cost' stores and warehouse clubs. Retailers cannot afford to ignore customer demands, so when thousands of shoppers began to complain about artificial additives in foods, supermarkets led the trend for 'additive-free' products. And some supermarkets have attempted to become more environmentally aware, to provide more information on labels or to provide better facilities in their stores. They know it makes good business sense. *SD*

Rice

Half the world's population lives off rice (*Oryza sativa*). It has been grown in China since around 3000 BC and gradually became the staple grain, taking over from millet. It was also grown in India very early on, but it took some time to move westwards, not reaching Egypt until 400 or 300 BC. From there it slowly became established in the Middle East and the Arabs finally took rice along North Africa and into Sicily and Spain.

In Europe rice is grown in northern Italy in the Po valley where it was introduced by the Venetians in the mid fifteenth century. It is also grown in Spain and Portugal. In Britain we eat about 1.25 kg (2.5 lb) of rice per person per year, an amount which a farmer in South China would consume in two days. In India over 300 different rice varieties are cultivated. It is believed that altogether throughout the world over 10,000 varieties of rice are grown.

Different types of rice are suited to different dishes. Patna rice is long-grained and used in savoury dishes, Basmati is even longer-grained. Both cook dry and separate, never sticky with starch, so these are perfect for Indian and Chinese dishes. Arborio rice, grown in Italy, cooks soft and creamy and is essential for making risotto. Short-grained rice is mostly used in the West for making sweet rice puddings, but in Japan short- grained rice which becomes sticky when cooked is perfect for making sushi. Other European short-grained rices may well be used for Spanish paella. Wild rice (Zizania aquatica) is not a rice at all but a reed-like grass which grows in shallow lakes and likes quite a cold climate: it is indigenous to Canada, Formosa, China and Japan. *CS*

Rickets

This is a crippling disease caused by deficiency of vitamin D, found in a few foods (fatty fish, for example) and also manufactured in the body by sunlight. Rickets prevents the bones hardening in childhood, thus causing the legs to be bowed under the weight of the body. It was common in Britain among working-class people living in cities during the industrial revolution. It is not now a problem in this country except in Asian immigrant communities where children may wear clothing which covers most of their skin even in the summer. (See Deficiency diseases; Vitamins.) *GC*

Roasting

A term usually applied to meat, to describe cooking on a spit or in an oven. Roasting is a safe method for cooking large cuts of meat because the oven can reach a high temperature, thus cooking the flesh right through to the centre. Roasting is generally done with added fat to prevent the meat from becoming dry: it often needs basting throughout the cooking, though fatty meats will happily cook in their own juices. *CS*

r

Roots

In the past it was primarily the vegetal food of winter which saved communities from starving. The wonderful thing about roots is that they need only be dug up when needed; also, once the frost has touched them, it turns the starch into sugars, which is why parsnips, for example, were formerly valued for their sweetness and used in dessert pies and tarts. The sweetest root of all is sugar beet, which was selectively bred and began to be cultivated in the midst of the Napoleonic wars and was a direct result of the British naval blockade which prevented the French from getting to their West Indian sugar plantations. Another root, the swede, was originally used as winter fodder for cattle. The orange carrot was bred in Holland in the seventeenth century. The Ancient World was only familiar with a purple carrot from Abyssinia, and somewhere the Arabs discovered a yellow carrot, both of which they took to Spain; several hundred years later the Dutch bred from them.

Gastronomically, root vegetables should be harvested small and barely cooked at all, steamed briefly or eaten raw. Baby turnips are a real delicacy served like this. Carrots make wonderful juice, one of the best ways of getting your beta-carotene, and its flavour is much improved by a dash of lemon juice and a pinch of celery salt. Root vegetables are a good source of fibre, some minerals and vitamins. *CS*

Roughage

(See Fibres.)

S

Salmonella

(See Food poisoning.)

Salt

Salt is a compound of sodium and chlorine (sodium chloride). Sodium is a mineral which like vitamins is essential: without it we die. The health of all the body's soft tissues depends on adequate and balanced supplies of the electrolytes sodium and potassium. Our diet and thus our bodies typically contain too much sodium and are relatively short of potassium.

All whole unprocessed plant foods are rich in potassium but are very short of sodium. In common with animals, humans have an inbuilt hunger for salt, probably evolved in response to the lack of sodium in nature.

Salt is also a preservative and salting has been used to stop perishable foods like meat and fish going bad for thousands of years. The traditional diets of marine nations like Portugal and Japan are very salty. Much processed meat such as ham and bacon is heavily salted, and canned vegetable soups and packaged breakfast cereals may contain up to or over a hundred times as much sodium as their raw materials.

The salt contained in a few slices of bread eaten each day is enough for health. Dietary guidelines usually recommend that we should halve our salt intake. Excess salt in the diet causes high blood pressure and thus increases the risk of stroke, and is probably the key dietary cause of stomach cancer. In America and most European countries the rates of stroke and stomach cancer have dramatically decreased in the last fifty years, the most likely explanation being increased use of industrial and domestic refrigeration in place of salt. (See Cancers; Stroke.)
GC

Saturated fats

Saturated fats are the unhealthy hard or hardened fats. They are the single main dietary cause of cardiovascular disease, and heart attacks in particular.

Production and therefore consumption of saturated fat has greatly increased in Britain in the last 150 years because of the industrialization of farming and food manufacture. Farmers breed 'fatstock' by penning animals and feeding them concentrates. The result is gross beasts whose fat is highly saturated. Methods of mass slaughter and meat manufacture originally devised over a century ago have turned fatty meat and its products into staple food. Processors turn unsaturated vegetable oils into saturated fats by means of the hydrogenation process in order to make cheap, stable, fatty (and often sugary) products.

Consequently, up to one-fifth (20 per cent) of calories consumed in Britain now is in the form of saturated fats. For good health, experts usually recommend a sharp reduction to a maximum of 10 per cent of the diet. The World Health Organisation has set a global target of 0 - 10 per cent of calories; which is to say, the less hard and hardened fat you eat, the better. (See Fat; Hydrogenation: Monounsaturated fat; Polyunsaturated fat.) *GC*

Sausages

The traditional British banger is considered part of our heritage, to be defended against the onslaught of the Euro-sausage at all costs. Unfortunately, the majority of British sausages are a far cry from the 'real' sausages that we can feel proud of. Pumped up with added water and additives, filled with rusk and disguised with colourings and flavours, the lean meat content of sausages can be minimal. What passes for meat is often fat, gristle and the less desirable parts of the animal. And not all the meat in a beef sausage need be beef: legally it can include pork, chicken, turkey or other animal meats.

Supermarket shelves now offer low-fat sausages. But don't think that you're likely to get a lot more lean meat. Instead some of the fat has been replaced by even more water. High quality butchers who pride themselves on their products are the place to look for really good sausages, which are made according to traditional methods using prime ingredients which now increasingly include interesting and unusual flavourings. *SD*

School meals

For many years the health of British children was protected by means of school meals made to specified standards laid down as law. Not now. In the 1980 Education Act the first Thatcher administration abolished nutrition standards for school meals, Mrs Thatcher herself claiming that modern British children are well-fed.

In 1983 the government commissioned 'The Diets of British Schoolchildren', a report based on a survey of over 3000 11 and 14 year-olds. When eventually published by the Department of Health in 1989, after a remarkable history of redrafting and delays, this showed that Mrs Thatcher was wrong. Most growing children from all backgrounds are stuffed with cakes, biscuits, chips, crisps and/or fizz, eat little fresh vegetables and fruit, and are often very short of vitamins and minerals crucial in early life, such as the B vitamins folic acid, calcium and iron.

Throughout the 1980s successive legislation privatized the provision of school meals, reduced the number of children able to eat cooked meals at school, and had the effect of gradually reducing the budgets for school caterers. As a result the general quality of food eaten by children continues to deteriorate. The combination of a fatty, sugary diet and a decline in sport and physical education is causing a steady increase in childhood overweight and obesity, and eating disorders are more common.

The seeds of adult health - and disease - are sown in childhood. Nutritional scientists predict that boys and girls who get used to fatty, sugary, salty foods are unlikely to change to a healthy diet, and are at high risk of heart disease, cancers and other serious diseases in later life.

In 1992 a small charity, the Caroline Walker Trust, published 'Nutritional Guidelines for School Meals'. Based on the findings of expert committees and written by Imogen Sharp, Director of the National Forum for Coronary Heart Disease Prevention, this report has been commended by relevant government departments and is now used by many education authorities and caterers as the basis for school meal specifications. If you are a parent or are interested in the health and welfare of children, check to see if the food available in your local school follows nutritional guidelines. (See Institutional food.) *GC*

Sea-weed

Sea-weeds, or sea vegetables as they are now known, have been traditionally eaten by coastal communities around the world. Over the last fifty years, these natural foods have been largely forgotten in Britain, but sea vegetables are now harvested from local sources around the Celtic fringes of Britain and Europe, and are available in health food shops in the UK.

Sea vegetables are highly nutritious, a good source of calcium, iodine and vitamins, and can contain twenty times as much iron as spinach. They are also good sources of alginates and other types of soluble fibre.

Different kinds of sea vegetable have a wide variety of uses. They can enhance flavour and add body to casseroles and stews, and can be used in salads, pastas and soups. And if soaked in water for five minutes, they can be eaten without cooking. Naturally they have a special affinity with fish.

Sea vegetables are widely used in Japanese cooking, especially sushi - rice and raw fish or vegetables wrapped in a sea vegetable called nori. It's delicious! *SD*

Seeds

These are dormant embryos waiting to be activated by warmth and water. If given both, a green sprout will begin to appear. The sprout contains vitamin C (ascorbic acid is always concentrated in rapidly growing tissue) and other vitamins and minerals. Sprouts after five or six days' germination also contain vitamins from the B group, including B12 and vitamins E, G, K and U. Thus seed sprouts have rich nutritional value. Three-tiered seed germinators are fairly cheap to buy so it is worth germinating your own seed sprouts. Try alfalfa, aduki beans, barley, fenugreek, lentil, mung bean and wheat seeds, all excellent in salads and sandwiches. *CS*

Sell-by date

This has now been replaced with 'best before' or 'eat by' dates to ensure that you know for exactly how long the food is safe to eat, if it has been stored correctly. (See Labelling.) *SD*

Slaughterhouse

Every year 3385 thousand cattle, 19,397 thousand sheep, 14,508 thousand pigs and 570 million poultry are slaughtered in the UK. A further 23 million poultry were exported in 1992 for breeding and ultimately for slaughter. At Christmas each year, 11 million turkeys are killed and 2 million geese, ducks and game birds.

The term 'slaughterhouse' was replaced by the French word ***abattoir*** after 1840, when public sensibilities began to emerge over the killing of animals for food. Until then the slaughter of livestock was done in town centres, behind butchers' shops or often in the street or alleyway.

There are 534 abattoirs in the UK at the moment. Six of them have a special licence to kill horses for human consumption (the meat is exported). Present routines of meat inspection are archaic, and most British slaughterhouses are attempting modifications to meet EC hygiene requirements, not least to raise the level of supervision.

Today's abattoirs are criticized for being both inhumane and unhygienic. Slaughter is basically still by the sticking and bleeding method: first the animal has to be stunned by a pistol in which a charge of compressed air drives a bolt an inch or two into the forehead. This method needs accuracy; if the animal is not stunned, a pithing rod is shoved in and out of the bolt-hole into the back of the brain. The animal is then hoisted by a back leg so that its throat can be cut and it bleeds out. A steer or cow will shed about 3.5 gallons of blood before it dies, which takes several minutes. Electric stunning is used for poultry, pigs and sheep: electrodes are placed either side of the head. The animal hangs from the stockman's pole, then a current passes through the brain. The legal stunning time by electric prod of seven seconds for pigs is only kept to when there is a vet or government inspector on the premises: often animals are inadequately stunned and therefore often conscious when their throats are cut. Religious law for Jews and Muslims decrees that animals must not be stunned before having their throats cut.

Death for animals is anything but sudden, efficient and quick for other reasons as well. They arrive parched and hungry after a long journey in cramped conditions. Once in the slaughterhouse they can smell the blood and sense the terror of the other animals. They often panic and struggle, making it more difficult for them to be stunned.

As to hygiene, meat is a highly putrefiable food which is produced in premises that serve also as latrines. Freshly cut flesh may be sterile but it can quickly be contaminated by ordure brought in on hides, wool and feathers. Fellmongers tell of cattle with 28 kg (over half cwt) of muck on their bodies being offered for slaughter. The rough processes of flaying, defeathering, disembowelling and drawing the intestines also sets up a miasma of bacterial contamination. The same electric saws are used to cut through the hide which is soiled by faeces and mud as to bisect the carcass, thus infecting the edible parts. There is inadequate policing by inspectors and vets. Killing animals appears to bring out a coarse brutality in the workers who make new workers undergo humiliating rites of acceptance by their group. Workers are paid on headage rates which means that they may hurry the process of killing and further ignore the hygiene and welfare regulations.

Note: The RSPCA is planning to introduce a Freedom Food symbol for farmers, abattoirs, hauliers and supermarkets who meet good standards of care. The Soil Association is also campaigning for better conditions. Their handbook on Animal Welfare is available for £2.50 (see Addresses).

Slimming

Slimming has become a national obsession, with up to 90 per cent of women claiming they have dieted in the past year. Yet for the majority there is no medical reason why they should be dieting. Most people find that any weight they do lose when slimming is quickly put back on again, sometimes with extra pounds. In fact there is now evidence that yo-yo dieting, where weight fluctuates up and down, is more dangerous for health than being slightly overweight. Only seriously overweight people are likely to benefit medically from weight loss.

However, a whole host of slimming products encourage would-be dieters to believe that the pounds can be shed easily and quickly. The truth is that long-term weight loss will only be successful if it is accompanied by a change in eating patterns which slimming products do little to promote. Therefore it is wise to be skeptical of any slimming product claims, particularly those which offer 'miracle' weight loss with no dieting or exercise. Most slimming products will do more to lighten your wallet than your weight. The best advice for those wanting to lose weight is the same as healthy eating for everyone. The diet should include plenty of fresh fruits and vegetables and starchy carbohydrate foods, while reducing fatty and sugary foods, including alcohol. That way you'll find it much easier to maintain a healthy weight and look after your health, while still enjoying your food. (See Body image; Weight.) *SD*

Smoking

In this context, smoking has two meanings. Smoking cigarettes kills around at least 100,000 people every year in Britain. The risk of cancers of the mouth and throat is greatly increased by the combination of alcohol and smoking. The risk of lung cancer, of which the chief cause is smoking, remains high but is somewhat decreased if smokers eat plenty of vegetables and other fresh foods rich in antioxidant nutrients and other protective factors. (See Alcohol; ACE.)

Smoking is also a food process. Smoked food contains carcinogenic chemicals; enjoy it once in a while, but don't make smoked food a staple part of your diet. (See Processing.) *GC*

Soups

Soups can be thick and creamy, chunky and substantial enough to act as a meal in themselves, or thin and clear as in consommé and the soups favoured by the Chinese. Soups can be served hot or chilled. It is very simple to make tasty, nourishing soups out of just a few vegetables and a dash of olive oil. Potato and leeks, for example, make an excellent winter soup, cut up and sweated in olive oil, simmered for 30 minutes or so in vegetable stock or water. A few mixed root vegetables, green beans and a little added pasta and tomato juice make a simple home-made minestrone. A quick and easy, highly nourishing soup can be made from small orange lentils, flavoured with onion and garlic. To buy packet or canned soup is a tragic waste of money, and nutritionally your home-made soup is going to be a winner. Blended soups and purées make excellent and nourishing baby food, without salt, and are a good way of encouraging children to eat vegetables. *CS*

Spices

Spices are best stored whole and dried. A small coffee grinder kept specifically for the purpose is an efficient way to grind spices as needed. If bought powdered, they have a tendency to lose aroma as the essential oils evaporate.

A–Z of common spices

Allspice So-called because it tastes like a mixture of nutmeg, cloves and cinnamon. It is the fruit of the Jamaican pimento tree and is used in pickles and some savoury dishes as well as in cakes and puddings.

Aniseed Used for sweets, aniseed also imparts a typical flavour to drinks such as raki, ouzo and Pernod (anise), which go well with fish.

Caraway A seed used in baking and cheese-making and also in sauerkraut (with juniper) and kummel liqueur.

Cardamom Aromatic seeds in small green or white pods essential for good pilau rice and other Indian dishes, and the aromatic ingredient in Arabic coffee.

Cayenne pepper A ground variety of red chilli, good with smoked fish and Welsh rarebits.

Celery seeds Ground together with salt, make celery salt for potato salad, tomato dishes and quail's eggs.

Chilli powder Ground red chillies with a wide range of flavours depending upon the variety used.

Cassia A bark which can be used in curries instead of cinnamon and in pickles and sweet mincemeat.

Chinese five-spice powder A mixture of Szechuan pepper, star anise, cloves and fennel seeds. A staple of Chinese cooking which needs to be used sparingly because of a pronounced liquorice flavour.

Cinnamon The bark is used in the form of sticks which can be ground or used whole to flavour liquids by infusion.

Cloves The very antiseptic dried flower-bud can cure toothaches but is also good in pickling, baking and Indian cookery.

Coriander Use the ground seeds as a spice or in pickles and in Indian food.

Cumin A fruit so small it is usually thought of as a seed which stimulates the appetite and is essential for authentic curry, chilli con carne and Munster cheese.

Fennel seeds Used in curries and for flavouring figs and sausages in Italy.

Fenugreek An important curry ingredient, the name means Greek hay.

Galangal Used in Thai and Asian cooking to give a gentle ginger flavour with camphor overtones.

Ginger Used in many Chinese and Indian dishes. The fresh root is preferable to powder except for cakes and puddings. It is an excellent remedy for colds, travel sickness and the morning sickness of pregnancy.

Horseradish The root ground with vinegar or cream brings out the flavour of roast beef and smoked fish to perfection. When using fresh root take great care to protect the hands and eyes.

Juniper Contains an alkaloid, juniperin, which imparts the berries' typical flavour to gin. Also used in sauerkraut, game cooking and rich marinades. Limerick ham is smoked over juniper branches.

Mace and nutmeg The nutmeg is a seed containing an alkaloid with psychedelic properties and is covered by a lace-like husk which has a similar flavour. Mace is used in pickling, Welsh rarebit and pound cake. Nutmeg is also versatile in both sweet and savoury dishes.

Mustard The seeds are polished and ground and mixed with water to form English mustard or with vinegars and spices for French mustard. The ground whole seeds are good in curries.

Paprika Made from the sweet capsicum, it is the essential spice for goulash but also works well with cream cheese and Spanish dishes where it is called pimenton.

Pepper Black peppercorns are the dried berries of the pepper vine which are picked while green. Green pepper can be preserved in vinegar. White peppercorns are picked when ripe when the red skin is removed and is far less aromatic but suitable for white sauces. An attractive mixture of different-coloured peppercorns is known in France as Mignonette.

Poppy seeds Very small: about 900,000 seeds make up 450 g (1 lb). It is used as a topping for bread and confectionery, in some curry dishes and also to make poppy seed cakes beloved of Austrians.

Saffron The most expensive spice. It takes over 70,000 crocus flowers, each with three stigmas, to produce 450 g (1 lb). Stigmas are removed by hand and dried to produce a spice with a wonderful yellow colour and delicious taste essential for bouillabaisse, paella and saffron cakes. Indians rarely use saffron to colour rice yellow, preferring either turmeric rhizome or, more commonly, artifical sunset-yellow food colouring.

Sesame seeds The oil gives a distinctive flavour to Chinese cooking and the seeds are used in Mexican, and Asian Oriental food. As a paste it is called Tahini and can make a delicious appetizer, especially Greek hummus, when it is combined with chick peas.

Szechuan pepper Comes from a Chinese tree and is quite aromatic.

Star anise The fruits of a small shrub. Part of Chinese five spice powder and can be used the same way as aniseed.

Tamarind The sticky, seedless pods of an African tree, tamarind brings a sour pungency to some curries.

Turmeric A bright yellow spice made from the ground rhizome of a member of the lily family used in piccalilli and most curry mixtures. Indians call it haldi. *MH*

Sporting diets

It's not just professional sports people who should be taking their diet seriously. Keen keep-fitters, those of you working out in gyms, regularly attending aerobics, playing local club sports like football, rugby and hockey, should all be looking into the area too. Just a few basic guidelines can help improve enjoyment, training and performance. (See Exercise; Nutritional needs.) *AU*

Steaming

This is the best method of cooking for all vegetables in order to ensure that they retain their nutritional value. When steamed they take hardly any more time to become tender than when boiled. Steamers are fairly inexpensive: you can choose from expanding stainless steel ones or traditional bamboo steamers as used in Chinese cuisine. Place the trimmed, washed vegetables in the steamer over fast boiling water and leave for the required cooking time. Times vary: mange-tout need about 4 minutes, fennel roots 10 minutes or so, new potatoes 20 minutes, and so on. Other foods requiring relatively brief cooking, especially fish, can benefit from steaming too. *CS*

Stir-frying

A cooking technique using a wok, that originated in the Far East, particularly in China. (See Frying.) *CS*

Stools

Solid human waste or effluent. Stool shape, size, nature and habit is evidence of good or bad health. Because the diet in industrialized countries is made up mostly of processed, refined foods, most people in Britain and other such countries are short of fibre. The result is cylindrical, small hard stools passed once a day only, or less often, with some effort. Over time this increases the risk of bowel diseases, including colon cancer.

A healthy, fibre-rich diet produces shapeless, large soft stools passed easily at least once a day. Such a diet protects against bowel diseases and also against general malaise caused by toxic substances accumulating in the gut. Diarrhoea, which is to say watery human effluent, is of course a symptom of disease. (See Bowel diseases; Fibre.) *GC*

Stroke

Once known as apoplexy, this is a disease of the circulation system. Blood vessels in the brain burst, destroying whatever bodily function is governed by the rupture. The result is commonly loss of speech and partial or complete paralysis which is sometimes reversible. Unlucky people may suffer a series of strokes before death. Stroke is in decline in Britain, America and other countries but is still very common, though unusual before middle age. It kills more women than men, for reasons not well understood.

High blood pressure (hypertension) is the key danger sign of vulnerability to stroke. Stroke is very common when traditional diets are very salty, as in Japan and Portugal. It declines when the use of mass refrigeration reduces the amount of salt used to preserve food. (See Blood pressure; Diet; Hypertension; Salt.) *GC*

Sugar

Sugar is a wonderful commodity - but for whom? It is the most profitable legal cash crop after tobacco. The economies of several countries, including Brazil, the Philippines, Cuba and Mauritius, depend on cane sugar which, as grown and exported from the West Indies, enriched Bristol and Liverpool. The world sugar trade is still centred in London.

Itself a preservative, sugar is uniform, stable, packs and travels well, makes fat palatable in the form of cheap goods like cakes, biscuits and confectionery, and together with water, additives and a dash of patented recipe is turned into soft drinks and colas.

No wonder modern food supplies contain so much sugar. Average consumption in Britain is up to 100 pounds a year, making up to a fifth or 20 per cent of calories. 'Not me' you may think, and it is true that sales of packet sugar continue to drop. But in Britain, over two-thirds of all the added sugar we eat is contained in manufactured foods, less than one-third is now added in home-cooking or at table. Look at labels: apart from 'sugar', any word ending in '-ose' indicates a type of added sugar.

As part of a whole nourishing package, sugars as an intrinsic part of fruit are fine. In manufactured foods, 'extrinsic' added sugars are 'empty calories' without nourishment. They certainly cause tooth decay and, especially in the form of 'sweet fat' confections concentrated in calories, contribute to obesity. For these reasons alone, dietary guidelines usually recommend that everybody should cut down on sugar. The WHO goal is 0 - 10 per cent of total calories, meaning that the less added sugar you consume, the better.

Some scientists who have been able to research the health effects of sugar, point out that sugared foods and drinks are liable to cause fluctuations in blood sugar levels which may eventually lead on to adult-onset diabetes. This is a minority view. A few individual researchers think that a sugary diet may be a cause of heart disease, gall stones, kidney stones, and colon cancer.

Certainly, the more sugar added to any diet, the less nourishment it contains; sedentary people in particular, are well advised to cut sugar out of their diet. (See Hypoglycaemia; Obesity; Tooth decay.) *GC*

Sweet potatoes

Sweet potatoes are unique. They are packed with the important antioxidant vitamins, C, E and beta-carotene, making them the richest single food source of all three. Until a few years ago these long, large tuberous vegetables were found only in specialist stores and markets. Now they grace the shelves of most large supermarkets.

Sweet potatoes are related to the morning glory plant and are native to the New World where they have been used for thousands of years. Columbus noted the sweet potato, grown by the Incas of Peru and the Mayans of Central America, in his diaries in 1493. Portuguese traders took them to India, Malaya, China and Africa, where they are still a staple.

When choosing sweet potatoes, go for firm, undamaged ones and scrub them clean. They can be cooked in a variety of ways and are delicious baked in their skins, mashed, roasted or added to casseroles and soups. Sweeter than ordinary potatoes, they can be pureed and added to cakes, scones or souffles. They are a good source of fibre and the red variety has the highest beta-carotene content. *AU*

t

Taboos

A recognized general prohibition of some food. (See Religion.) These are not only religious, they are also social; we only have to think of the British refusal to eat horse, dog or cat, for example, while the Chinese eat all three. Nor do they have to be about food, they can relate to table manners. For example, we think it a social gaffe to eat asparagus with a knife and fork, but Americans think it polite.

Every nation and class are bound by taboos and strictures over the preparation, cooking, eating and clearing-up of food, not only what culinary implement to use, but how to dress and what language to use while the meal is continuing. (See *The Rituals of Dinner* by Margaret Visser for an exhaustive study of the subject.) *CS*

Take-aways

The take-away meal has earned itself an undeservedly bad reputation and is often referred to as junk food (see Junk food). In fact, if chosen with care, take-away food can be nutritious and in line with current advice on healthy eating.

• A burger in a bun with lettuce and tomato served with a small portion of fries and an orange juice, with a trifle for dessert, provides 35 per cent of the energy from fat and over 50 per cent from carbohydrate, which is bang on line with current advice. Some burger places serve flame-grilled chicken. This in a bun with a salad garnish and a vanilla shake again has 35 per cent of the energy coming from fat and 50 per cent from carbohydrate. The chicken and burger contain protein, the bun, starchy carbohydrate, the orange juice vitamin C and the shake calcium.

• Jacket potatoes are becoming more widely available and make a good choice if filled with chilli, baked beans or cottage cheese.

• If going to a kebab house, choose a shish kebab which is just lean meat with peppers, tomatoes and onions on a skewer in a pitta. Donner kebabs are much fattier and best avoided.

• In Indian take-aways go for simple dishes which are not fried or covered in creamy sauces. Chicken tikka with rice, dahl and a yogurt sauce is a good example. A chicken korma, on the other hand, is packed with fat, and if eaten with naan and fried rice will be loaded with calories and not at all balanced.

• In Chinese take-aways the same rules apply. Go for plain, unfried dishes. Surprisingly, sweet and sour dishes are a good choice. Whilst they contain sugar, they are low in fat. Again, eat with plain boiled rice rather than fried rice or noodles.

• Save fish and chips for a treat and when faced with a huge pizza menu, go for simple ones without extra cheese, salami, eggs and so on. *AU*

Tartrazine (E102)

Tartrazine or E102 is probably the most reactive of all the food colours. After caramel it is one of the most commonly used colours and has been shown to increase the histamine level of normal adults when large doses are given. But there is much dispute as to the level of adverse effects in the community. It can be replaced with nutritionally beneficial carotenoids and is certainly best avoided for children before adolescence. (See Colours.) *MH*

Taste

For most of us taste is a deceptive servant. For *Food File*, school-children were given the choice between a cheap synthetic strawberry-flavoured jelly and one made from real strawberries. Almost all chose the synthetic because that is what they were used to. We are constantly being indoctrinated with special flavours which give us a standard which may or may not be appropriate. Make tomato soup out of tomatoes and compare it to the Heinz variety: both are excellent but very different.

Mouth feel as well as sight, smell and taste, helps to distinguish different foods, for example, margarine from butter.

Different areas of the tongue detect the four key tastes which are sweet, sour, salt and bitter. To these must be added a relatively recent discovery and that is umami or deliciousness. This triggers a separate response in the brain and is caused by glutamates. The biological purpose is that mother's milk is rich in glutamates and this provides a bonding which is quite specific and makes the baby happy. *MH*

Tea

(See Coffee and tea.)

Tempeh

Pronounced 'tempay', this is a delicious miracle food. It is made from soya beans which have been fermented by the introduction of a powdered culture over a two-day period. Fermentation means that the beans have been rendered virtually pre-digested, reducing the raffinose and stachyose that provoke intestinal gas. Fermentation also releases delicious aromas and flavours of the kind found in cheese, yeasty bread and beer. It is thought that the process could go back as far as 2000 years to China, at which time the Chinese were inoculating dehulled soy beans with wild moulds as a stage in the making of soy sauce. Others think that tempeh originated in Java a thousand years ago, where it is still a staple food.

You will find packets of frozen tempeh in most health food stores. To cook, thaw, then cut into cubes and fry in olive oil and garlic, or stir-fry with ginger, chilli and green beans or peppers. Tempeh is as high in protein as beef or chicken but contains only 157 calories per 100 g (4 oz) it has no cholesterol and no fat. It has all eight essential amino-acids as well as being rich in minerals and vitamins, particularly B12. Best of all, it tastes fabulous, which is why it is a miracle food. *CS*

Toddlers – encouraging healthy eating

Encouraging children to adopt good habits is not always easy but it's best to start young, and food habits are no exception. Here are a few tried-and-tested hints which should help prevent mealtimes becoming a battle-ground:

1. Get your children into the habit of eating breakfast and other meals by eating with them. The atmosphere round the table is important in making mealtimes enjoyable for everyone.
2. Young children, particularly, can be tempted by the way that food is presented. Different shapes, sizes and textures all increase appeal so, for example, try making a face on shepherd's pie or pizza using peas, slices of tomato and other vegetables.
3. Involve your children in making meals, as most love to eat anything they have helped make themselves.
4. Try not to use foods like sweets and crisps as rewards or treats.

Some toddlers can be fussy eaters or appear to survive on very little. This is not unusual and is unlikely to do your child any harm in the long term. Try not to overreact or let your child know you are anxious otherwise you're more likely to find that eating becomes a battle of wills. *SD*

Tofu

A curd made from soy beans, a staple food in both China and Japan for many thousands of years. Tofu, in fact, has the same importance for the peoples of East Asia as eggs and dairy products do for us in the West. But unlike dairy produce, tofu happens to be an incredibly healthy food as it is high in protein and in linoleic acid, an essential fatty acid, thought to be vital in dispersing cholesterol from the bloodstream.

Tofu can be bought in packets, in which case drain before use and leave to firm up a little. Sold loose in Chinese stores, it is likely to be home-made and of excellent quality. If smoked, it only needs to be taken from its packet, sliced and stir-fried. Follow the recipe ideas for Tempeh. Just add flavourings and mixed vegetables, cook and serve as a real treat. *CS*

Tomatoes

The tomato (*Lycopersicon esculentum*) is today one of the most pervasive flavourings worldwide, although after they were discovered in the New World they were viewed with great suspicion, thought to be either poisonous or an aphrodisiac. The most popular canned vegetable, tomatoes can also be bought pureed into a paste, processed into soup, made into a sauce or sun-dried. Fresh tomatoes are available all the year round, yet a really good flavour is like the quest for the Holy Grail. Only in the summer months, freshly picked in the Mediterranean sun, do tomatoes ever taste how they should. The first tomatoes were yellow, hence the Italian word for tomato, pomodoro ('golden apple'). Yellow tomatoes have only lately crept back into our seed catalogues.

There are, in fact, hundreds of varieties, which can usefully be divided up into round, plum, cherry, yellow and large. Some need to be grown under glass while others will happily thrive outdoors even in northern climes for the short summer season. Tomato skins and seeds are indigestible and many recipes tell you to remove them, otherwise they travel right through the gut unchanged. Nutritionally, tomatoes are a good source of vitamin A and C, are high in fibre, potassium and folic acid (thus a good food to eat throughout pregnancy). The highest vitamin content is in the jelly which surrounds the seeds. *CS*

Tooth decay

Almost everybody in Britain has had or will have some rotten teeth. Tooth decay, also known as dental caries, is caused by processed (refined) sugar and by sugared food and drink. There is no other important cause. Otherwise harmless bacteria naturally present in the mouth feed off sugar embedded in crevices in and between teeth, and acids produced by these bugs attack the teeth themselves. Processed starchy food can contribute to tooth decay if it is sticky, and especially if it is also sugared, as can fruit juices, especially if they are sweetened. However, there is no good evidence that sugar as naturally present in whole fruit is a significant cause of tooth decay.

Tooth decay is painful and expensive to treat. In adult life continual dental treatment is liable to lead on to bleeding and receding gums, bad breath, loss of teeth and self-respect, general malaise, and overdrafts.

The British Department of Health and the World Health Organization recommend that everybody in affluent countries like Britain would do well to reduce their sugar consumption, if only for the sake of their dental health. These recommendations have also featured in the great majority of authoritative expert reports published since the 1960s concerned not just with diet and tooth decay, but also diet and the prevention of major non-infectious diseases. (See Sugar.) *GC*

Trading standards

Trading standards officers are the consumer's defence against malpractice. If you find misleading labels or advertisements or substandard food you should complain to your local council's Trading Standards or Environmental Health or Consumer Protection department who have the powers to investigate, to persuade and if necessary to prosecute. Their telephone number is listed under your local council or Town hall. *SD*

Trans-fatty acids

Saturated, monounsaturated, polyunsaturated: these are all now familiar from food labels.

The message of the Health Education Authority and other bodies, amplified by food advertisements, is that saturated (hard) fats are bad for you, and unsaturated (soft) fats and (liquid) oils are good in moderation. For good health it is advisable to cut your consumption of fat generally, and also to switch from saturated to unsaturated fats. Some polyunsaturated fats are 'essential', meaning that the body needs them in small quantities, much like vitamins, for health and life itself.

You may also have heard of 'trans-fats', or 'trans-fatty acids', although there is no mention of them in advertisements or on labels. In 1984 a report of the Department of Health's Committee on Medical Aspects of Food Policy (see COMA) recommended that trans-fats should be grouped with saturated fats as bad for heart health, and that the trans-fat content of processed foods be identified on labels. This recommendation got nowhere and was dropped.

Trans-fats are not saturated fats. They are a type of polyunsaturated fat whose chemical structure is altered (some would say perverted) in the course of manufacture notably of margarines, baked good such as cakes and biscuits with long shelf-lives, and any processed product containing hydrogenated fats or oils (which are identified on labels). Over 2 per cent of the calories typically eaten by people in Britain are trans fats. A diet made up of fresh whole foods together with some processed products such as bread contains virtually no trans fats.

Although it is early days yet, recent research by independent scientists, notably in America, quite strongly suggests that trans fats are very bad for the health. Evidently they block metabolism of essential fats in the body and thus are liable to create a deficiency state; this in turn can cause relatively rapid blocking of the coronary and other arteries. A radical theory is that trans fats more than saturated fats are the key dietary cause of heart disease. Significantly, heart attacks became colossal epidemics in Britain, America and other industrialized countries in the 1950s, twenty or thirty years after the general introduction of margarines and other hydrogenated products containing substantial amounts of trans fats. Major margarine manufacturers have now been impressed by the evidence, and are findings ways and means to reduce trans fats in their products. (See Essential fats; Fats; Saturated fats; Polyunsaturated fats.) *GC*

U

United Nations

The United Nations (UN) and its constituent agencies advise and co-ordinate national and international policies of member states. Generally speaking, the poorer a country the greater the influence of the UN which is usually perceived as a benign influence but is identified by some critics as an instrument of the USA and of the 'new world order' seeking to make the world safe for multinational business in, among other things, legal arms and drugs, and processed food and drink. (See FAO; GATT; WHO.) *GC*

V

Vanilla

Vanilla is the aromatically flavoured pod of one of seventy species of the genus, a member of the orchid family. It is tropical and a key export from Madagascar which produces 20 - 30 cms (8 - 12 inch) pods from the delectable *vanilla fragrans, syn planifolia*. The name comes from the Spanish word *vainilla* which means little sheath, the shape of the fruit.

Put half a dozen vanilla pods into a jar and cover with sugar for use in desserts and baking and they will remain good for several years. When making custard, stirring a vanilla pod into the mixture is generally enough to give the required flavour.

Read labels carefully on vanilla flavoured products to avoid the second-rate taste of the synthetic substitute, vanillin. *MH*

Veal

The meat from calves. Because of the desire for 'white' veal, this meat is all too often produced by taking the calves away from their mothers when they are a few days old and keeping them in 60 cm (24 inch) wide wooden crates, so narrow that the calves can neither turn around, nor turn their heads to groom themselves. The floors are slatted, so their leg joints become malformed. They are fed on a liquid diet which is deficient in iron, lacking the fibre that ruminants crave for; often they gnaw the wooden bars or eat their own hair as a substitute. They stay in these crates on this diet for fourteen weeks until they are taken to slaughter, often too weak to be able to stand up and many suffering from anaemia. This method is to ensure that the carcass meat is pale and bloodless, thus giving the chef a meat which cooks white.

Although this rearing method has been banned in the UK, two-thirds of our calves are exported to France and Holland where this is the only method used. The carcass meat is exported back to us as white veal for hotels and restaurants, and also to food manufacturers to make veal, ham and egg pies. There is a humane alternative method of rearing, where calves are penned in groups of twenty on deep straw in covered yards. Increasing numbers of confirmed meat-eaters choose to avoid eating veal and hopefully that trend will continue. *CS*

Vegetables

A plant or part of a plant used for food, other than a fruit. Vegetables can be divided up into different categories:

1. Leafy: the darker green the leaf, the more vitamins and minerals it contains. Therefore the outside leaves are more nutritious than the lighter green ones at the heart.
2. Seeds in a pod: vegetables such as legumes (peas, beans, etc.)
3. Fruits: some vegetables are really fruit, like the melon, marrow and cucumber family, where the fruit encases the seeds, or the pepper and aubergine family which are fruits growing from small shrubs.
4. Roots: rhizomes and tubers that grow underground, such as potatoes, ginger, turnips.
5. Stems: vegetables such as asparagus and celery.
6. Water plants like watercress and the water chestnut.
7. Sea-weeds also count as vegetables and are highly nutritious.
8. Mushrooms and fungi.

We tend to separate the grass seeds, like wheat, oats and rye, from vegetables and call them cereals.

Our consumption of vegetables is the lowest in Europe. Latest research shows that nutrients in vegetables and fruit play a protective role in fighting disease, so several portions of vegetables a day are recommended. (See A.C.E.) *CS*

Vegetarians

The word was coined in the late 1840s when the Vegetarian Society was founded; it was taken from the Latin, *vegetus*, and meant lively and energetic. The Society used it in those early days, and still does, to mean an abstention from meat, fish and fowl, to abstain from the flesh of all sentient creatures and to live off plants, fruits, vegetables and grains. There is no need to kill another creature in order for human beings to survive, in fact nutritional research in the last two decades points irrevocably to the fact that people can be far healthier on a plant diet than one which relies partly on animal protein. The same research also states that the vegan diet, that is, one without eggs and dairy produce, is also marginally more healthy than the vegetarian one.

Today, the word 'vegetarian' is undergoing a change of meaning; as more and more people eat less meat, younger people now often use it to denote the fact that they abstain just from red meat. Perhaps it shows that there is a need for a new word which will mean abstention from red meat, or a new word for the millions of people in the UK and the US who now only use a sliver of meat at certain times for flavouring, who have a real love of vegetables, yet who dislike the word vegetarian, as for them the connotation is inelegant. *CS*

Very low calorie diets

A very low calorie diet is a weight loss plan in which normal meals are replaced with a special formula diet. The formulas are usually in drink form and provide all the nutrients necessary for a healthy adult, but are very low in energy. Providing 500 calories or less a day, very low calorie diets were designed to produce rapid loss of fat without affecting lean tissues such as muscle. Initial fears over safety were due to problems with early formulas, some of which led to deaths in America.

Today's versions are safe providing they are followed under the supervision of your doctor. This is vital since they are unsuitable for people with heart disease, or vascular, kidney and liver problems. They must only be followed for the time stated by the manufacturer and must not be used by pregnant women, adolescents or children.

There is no doubt these diets can be effective in the short term but long-term results are poor. A major criticism is that very low calorie diets do nothing to re-educate the eating habits which helped contribute to obesity in the first place. *AU*

Vinegars

The non-brewed variety beloved of fish and chip shops is merely dilute acetic acid of between 3 and 4 per cent, possibly coloured with a little caramel, to give a natural look. It is best avoided.

In Britain vinegars are traditionally made by putting a naturally fermented alcoholic drink into a vat containing some 20,000 gallons with a base of a web of lathes upon which are 3.3 m (14-foot) layers of sterilized birch twigs. Each vat uses about 2 tonnes of twigs. The twigs are steamed for forty-eight hours before use and then soaked with a working culture containing the bacterium Acetobacter. When this is well established on the birch twigs the alcohol is added and circulated for two to three weeks to provide the oxygen necessary for the Acetobacter to convert alcohol into acetic acid.

For the best vinegars the resulting product is stored in oak casks or vats and allowed to mature, producing a subtle flavour which will improve over years.

Malt vinegar comes from beer, cider vinegar from cider and wine vinegar from wine. Of the straight vinegars my preference is for a good, uncoloured cider vinegar. When pickling go for one with at least 5 per cent acetic acid to help the preservation process.

Balsamic vinegar, if properly made, is expensive but wonderful in small amounts. In Italy it is called Aceto Balsamico di Modena. It should be made from the reduced must of the white Trebbiano grape and aged in a system similar to the sherry solera in a series of wooden casks of ever- diminishing size. It is darkly aromatic and a small amount with olive oil and seasoning makes an excellent (and fashionable) dressing for salads.

For Italian and Chinese cookery, rice vinegar is made from sake must which is what remains after the drink has been decanted.

Many beneficial properties are ascribed to cider vinegar which is also much used by farmers and horse breeders to keep their animals healthy. *MH*

Vitamins

Vitamins are essential for life. We need them in small amounts to ensure good health and growth. They are a group of non-related carbon-based substances which are necessary to make the various systems in the cell work. We have long known that they prevent deficiency diseases like scurvy and rickets. We now also believe that antioxidant vitamins (vitamins C, E and the carotenoids) can ward off degenerative diseases as well as maintain optimum health. (See A.C.E.)

Recommended daily amounts (see table below) are based on the minimum amounts needed to prevent deficiency diseases in adults. Optimal levels are a matter of keen debate. Fresh fruit and vegetables, nuts and seeds are good sources for most vitamins.

Recommended Daily Allowances (RDAs) are obligatory for use in nutritional labelling of foods in the EC. The UK developed its own system based on Reference Nutrient Intake (RNI) but the EC has decided that since RDAs are what we are all familiar with, they are what we will see on labels. *MH*

Vitamin	*RDA*	*Upper Safe Level*	*Function*
Vitamin A	800μg	9000 μg (except for pregnant women 800μg)	Essential for vision growth, reproduction, the immune system and cellular development
Vitamin D	5μg	50μg	Keeps the minerals in balance, utilizes calcium to build bones and prevent rickets
Vitamin E	10mg	2000mg	Reproduction and as an antioxidant.
Vitamin C	60mg	1g	Antioxidant. A deficiency causes scurvy. Helps absorption of iron and assists wound healing
Vitamin K	none	Safe. There is normally enough in a balanced diet	Necessary as a blood clotting factor
Beta carotene	none	15mg is generally recognized as sensible. High doses can turn skin yellow but are not toxic	Antoxidant free radical scavenger which might protect against some forms of cancer, such as that of the lung and other degenerative conditions
Thiamin	1.4mg	500mg	Needed for carbohydrate metabolism
Riboflavin	1.6mg	Safe	Catalyses oxidation-reduction reavtions
Niacin	18mg	Upper safe levels of niacin as nicotinamide 2000mg, as nicotinic acid 500mg, but not in a sustained release form	Used for fatty acid metabolism and tissue restoration
Vitamin B_6	2mg	50mg	Used for utilizing proteins and fats
Folacin	200μg	400μg for the potentially pregnant (larger intakes are safe but can mask the effects of vitamin B_{12} deficiency).	Essential to the correct development of the foetus, and in protein metabolism. Deficiency causes poor division
Vitamin B_{12}	1μg	200μg	Prevents anaemia
Biotin	0.15mg	Safe	Used for carbohydrate and fat metabolism
Pantothenic acid	6mg	Safe	Releases energy from carbohydrates, creates and breaks down fatty acids

W

War

In modern wars both soldiers and civilians have tended to be healthier than in peacetime. This is because in wartime, governments do their best to ensure that young adults, at least, are fit to fight and support the war effort. The science of nutrition developed in the early years of this century in response to the appalling discovery, initially by the British government, that a high proportion of young men then called to arms were stunted and feeble, unable to carry a pack and a rifle. Many suffered deficiency diseases, especially rickets.

Consequently, nutritionists in the 1930s persuaded the British government of the day that the whole nation, especially the working classes who supplied most fighting men and factory workers, should be fed plenty of food to specified minimum nutritional standards. During the 1939 - 45 war the British people as a whole became fitter and slimmer, and rates of tooth decay, diabetes and heart disease dropped. This was partly a result of wartime food policy, which included encouragement of allotments to grow potatoes and vegetables, and partly because of shortages causing rationing of some fatty and sugary foods.

The food supplies of other countries shifted in the same direction during the war, with similar results. During the 1950s and 1960s researchers in America, Australasia and Scandinavia concluded that the 1939 - 45 war among other things amounted to a vast nutritional experiment, showing that post-war industrial food supplies had gone wrong, and contained far too much fat and sugar.

This remains true. And modern push-button wars can be fought by sedentary people. While American astronauts are fine figures of men, because every extra pound of weight is a load on their craft, American soldiers who rained death on Iraq in 1991 did so from the military equivalent of armchairs, and were often out of shape. In conventional wars, though, fit soldiers have an advantage, which may be one lesson from the Vietnam war. (See Rickets.) *GC*

Water

In recent years we have become much more concerned about the quality of our drinking water, and sales of bottled mineral water and water filters have boomed. Water companies tell us that our water meets very high standards but a number of well-publicized cases of contamination of drinking water have fuelled consumers' concerns.

Some British drinking water fails to meet EC standards, particularly on the grounds of nitrates from agricultural fertilizers and some pesticides. There may also be contamination from other chemicals and from lead, particularly old pipes. The UK government has argued that it will cost too much to ensure that all drinking water meets the EC's standards and have asked for standards to be lowered. Many consumer and environmental organizations think that the polluter, rather than the consumer, should pay to clean up water supplies.

Water is also an important ingredient in food processing. It is a cheap ingredient, but loopholes in labelling laws mean you cannot always tell how much water foods contain. Manufacturers of foods such as sausages, poultry, fish products and bacon do not have to specify exactly how much water is in the food. For example, one-fifth of a can of ham can be water - but you won't find anything on the label to tell you so. *SD*

Weaning

Babies will be ready to start on solid food at any time between three and six months. All babies are different, some take to it quickly and like anything and everything, while others are more choosy.

It's important not to rush to try and 'force-feed' your baby when weaning. Most babies know when they have had enough to eat, so don't spend a lot of time persuading yours to take food. Babies soon learn the effect that refusing food can have. But if you give encouragement and attention there's a better chance that mealtimes will be enjoyable and relaxed, and not a battle of wills.

Fruit or vegetable purées (with no added salt or sugar) make good first foods, also potato, carrot, yam, plantain, spinach, apple and banana. Or you can make a thin porridge from rice, cornmeal, sago or millet, for example. Just a small teaspoon is enough at first. You should avoid wheat-based foods, cows milk, eggs, citrus fruits and nuts until your child is at least six months old as all these foods can cause allergies. (See Allergies; Baby foods.) *SD*

Weight

Our national obsession with slimming is largely responsible for the distorted view so many of us hold over what constitutes healthy body weight. It's certainly not the one promoted by the media and characterized by waif-like fashion models.

One of the most reliable ways of determining if we're at a healthy weight for our height is to use the Body Mass Index equation. This involves dividing our weight in kilograms by our height in metres squared. In other words, W/H^2. If the figure obtained is less than 20 this indicates being underweight to an extent which in the long term can be a hazard to health. Between 20 and 24.9 is desirable, 25 - 29.9 is moderately obese and over 30 is severely obese, which can also endanger health.

It's important to take into account basic body shape when considering weight. If you're basically a pear shape then no amount of dieting is going to make you into a long lean ectomorph like Twiggy. It's absolutely possible, though, to be a healthy pear in the 20 - 24.9 BMI band. *AU*

Whole foods

Whole foods or whole food are foods from which nothing is taken out and to which nothing is added. Whole foods are whole grains, sun-dried fruit, pulses, nuts and seeds; they are foods which have been grown organically without artificial fertilizers and pesticides. Whole foods have not been refined, processed, packaged, canned, frozen or pre-cooked. The term 'whole' in itself has connotations of completeness, lack of flaws and injuries, of, indeed, health itself. Just as the word 'wholesome' suggests spiritual, moral and physical worth, so the term 'whole foods' carries with it a bag full of positive images. *CS*

Wine

I have always felt that a reasonable intake of wine was doing me good and research now shows that red wines are a rich source of polyphenols which are powerful antioxidants. The Bulgarians have even prepared a product from their Cabernet Sauvignon wine which has been studied for its decontamination effects, protecting against irradiation.

The *New England Journal of Medicine* reported a trial in which it was clear that moderately high levels of alcohol consumption, around 21 units or more a week, increased the high-density lipoprotein cholesterol (HDL) which has a protective effect against coronary heart disease. They also warn that the difference between moderate and large intakes may be the difference between preventing and causing disease.

We therefore have to walk a happy tightrope between having a healthy intake of wine and consuming so much that we are in danger of developing liver failure, some cancers and brain damage. The protective effect seems stronger for men than for women but may help to account for the low levels of coronary heart disease in southern Europe where the glorious combination of wine, garlic, fresh fruits and vegetables seems to protect many from heart disease. (See Mediterranean diet.) *MH*

Wound-healing

Are you well or ill? You can easily check most of the common signs of health and disease by yourself. One sign of health is the speed at which wounds heal. As a rule, the faster your wounds heal, the healthier you are. Check by comparison with the past, or with friends and members of your family.

The nutrient with a special role in wound-healing is zinc. This is why ointments whose active ingredient is zinc are commonly used for cuts and grazes. Major wounds caused by injury or surgery are likely to heal faster and better if treated with zinc supplements taken by mouth. (See Zinc.) *GC*

y

Yeast extract

Yeast is a by-product of brewing. The grains are rich in protein and B vitamins. The old British product, Marmite, was originally intended to rhyme with meat so highlighting its value as a nutritional substitute for meat protein. In fact Marmite, with 40 per cent protein, contains marginally more than meat-derived Bovril. The problem is the massive proportion of salt, 4.5 and 4.8 g per 100 g respectively, equivalent to more than 11 per cent salt. Therefore only the low sodium variety should be used sparingly for babies. *MH*

Yogurt

Yogurt is made from fermented milk and is a good source of calcium and protein. Its health-promoting properties were thought to account for the longevity of Bulgarian peasants. But whatever the truth, the products on supermarket shelves are a far cry from the curdled milk product originating in the Balkans.

Since they latched on to its healthy image, yogurt has been a huge money-spinner for the food industry. This simple food is now available set, stirred, low-fat, live, creamy, Greek-style and flavoured with everything from strawberry to toffee.

But watch out for added sugars and additives, particularly in some children's brands, and don't be taken in by claims for live yogurt. There is no real evidence that the cultures they contain stay 'live' long enough to colonize the gut. And for any benefit you'll need to eat several pots a week. *SD*

Z

Zinc

Zinc is a rather brittle bluish metal which is present in all tissues and necessary for over seventy of our enzyme processes including those that produce RNA, DNA and protein. Zinc is 100 times more concentrated in semen than in blood plasma. Oysters contain between 8 - 90 mg of zinc per 100 g (4 oz) massive concentrations which might give the hopeful scientific backing for their supposed aphrodisiac qualities. However, zinc is much more valuable as a wound healer and anti-infective, whilst playing a vital role in giving us a sensitive sense of taste. Regular consumption of more than four times the RDA (recommended daily allowance) of 15mg of zinc can cause a shortage of copper and reduce the immune response. *MH*

Zest

The peel of orange of lemon used as a flavouring, or the oil squeezed from the peel to add piquancy to food and drink. The word is often used figuratively to convey a keen relish or enjoyment and what better entry to end on - even if we have to cheat with the alphabetical order. Understanding more about the food we eat, and following some of the simple tips in this guide, should increase our zest for life and enable us to eat well with gusto and enthusiasm. *AU*

World in a Stew

Compiled by Eliza Stephens with Patricia Llewellyn
Recipes adapted by Robert Muir

All recipes serve four unless otherwise stated

THE AMERICAS

The food of the Americas is an exhilarating mix of ingredients and cultures from all over the world. The Americas are home to some of the world's most versatile ingredients and some of the most racially mixed populations in the world.

Every country is different: different climates, different ingredients and different people. Looking at the food eaten today is an excellent way of looking into the past. The five countries covered in this section serve as a small taster of the food from this vast continent.

THE AMERICAS

UNITED STATES OF AMERICA

The United States of America is an immense country with a huge range of culinary influences. The original American indians, like the Hopi, Navajo and Pueblo tribes of the southwest gave a great tradition in corn, bean and chilli cooking. The year 1604 saw the arrival of the first Europeans, who were soon followed by people from all over the world. Today American food is a true melting pot of ingredients and cooking methods. Every state in the Union has its own unique cooking styles, making the best of the local ingredients and the traditions of the various groups of people who settled there.

One of America's most delicous regional cooking styles comes from the southern state of Louisiana, home of the Cajun people. For the second series of Food File, Louisiana-born Alicia Zervigon prepared the tradional Cajun dish Chicken Gumbo.

The Cajuns were actually the Acadians, a group of people who left France in the seventeenth century and settled in Nova Scotia, Canada. In 1755 they were driven out of their homes by the Beastly British, as Alicia called them, and came to settle thousands of miles further south in the Bayou country of Louisiana. Cajun food is a mixture of French, Amerindian, Italian and African.

The Cajuns were poor people who lived mainly as farmers and shrimpers, with no time to spend all day cooking. Chicken Gumbo was the perfect meal for them: they could put all the ingredients into one pot in the morning and leave it to cook all day, ready for when they returned home in the evening.

Chicken Gumbo

Gumbo is the African name for okra which is used in this dish as a thickening agent. The Cajun spices give this recipe a real zing. It's cheap, easy to make and nutritious. Ideal for large gatherings and perfect with cornbread. The peppers, celery and onion combine in this dish to create the classic Cajun 'trinity', the basis of many dishes in their kitchen.

INGREDIENTS

Serves six

8 tablespoons olive oil
2 green bell peppers, chopped
½ head celery, roughly chopped (including leaves)
450 g (1 lb) onions, sliced
225 g (8 oz) smoked gammon or smoked bacon piece, cut into chunks
2 chicken quarters
3 cloves garlic, crushed
450 g (1 lb) okra, topped and tailed and cut in half
2 tablespoons Cajun seasoning (see below)
2 bay leaves
2 teaspoons oregano
salt

METHOD

(1) Pour the olive oil into a large pot and sauté the peppers, celery and onions until soft.

(2) Add the meat, garlic, okra, Cajun seasoning, bay leaves and oregano and mix thoroughly. Cover with water and bring to the boil.

(3) Boil for 10 minutes, then turn down the heat, cover and simmer for approximately 2½ hours, adding more water if necessary (remember this is a soup).

(4) Towards the end of the cooking time, the chicken should have fallen away from the bones. If not, separate with a fork and return, with the bones, to the soup. Add salt to taste. Serve on top of a little boiled rice.

VARIATION

For a change, or if you don't eat meat, try using pumpkin and root vegetables such as potato, carrot and parsnip instead of the meat. Cook for just 1 hour, and 15 minutes before the end, add some chopped spinach leaves.

CAJUN SEASONING

'Cajun seasoning' can be bought from specialist shops ready mixed. If it is not available or not very good, you can make your own using the following mixture instead:

1 teaspoon salt
1 teaspoon white pepper
1 teaspoon black pepper
1 teaspoon cayenne pepper
1 teaspoon poultry seasoning
1 teaspoon dried basil
1 teaspoon cumin

Cornbread

Eat this with your soups or stews and you'll see why it is so popular all over America.

INGREDIENTS

Serves four to six with a meal.

140 g (5 oz) fine cornmeal
140 g (5 oz) flour (use a mixture of wholemeal and plain white)
1 ½ tablespoons baking powder
1 teaspoon salt
2 tablespoons brown sugar
2 tablespoons sunflower oil
300 ml (½ pt) milk
50-100 ml (2-4 fl oz) water, depending on the flour

METHOD

(1) Preheat oven to 200°C/400°F/gas mark 6 and heat your oiled 25 x 15 cm (10" x 6") baking tin in the oven while you make the batter.

(2) Mix all the dry ingredients together in a mixing bowl. Gently whisk in the oil, milk and water bit by bit until the batter is thin and pourable.

(3) Pour the batter into the baking tin and cook in the oven for 30 minutes or until the bread is brown on top.

(4) Remove from the oven, run a knife around the edge of the tin and transfer to a bread board for serving.

Baked Beans

A real winter warmer, with enough left over for beans on toast in the morning. The delicate sweetness of the maple syrup and the long slow cooking make this dish delicious.

INGREDIENTS

Serves four

450 g (1 lb) dried beans (baricot, pinto)
225 g (8 oz) slab of bacon
3 tablespoons maple syrup
1 teaspoon dry mustard
½ teaspoon salt
1 teaspoon ground black pepper

METHOD

(1) Soak beans overnight in a large bowl filled with water.

(2) Drain the beans and place in a large saucepan with fresh water to cover. Bring to the boil, cover and simmer over low heat for 45 minutes.

(3) Drain the beans, reserving the bean water.

(4) Preheat oven to 130°C/250°F/gas mark 1-2. Put bacon in casserole, cover with beans.

(5) Mix 600 ml/1 pt of the bean water with maple syrup, mustard, salt and pepper; pour it over the beans.

(6) Cover the casserole and bake in the oven for about 6 hours. Serve with corn bread and salad.

THE AMERICAS

BRAZIL

The cooking of Brazil is a mixture of African, Amerindian and Portuguese. Brazil is a huge country covering almost half of South America.

Brazilian food can be divided into two major groups: the spicy African-based food of the tropical north, said to be some of the best in South America; and the milder Portuguese-influenced food of the more temperate south. Unlike Mexico and Peru, whose food is still strongly based on the ancient traditions of the great Aztec and Inca civilisations, Brazil's food is based on the period of history since the arrival of the Portuguese.

The Portuguese came to Brazil in the sixteenth century and began importing millions of people from West Africa to work as slaves on the sugar plantations. Brazil's climate and geography are similar to West Africa's and the Africans found that they were able to grow and prepare many foods from their homelands. Today, palm oil, a traditional African cooking oil, is used extensively in Brazil, giving food a characteristically yellow colour and nutty flavour.

The Brazillians love stews. Whether it is the spicy African-based prawn and coconut stews from the Bahai region in the North, or the Brazillian national dish, Feijoada, from Rio de Janero in the South, stews are central to Brazilian life.

Feijoada

'Feijoada means beans, stew of beans.'

Monica Nicholson lives with her husband and two children in Hertfordshire. Born in Brazil, Monica was taught to cook Feijoada by her grandmother when she was a child and she enjoys cooking it for her family and friends in Britain today. She says:

Feijoada is mainly a stew of black beans and different kinds of dried and smoked meats. The addition of pigs' trotters, tails and ears give the Feijoada its special flavour. Without them you would just have beans and pork, not Feijoada.

Feijoada started with the slaves in Brazil. Any meat left over from the Senor's house on the farm was taken to the kitchen to make stew.

Unfortunately, since the 1970s, the poor in Brazil can't afford to eat Feijoada anymore. They say that if they can even get the beans, they are lucky.

Monica serves her Feijoada with the traditional accompaniments of Brazilian Rice, Farofa (cassava flour), Couve (spring greens), and Malho de Pimenta e Limao, a chilli and lemon sauce. With all these extras, Feijoada becomes Feijoada Completa and is a perfect meal for a large gathering.

Feijoada Completa

INGREDIENTS

2 pig's ears
1 salted pig's trotter
1 pig's tail
225 g (8 oz) smoked bacon, cut into large chunks
225 g (8 oz) smoked pig's ribs, separated
225 g (8 oz) smoked pork sausage
450 g (1 lb) pork loin
4 tablespoons olive oil
2 onions
2 cloves garlic, minced
bay leaf
450 g (1 lb) dried black beans, soaked overnight
salt and pepper

METHOD

(1) Soak the pig's ears, trotter and tail overnight.

(2) Cut off the ear joint, leaving only the flap, and split the trotter. Put all the soaked meats in a large saucepan, cover with water, bring to the boil and then simmer until the meat is tender - (about 1¼ hours).

(3) In another saucepan, put the smoked bacon, smoked ribs and smoked pork sausage. Pour boiling water on to the smoked meats and simmer for about 30 minutes to lose some excess fat.

(4) Drain all the meats and wipe dry. Slice the ears into strips, chop the tail into 5 cm (2") pieces and slice up the smoked pork sausage. Fry the pork loin gently in 2 tablespoons of the olive oil.

(5) In a casserole, sauté the onions in the remaining olive oil with the garlic and bay leaf. Add the ears, trotter, tail and black beans and stir for a few minutes before covering with water and cooking for an hour until the beans are nearly tender.

(6) Add the smoked meats and pork loin and continue cooking for another 30 minutes. Mash up a few ladles of beans then return to the casserole and cook for a few more minutes to thicken up the stew. Add salt and pepper to taste. Serve with Brazilian Rice, Farofa, Couve and Molho de Pimenta E Limao and sliced oranges.

Brazilian Rice

INGREDIENTS
450 g (1 lb) long-grain rice, uncooked
1 onion, chopped
2 cloves garlic, minced
½ bay leaf
1 tablespoon olive oil
salt

METHOD
(1) Rinse the rice several times to remove the starch.

(2) Sauté the onion, garlic and bay leaf in the olive oil for 5 minutes until the onion is softened. Add long-grain rice and continue cooking for a few minutes, stirring continuously.

(3) Add water to cover, plus a little salt, and bring to the boil. Reduce the heat, cover, and simmer for 12-15 minutes.

Farofa (Cassava)

INGREDIENTS
1 onion, finely sliced
1 tablespoon olive oil
1 clove garlic, minced
2 rashers fatty smoked bacon, finely chopped
110 g (4 oz) cassava flour (available from Spanish and Portuguese delicatessens)

METHOD
(1) Sauté the onion in the olive oil until softened, then add the garlic and the bacon bits.

(2) Cover with cassava flour and stir continuously over a medium flame until the cassava turns a golden brown.

(3) Sprinkle on to the Feijoada.

Couve (Spring greens)

INGREDIENTS

225 g (8 oz) spring greens, kale or green cabbage, stems removed, leaves shredded
4 tablespoons sunflower oil

METHOD

(1) Plunge the spring greens, kale or green cabbage into boiling salted water, drain and dry.

(2) Heat the sunflower oil in a frying pan and fry the vegetables for 2-3 minutes, stirring continuously.

Molho de Pimenta e Limao (Chilli and lemon sauce)

INGREDIENTS

3 chilli peppers
½ teaspoon salt
1 onion, finely sliced
1 clove garlic
juice of 1 lemon
1 tablespoon bean liquor (kept after cooking black beans)

METHOD

(1) Pound the chilli peppers, salt, onion and garlic into a paste.

(2) Add the lemon juice and bean liquor.

THE AMERICAS
JAMAICA

The island of Jamaica is one of over 200 islands which make up the chain of tropical islands called the Caribbean, running from Florida in the north down to Venezuela in the south. Jamaica lies towards the north, near the islands of Cuba and Haiti.

Jamaica has an abundance of tropical fruits, a passion for root vegetables and its people are addicted to one of the hottest chilli peppers in the world, the Scotch bonnet. These small lantern-shaped red and yellow chillies produce a blast of heat of nuclear proportions. The food of this region rests firmly on its lush tropical climate, surrounding blue Caribbean sea and the history of the people who have lived there.

BRIEF HISTORY OF THE CARIBBEAN

The original inhabitants of the islands included the Amerindian tribes of the Arawaks and the Caribs. The Arawaks were peaceful people. They were great farmers and brought chilli, maize, cassava, sweet potatoes and yams to the islands from South America. They enjoyed hunting in a rich Caribbean sea teaming with huge red snappers and many other fish. The Caribs were not great farmers and relied on hunting meat and fish. They were a war-loving people and soon wiped out the gentle Arawaks.

The arrival of Christopher Columbus in 1492 opened up a new world to the power-hungry Europeans and they took to it like wild fire. Ship after ship of Spanish and Portuguese arrived bringing with them sugar cane, rice, coffee, pigs, salt cod, breadfruit, mangoes, limes and oranges. They soon almost completly wiped out the Caribs and the other tribes living on the islands, either by working them to death as slaves on the new sugar plantations or killing them outright, claiming they were possessed by the devil and were cannibals. The resulting shortage of labour meant that first the Spanish and then the Portuguese started importing slaves from West Africa, who brought with them new foods like okra, akee and callaloo, a tasty spinach-like vegetable.

After the abolition of slavery, many people from China and India also came to the area to live and work, bringing with them their own styles of cooking.

Today most of the Caribbean islands are independent, although some still have European governors. The population is mainly African in origin with significant numbers of Chinese, Indian and some European. Its food is an exciting mixture of these, together with native Amerindian influences.

Mary Donaldson's
Lamb Curry Rice and Peas

Mary Donaldson was the first person to take part in World in a Stew and her West Indian cooking has made her one of the legends of the Notting Hill Carnival where, for the last nine years, she has been preparing traditional Jamaican dishes for over 500 people. When Mary was a small child she had to stand on a stool while her mother taught her how to prepare curry. She says, 'In Jamaica, as soon as you can eat, you eat curry, rice and peas and once tasted you will always come back for more.'

The recipe for Mary's curry originally came to Jamaica with the Indian workers but its ingredients make this a very Caribbean speciality. The chillies came over with the Arawak Indians; the allspice or 'Jamaica pepper' is native to the islands and today Jamaica is the world's largest producer; the tomatoes and red pepper come from South America, the soy sauce from China, the curry powder from India and the rest was brought over with the Europeans. The heat of this dish comes more from the black pepper than the Scotch bonnet chilli, which is kept whole and removed before serving. The dish is perfect, and well-balanced nutritionally when served with Mary's 'Rice 'n' Peas'. A fruit salad of mango and limes will round the meal off nicely.

Lamb Curry

INGREDIENTS

Serves four to six

900 g (2 lb) lamb, cut into small pieces
1 ½ tablespoons mild curry powder
1 teaspoon chilli powder
2 teaspoons ground allspice
2 tablespoons soy sauce
2 cloves garlic, finely chopped
2 teaspoons ground black pepper
225 g (½ lb) onions, chopped
sprig of thyme
2 tablespoons oil
bay leaf
1 Scotch bonnet chilli
225 g (½ lb) tomatoes, quartered
1 red bell pepper, deseeded and chopped
300 ml (½ pint) water

METHOD

(1) Put lamb in a bowl, add curry powder, chilli powder, allspice, soy sauce, garlic, black pepper, onions and thyme. Knead the lamb and powders, then leave to marinate for an hour.

(2) Heat the oil in a saucepan over medium heat. Add the meat mixture and cook for 10 minutes.

(3) Add chopped red pepper, tomatoes, bay leaf and Scotch bonnet (whole) and water and cook for 1 hour. If it starts to dry out, add more water.

(4) Remove Scotch bonnet chilli pepper before serving. Serve with Rice 'n' Peas.

Rice 'n' Peas

In this famous dish, the peas are in fact beans! In Jamaica, red kidney beans are used, elsewhere in the Caribbean, they use gungo (pigeon) peas.

INGREDIENTS

Serves four to six

450 g (1 lb) long grain rice
400 g (14 oz) can red kidney beans, drained
400 g (14 oz) can of coconut milk or 55 g (2 oz) creamed coconut mixed with
600 ml (1 pt) hot water
110 g (4 oz) spring onions, chopped
1 clove garlic, finely chopped
1 teaspoon of ground black pepper
1 teaspoon of salt

METHOD

(1) Rinse rice several times, place in a saucepan, add kidney beans, can of coconut milk, crushed garlic, black pepper, salt and the chopped spring onions and mix well.

(2) Add water to cover rice with an inch shelf over the rice, bring to vigorous boil then cover with foil and lid.

(3) Turn heat down very low and cook for 25 minutes. The rice should be soft and fluffy. Serve with lamb curry and salad.

Jamaican Pepperpot

This is a soup containing meat and vegetables, not to be confused with the traditional Caribbean 'pepperpot' which is a stew containing meat but no vegetables.

INGREDIENTS

450 g (1 lb) spinach, washed and torn roughly
225 g (½ lb) salt beef, cubed
3 cloves garlic, bruised and coarsely chopped
5 spring onions, sliced lengthways and chopped in 5 cm (2") lengths
3 fresh green chillies, deseeded and chopped
1 Scotch bonnet chilli, whole
110 g (4 oz) okra, topped
1.8 ltr (3 pts) water
30 g (1 oz) creamed coconut, chopped
225 g (8 oz) crabmeat
salt and pepper to taste

METHOD

(1) Put everything up to and including the water in a large saucepan, bring to the boil and simmer covered for 1½ hours

(2) Add the coconut, crabmeat and seasoning and simmer for 15 minutes.

THE AMERICAS
MEXICO

Mexican food is unique and delicious. The now famous tacos, enchiladas, guacamole, salsas and refried beans all have their roots in a dramatic period of Mexican history.

When the Spanish reached Mexico in 1517, they were amazed at what they found. In contrast to the native inhabitants of the Caribbean, who relied on basic farming and hunting, Mexico was the home of the incredible Aztec and Mayan civilisations. By 1519, the Spanish conquistador, Hernando Cortes, had invaded the Aztec capital city, Tenochtitlan, and found a society as advanced as any in Europe with a cuisine to match. These amazing people were great cultivators of crops, they understood the principles of a balanced diet and were conservationist.

Corn, squashes and beans formed the backbone of the Aztec diet. They grew beans up the stalks of the corn and the squashes in between. This not only insured a nutritionally-balanced diet, but also maintained the fertility of the soil. They kept bees for honey, domesticated the native turkey and were careful not to overhunt wild animals by regulating their hunts. Their favourite flavouring was of course the wonderful chilli pepper and today Mexicans still use three or four different varieties in a single dish.

It has been said that modern Mexican cooking means Aztec plus pigs, but many of the foods brought over by the Europeans have been readily absorbed into Mexican cooking. Coriander is now a favourite herb, onions and garlic are used extensively, rice is now a major staple and citrus fruits add a new zest to their food. The arrival of lard from the pigs also instigated a completely new method of cooking. Before pigs, all food was either boiled, steamed or roasted. Lard meant frying, and if you look in most Mexican cookbooks, you will see that wherever a recipe calls for fat, it is nearly always lard.

Chillies are the pride and joy of Mexican cooking and are eaten at every meal. They grow abundantly in Mexico and are available in many different sizes, shapes and colours. Although many people tend to think of chillies as merely hot, there is much more to them than that. Mexican chillies have a wide range of heats and flavours: some are very hot and others almost sweet. The heat of chillies is measured on a special scale and they are categorised according to their Scoville Heat Units. The hottest chilli in the world, the habanero, gets 10/10 whereas a mild sweet bell pepper gets 0/10. When combining chillies into a single dish, it is the flavour rather than the heat of the chilli that counts. A wide variety of Mexican chillies and chilli information is available by mail order from The Cool Chile Company (see Address section).

Mole Poblano
(Spicy Chocolate Chicken)

Mexican-born Graciella Sanchez and her British husband live in London with their large family. She prepared for us Mexico's national dish, Mole Poblano. There are many different versions of this ancient dish. The word 'mole' means chilli sauce and 'Poblano' refers to the Puebla region of Mexico where this version originates.

Mole Poblano contains two other classic Mexican ingredients: chocolate and peanuts. The cocoa bean originally came from Yucatan in the Mayan region of Mexico. It was greatly prized by both the Aztecs and Mayan people. Not only was it used in their cooking and as a drink but also as money: if you had chocolate you were very rich. The small amount of chocolate added to the Mole Poblano is used to darken the colour of the sauce and sweeten it slightly - delicious. Mole Poblano is Mexico's 'Sunday lunch' and is served with rice, beans and the very Mexican, soft corn or wheat tortilla.

INGREDIENTS

1.6 kg (3½ lb) chicken, skinned and chopped into 8 pieces
5 tablespoons wine vinegar
1 teaspoon salt
1 teaspoon ground black pepper
1 teaspoon sugar
6 cloves garlic, crushed
3 mulato chillies
3 ancho chillies
2 pasilla chillies
3 chipotle chillies
1 ltr (1¾ pts) boiling water
55 g (2 oz) sesame seeds
55 g (2 oz) flaked almonds
1 wheat tortilla
3 onions, quartered
½ teaspoon aniseed
30 g (1 oz) plain chocolate, grated (the best chocolate to use contains about 70% cocoa solids)
2 tablespoons tomato purée
7 cm (3") piece of cinnamon
6 cloves
10 peppercorns
110 g (4 oz) raisins
1 chicken stock cube
5 tablespoons oil

METHOD

(1) Put the vinegar, salt, pepper, sugar and half the garlic in a bowl and mix together. Add the chicken pieces and marinate for 1 hour.

(2) Dry fry the chillies (i.e. fry without oil) for a few minutes until soft, then remove stems and deseed. Cover with the boiling water and leave to soak for an hour.

(3) Dry fry the sesame seeds and almonds until they start turning brown and reserve. Dry fry the tortilla for a minute or two, turning occasionally until it goes brittle and reserve.

(4) Put the chilli mixture, ¾ of the nut mixture (reserving the rest for garnishing), the tortilla (broken-up) the reserved garlic and the rest of the other ingredients (except the oil) in a liquidiser and mix to a paste.

(5) Put the oil in a heavy casserole dish and lightly brown the chicken pieces for about 5 minutes, turning occasionally. Remove and reserve. Add the liquidised paste to the casserole and fry for a few minutes, then return the chicken pieces to the casserole and cook in a preheated oven (180°C/350°F/gas mark 4) for 1¾ hours. Garnish with the remaining nuts and serve with refried beans, rice, tortillas and a cucumber salad.

The following recipes are everday fare for Mexicans, served wrapped in tortillas.

Refried Beans

INGREDIENTS

225 g (8 oz) dried beans (pinto or kidney)
3 tablespoons oil or lard
1 onion, sliced
1 onion, finely chopped
1 clove garlic, finely chopped
grated Cheddar cheese to garnish

METHOD

(1) Soak beans in plenty of water overnight.

(2) Drain the beans and put them in a saucepan with 1 ltr (1¾ pt) fresh water, 1 tablespoon of the oil and the sliced onion. Bring to the boil over high heat then reduce heat to low and simmer covered for 2 hours.

(3) Heat the remaining oil in frying pan, add finely-chopped onion and garlic and sauté over medium heat for 4 minutes.

(4) Turn heat to high, add some of the cooked beans, and mash and cook until they begin to dry. Then add some more beans and repeat until all the beans have been added and the mixture is a puree.

(5) Put beans on a serving dish and garnish with grated cheese. Serve with Cos lettuce leaves, radishes and tortilla chips.

Salsa

A refreshing tomato salsa with a hidden bite.

INGREDIENTS

450 g (1 lb) tomatoes
1 onion, finely chopped
1 tablespoon fresh coriander, finely chopped
1 small green chilli, seeded and chopped (optional)
pinch of salt
pinch of sugar
pinch of pepper

METHOD

(1) Put tomatoes in a bowl and pour enough boiling water over them to cover - this is the key to peeling tomatoes easily. After 15 seconds, drain the tomatoes, run some cold water over them, make a nick with a knife to break the skin and start peeling.

(2) Cut the tomatoes in half, remove the seeds and chop the flesh finely.

(3) Put the tomato flesh and the rest of the ingredients in a bowl and mix gently.

Guacamole

An ever-popular Mexican taste sensation.

INGREDIENTS

3 ripe avocadoes
½ onion, finely chopped
1 small green chilli, seeded and finely chopped
1 tomato, peeled, seeded and coarsely chopped
1 tablespoon fresh coriander leaves, finely chopped
pinch of salt
pinch of pepper

METHOD

(1) Halve the avocadoes and remove the stones. Scoop out the flesh, put in a bowl and mash with a fork.

(2) Add all the other ingredients and gently mix together. Cover with clingfilm and refrigerate for 1-2 hours.

THE AMERICAS

PERU

The land of the Incas and the Andes, home of corn, aji (chillies) and the potato, Peru lies along the western coast of South America. Dry, arid, desert-like plains run along the Pacific coast line. The massive Andean mountain range cuts right through the centre, and lush tropical valleys run to its eastern borders. The food of Peru is a mixture of old and new. The indigenous Quechua Indians or Incas, the Spanish invaders and black Africans brought over as slaves, have all strongly influenced the food of this region.

The Quechua Indians or Incas, were 'Sun worshippers'. Their favourite chilli was called 'mirisol', meaning looking at the sun, and many traditional Peruvian dishes are sunshine yellow.

The Andes is the second highest mountain range in the world, reaching heights of 20,000 feet. The Quechua Indians made use of the vast temperate regions of the Andes by terracing the mountainside for growing crops. The altitude of these terraces also affects crop growth, and although corn cannot be grown successfully above 11,000 feet, potatoes and the other staple grain of that region, quinoa, thrive.

The other significant effect of living at high altitudes is that the higher the altitude, the lower the boiling temperature of water is. This means less energy is required to cook food by this method.

In our search for new ways with familiar foods, it is really Peru's use of the potato that we have most to learn from. The Quechua Indians even developed a method of 'freeze drying' potatoes which meant they could be stored for long periods of time. The potato, solanum tubersum, wasn't introduced into Europe until the sixteenth century and even then was treated with suspicion. Potatoes grow anywhere where it's not too hot or too cold, and today they are an important staple wherever they do grow. These days, many people in Britain associate potatoes with Ireland, but the Peruvians were using them in their kitchens for hundreds of years before potatoes ever made it into an Irish stew.

Papas a la Huancaina

(Spicy Potatoes in a Cheese Sauce)

The most basic potato dish of Peruvian mountain people was simply boiled potatoes with aji (chilli) and herbs. The arrival of the Spanish conquistadors in the sixteenth century meant the arrival of cheese: they taught the Peruvians the art of cheese-making, which was happily combined with their basic potato dish to give Papas a la Huancaina.

INGREDIENTS
675 g (1½ lb) potatoes, scrubbed
1 onion, finely sliced
2 fresh chillies, deseeded and finely chopped
juice of 1 lemon
225 g (8 oz) Caerphilly cheese, grated
150 ml (¼ pt) single cream
½ teaspoon chilli powder
½ teaspoon turmeric
4 tablespoons olive oil

METHOD
(1) Boil the potatoes in their skins until cooked. Drain and chop into largish chunks. Place in a serving dish and keep covered in a warm place.

(2) Meanwhile mix together the onion, chillies and lemon juice and reserve.

(3) Mix the cheese, cream, chilli and turmeric. Heat the olive oil in a small, heavy saucepan for a few minutes over a low heat. Add the cheese mixture and cook, stirring constantly until the cheese has melted.

(4) Pour sauce over the potatoes. Drain the onion and chillies and arrange them on top of the potatoes.

(5) Serve with hard-boiled eggs, olives, prawns and on a bed of lettuce.

Ceviche (Marinated raw fish)

It is not just the Japanese who eat raw fish! Do make sure that the fish you use is absolutely fresh.

INGREDIENTS
450 g (1 lb) plaice fillets, skinned
juice of 6 lemons
1 Scotch bonnet chilli, finely chopped
1 onion, finely sliced
2 cloves garlic, bruised
salt and pepper to taste

METHOD
(1) Chop the fish into bite-sized chunks and place in a non-metallic dish.

(2) Mix the lemon juice, Scotch bonnet chilli, onion, garlic, salt and pepper together.

(3) Pour the mixture over the fish, cover the bowl and chill in the fridge overnight.

(4) Drain the fish and place on lettuce leaves. Serve with sweetcorn and boiled potatoes.

Aji de Gallina
(Chicken in Spicy Nut Sauce)

A classic Peruvian dish.

INGREDIENTS

1.4 kg (3 lb) chicken, quartered
110 g (4 oz) walnuts
110 g (4 oz) fresh breadcrumbs
300 ml (½pt) milk
2 tablespoons chilli paste or 6 small dried red chillies, deseeded
2 tomatoes, skinned and deseeded
900 g (2 lb) potatoes, peeled
2 cloves garlic, crushed and chopped
2 medium onions, finely chopped
4 tablespoons olive oil
450 ml (¾ pint) stock
55 g (2 oz) parmesan

GARNISH

3 hard-boiled eggs, quartered
black olives
1 large chilli, deseeded and cut into threads

METHOD

(1) Put chicken in large saucepan, cover with boiling water and simmer for 45 minutes.

(2) Remove chicken and leave to cool, strain stock and reserve.

(3) Discard skin and bones from chicken, shred the meat and reserve.

(4) Put walnuts in a blender and grind fine, add breadcrumbs, milk, chilli paste or chillies (finely chopped) and tomatoes and blend to a purée.

(5) Boil the potatoes until tender.

(6) Heat a large deep frying pan, add olive oil, then sauté onions and garlic until soft and translucent.

(7) Add the purée, bring to the boil and simmer for 5 minutes.

(8) Add the chicken, stock and parmesan and simmer until chicken is heated through.

(9) To serve, place sliced potatoes in a large warm casserole dish, cover with chicken and sauce. Decorate top with eggs, olives and chilli strips.

CHINA: SZECHWAN REGION

The Chinese base their cooking around a balance of colours, textures and what is known as 'The Five Flavours': salt, sweet, bitter, sour and spicy hot. The different regions of this huge country have distinctive styles of cooking. The Szechwan region lies in the south-west, a fertile region isolated from the rest of China by the great Yangtze river and surrounding mountain ranges. The name Szechwan means four rivers and the region's subtropical climate, extensive irrigation systems and fertile soil provide enough food for the 100 million people living in this highly populated region.

The Szechwan diet is based on rice, wheat, vegetables; and soyabeans for protein. Meat plays a minor role in the diet, used more as a seasoning than a food source. Not only is meat production an inefficient use of valuable land, but the people of Szechwan have been influenced by vegetarian beliefs brought over with the Buddhists from India. When meat is used, it is normally pork, chicken or duck. Szechwan is a land-locked area with a good supply of freshwater fish coming from the rivers, irrigation systems and specially-built ponds. Forests provide the Szechwanese with some of the best mushrooms and fungi in China.

Szechwanese food is hot and spicy. Szechwan peppercorns and the extensive use of hot chillies give the food its distinctive numbing, spicy, hot flavours, as in Hot and Sour Soup. Soy sauce, rice wine, ginger, garlic, vinegar, sugar and spices such as star anise are all common in the cooking of this region.

Most Chinese restaurants in this country cook Cantonese food, but Szechwan cooking is becoming increasingly popular as we become more accustomed to all these new and exciting spicy flavours.

Chinese or Asian supermarkets are a good source for the more unusual ingredients in these receipes, and their stocks are often fresher and cheaper too.

Pock-faced Ma's Bean Curd

This famous Szechwan dish is said to be named after the woman who made it in the Szechwan capital of Chengdu. Whether she was spotty or not, her food was wonderful.

INGREDIENTS

225 g (½ lb) lean, minced pork or beef
1 tablespoon minced ginger
6 spring onions, finely chopped
6 cloves of garlic, finely minced
4 tablespoons soy sauce
1 tablespoon sesame oil
1 tablespoon rice wine
1 tablespoon hot pepper flakes in oil

1 tablespoon white sugar
4 cakes bean curd/1 box fresh bean curd cut into 1-2 cm (½ - 1") cubes
1 teaspoon roasted, ground Szechwan peppercorns
120 ml (4 fl oz) water or stock
4 tablespoons peanut oil

METHOD

(1) Marinate the minced meat with half the spring onions, half the minced ginger, 2 tablespoons of the soy sauce, the sesame oil and rice wine. Mix well and leave for 30 minutes.

(2) Prepare all the other ingredients and place within easy reach from the stove.

(3) Heat the peanut oil in the wok over a high flame until a haze forms. Add the garlic and the rest of the ginger and stir fry for 30 seconds. Be sure not to burn the garlic. Add the hot pepper flakes in oil and stir fry for a further 20 seconds.

(4) Add the meat and its marinade, stir fry for one minute, breaking up any lumps, then add sugar and cook for a further 30 seconds.

(5) Stir in the remaining spring onions, soy sauce and water.

(6) Add the bean curd, being careful not to break the cubes. Lower the heat and simmer for 2 more minutes.

(7) Add the ground Szechwan peppercorns, stir in and then test for salt.

(8) If the sauce is a bit runny, thicken it with 1 teaspoon cornstarch dissolved into 3 tablespoons water. The sauce will thicken and become clear on simmering. Serve your delicious Pock-faced Ma's Bean Curd with rice, stir-fried beansprouts and a green salad.

Braised Szechwan Chicken

INGREDIENTS

Serves 4

900 g (2 lb) chicken pieces (thighs, legs, and breasts cut in half)
5 cm (2") fresh ginger, peeled and cut into 5 slices
4-8 dried, whole, deseeded, chilli peppers
7 whole star anise
20 spring onions
25 dried Chinese mushrooms (or as many as you can afford)
4 heaped tablespoons Chinese Black fungus or Tree fungus
250 ml (9 fl oz) rice wine
10 tablespoons dark soy sauce, 6 tablespoons peanut oil, 2 tablespoons sesame oil

METHOD

(1) Put mushrooms in a bowl, cover with boiling water and leave to soak for 20 minutes. Reserve the soaking liquid and cut mushrooms up into quarters.

(2) Put the Tree fungus in another bowl, pour over some boiling water, leave to soak for 15 minutes, drain, wash well and chop roughly.

(3) Skin, wash, prepare and dry the chicken pieces.

(4) Place the chicken in a bowl with half the rice wine and 10 of the spring onions, roughly chopped. Leave to marinate for at least 30 minutes.

(5) Heat oil in a large saucepan over a high heat. When oil is hot, add ginger, chilli, star anise and sugar and stir for 1 minute.

(6) Add the chicken and its marinade to the saucepan. Cook for 5 minutes until quite firm.

(7) Add the remaining rice wine and soy sauce and cook for a further 3 minutes.

(8) Add the remaining 10 spring onions, mushrooms and their soaking water, plus extra water to cover the chicken. Bring to the boil and simmer for 1½ hours until the chicken is very tender.

(9) Fifteen minutes before the end of cooking, add the prepared Tree fungus.

(10) Transfer to the cold serving bowl, mix in the sesame oil, and leave to cool slightly. (This lets the flavours come out.) Serve with rice and green salad.

Stir-fried Beansprouts

Beansprouts are sprouted Mung beans. They add a refreshing bite to any meal.

INGREDIENTS

450 g (1 lb) fresh beansprouts, washed and dried
1 teaspoon salt
1 tablespoon soy sauce
1 tablespoon rice wine vinegar
8 spring onions, roughly sliced
2 tablespoons peanut oil

METHOD

(1) Heat the peanut oil in a wok over a high flame until a haze appears. Add the beansprouts and spring onion and stir fry vigorously for 1 minute.

(2) Add salt and soy sauce and stir fry for a further minute.

(3) Add the rice vinegar and stir fry for another minute. Check the beansprouts are cooked but still crunchy - be sure not to overcook. Serve with other Chinese dishes, rice and a green salad.

ETHIOPIA

'In Britain, when people hear the word Ethiopia, all they think of is famine, but there's much more to it than that. Ethiopia is a rich and ancient culture, and I think the food is the best in the world,' says Bethelhem Yohannes.

Bethelhem came to London from Ethiopia, in north-east Africa, three years ago. She is studying for a degree in hotel management and in her spare time helps with the cooking at her brother's restaurant. Cooking is a valued skill in Ethiopia ... all women strive to cook well - in fact, one of the first things a man will ask about a prospective wife is how well she cooks. If she can't, getting a husband can be difficult, especially when it comes to Doro Wat.

Doro Wat is always eaten on special occasions in Ethiopia. It is a chicken and egg stew made with a mix of different spices, turning the dish a deep red colour. The ghee (clarified butter) can be bought from Asian supermarkets.

The essential flavouring for most Ethiopian food is berbere (pronounced burberry), a hot, volcanic mixture made from a range of spices such as cardamom, cinnamon, cloves, garlic and plenty of ground chillies. It is Ethiopia's garam masala. All households have their own special recipe and it is used in a wide range of dishes to add both flavour and colour.

Most Ethiopian foods are served with enjera, a flat, pancake-like bread which acts as tablecloth, plate, and even cutlery. It is made from teff, a cereal grain related to millet which is Ethiopia's staple food. The teff is ground to a powder, made into a batter and allowed to ferment for three to four days before being cooked on a flat, clay griddle. While it cooks, bubbles of fermentation break through the pale-gold batter leaving the surface full of holes, not unlike the surface of a crumpet. It has a mild, lemony flavour that goes perfectly with the spicier stew.

Ethiopians eat from a communal platter and always with the right hand. The enjera is placed on a large wicker basket-table which the diners sit round. Portions of food are placed near each diner on the enjera and the meal is then eaten by tearing off pieces of the bread and using it to scoop up the food. Diners always eat from their own side of the dish, otherwise one is considered greedy. Feeding each other is part of the meal, making a parcel from the enjera and a few choice morsels before popping it into a neighbour's mouth if they seem to be 'holding back'.

Doro Wat

'A party is not a party without a Doro Wat.'

INGREDIENTS

1.4 kg (3 lb) chicken, skinned and jointed
juice of 1 lemon
900 g (2 lb) onions finely chopped
6 tablespoons ghee (clarified butter)
4 cloves of garlic, finely chopped
5 cm (2") ginger, peeled and finely chopped
100ml (4 fl oz) red wine
250ml (9 fl oz) water

BERBERE

Ethiopians use a mixture of spices called Berbere. The
mixture of spices listed below is as near an approximation as is possible using the ingredients available in Britain.

2 tablespoons chilli powder
2 tablespoons paprika
a pinch each of ground ginger, cardamom, coriander, fenugreek, nutmeg, cloves, cinnamon, allspice, basil and oregano

METHOD

(1) Put chicken in a bowl, add the lemon juice, salt and two cups of water and leave to stand for 30 minutes.

(2) In a heavy pot, fry the onions without oil for 15 minutes, stirring often to prevent them burning, until they go soft and dry.

(3) Add ghee, then garlic and ginger. Cook for 4 minutes, add all the spices, stir and cook for 4 more minutes.

(4) Add the dry chicken pieces, the wine and the water. Cover and cook over a low heat for 45 minutes to an hour, or until tender.

Yemisser Seletta (Lentil salad)

The more fiery Ethiopian dishes are wonderfully set off by salads like this one.

INGREDIENTS

225 g (½ lb) puy lentils if possible, otherwise any green or brown lentils, washed
2 tablespoons olive oil
3 tablespoons red wine vinegar
½ teaspoon salt
black pepper
6 shallots, peeled and quartered
2 fresh chillies, destemmed, deseeded and cut into thin strips

METHOD

(1) Put the washed lentils in enough salted, boiling water to cover them by 7 cm (3"). Turn heat to low and simmer uncovered for 30 minutes.

(2) Drain the lentils in a large sieve and run under cold water. Drain and reserve.

(3) Mix the oil, vinegar, salt and pepper in a salad bowl with a whisk.

(4) Add the lentils, shallots and chillies to the bowl and mix thoroughly. Leave to marinate for an hour before serving.

Yataklete Kilkil
(Fresh vegetables with Garlic and Ginger)

INGREDIENTS

225 g (½ lb) small new potatoes, scraped
225 g (½ lb) carrots, quartered and cut into 5 cm (2") pieces
225 g (½ lb) French beans, topped and tailed
2 onions, peeled and coarsely cut
1 bell pepper (red or green), seeded and cut into thin strips
2 fresh chillies, destemmed
50 ml (2 fl oz) olive oil
4 cloves garlic, finely chopped
2 cm (1") ginger, finely chopped
salt and pepper
1 bunch spring onions, halved lengthways and cut into 5 cm (2") pieces

METHOD

(1) Add the potatoes, carrots and beans to enough boiling water in a saucepan to cover them. Bring back to boil, then boil uncovered for 5 minutes.

(2) Drain in a large colander and run cold water over them to stop them cooking. Leave to drain completely.

(3) In a heavy saucepan, heat the olive oil over medium heat until a light haze appears. Add the onions, pepper and chillies and sauté for 5 minutes, stirring often. Add the garlic, ginger and salt and pepper to taste and cook for a further minute.

(4) Add the reserved vegetables and the spring onion to the pan, mix well, then reduce heat to low and cook for 10 more minutes.

FRANCE

France has a reputation for having the most sophisticated cuisine in the world. Its culinary history is peppered with the names of famous chefs, rich sauces and elaborate patisserie. But this is French 'haute cuisine', a tradition that has developed through the centuries in the kitchens of kings and the restaurants of the rich. It is a classical style characterised by definitive recipes and strict principles.

France's country cooking is quite different in approach, although just as much part of its gastronomic reputation. Its recipes demonstrate a strong affection for local culture and make the most of regional specialities. Country cooking also has its so-called 'classic' recipes, but rather than being concerned with technique, it relies more on the availablility of local ingredients. A coq au vin, for example, is a dish that is cooked all over France, but in Alsace it will be made with a white wine and in Burgundy, of course, with red.

Each region of France has its own distinct culinary characteristics, but it is Provence that has the most highly-flavoured foods. Its cuisine is mainly based on garlic, olive oil and tomatoes which turn up in some of the region's most famous dishes. Tomatoes were regarded with suspicion in France until the nineteenth century, but the tomato's assimilation into Provencal cooking must have been extremely rapid since most of today's recipes seem to contain them.

Provençal cooking has evident Italian influences, especially in Nice. Nice was part of the Italian kingdom of Sardinia, Liguria and Piedmont until 1860, and the Italian presence is still evident: the Niçois's favourite snack pissaladiere, made with tomatoes, anchovies and onions, is barely distinguishable from its Italian cousin, the pizza.

Cassoulet

A famous stew, steeped in tradition, popular all over France but originating in the Languedoc region.

INGREDIENTS

900 g (2 lb) haricot beans, soaked overnight
110 g (4 oz) streaky bacon
1 onion, stuck with 3 cloves
4 cloves garlic
225 g (½ lb) carrots, sliced
bouquet garni
10 black peppercorns crushed
1 duck, quartered
225 g (½ lb) lean pork, cubed
5 cloves garlic
2 onions, chopped

400 g (14 oz) tin tomatoes, chopped
2 chorizo sausages
225 g (½ lb) garlic sausage (smoked)
110 g (4 oz) dry breadcrumbs
salt and pepper

METHOD

(1) Place all ingredients up to and including peppercorns in a large saucepan, just cover with water and bring to the boil. Remove scum, turn heat to low and simmer for 1 hour.

(2) Meanwhile, put duck in the oven for 30 minutes, then place under grill, skin side up, for 5 minutes to brown. Remove duck and reserve.

(3) Place the duck fat and juices in a frying pan over a medium heat. Add the pre-cubed pork and brown, then reserve the meat with the duck.

(4) Add the onions and garlic to the frying pan and sauté for 10 minutes, stirring often.

(5) When the beans are ready, remove the onion and bouquet garni.

(6) Preheat the oven to 130°C/250°F/gas mark ¼. Now build (preferably in a large earthenware casserole) the cassoulet. Place beans at the bottom, followed by the meats (including sausage), tomatoes and onion and continue building, ending with a layer of beans.

(7) There should be enough liquid to not quite reach the top of the beans. Add more boiling water if necessary. Place in oven (covered) for 2 hours.

(8) Turn oven up to 170°C/325°F/gas mark 3. Remove lid, check that the beans are not drying out, then add a layer of half the breadcrumbs and return to oven.

(9) After 30 minutes, break the crust that forms, and stir into the beans. Add the remaining breadcrumbs and return to the oven for a further 30 minutes.
Serve with copious amounts of robust red wine.

Onion Soup with Croûtes

INGREDIENTS

Serves 4

Soup

30 g (1 oz) butter
1 tablespoon sunflower oil
450 g (1 lb) onions, thinly sliced
1 tablespoon flour
900 ml (1½ pt) stock, either meat or vegetable, made fresh or from stock cubes

Croûtes

6 slices crusty French bread, brown or white, cut about 2½ cm (1") thick
2 teaspoons olive oil
55 g (2 oz) grated cheese (Cheddar, Gruyere, Parmesan or a mixture)

METHOD

To make the soup:
(1) Melt the butter and the oil in a large saucepan over a medium heat. Add the onions, stir and cook, uncovered, over a low heat for approximately 30 minutes, stirring every few minutes, until the onions turn a deep, golden brown and are caramelised.

(2) Add the flour and stir constantly for 1 or 2 minutes. Remove from heat.

(3) Make the stock by crumbling the stock cubes into boiling water, following the instructions on the packet.

(4) Stir the hot stock into the onions, return the pan to a low heat and simmer, uncovered, for 30 minutes. Season the soup with salt and pepper to taste.

To make the croûtes
(1) While the soup simmers, preheat the oven to 170°C/325°F/gas mark 3.

(2) Put the slices of bread on a baking sheet and bake for 15 minutes.

(3) Remove from the oven and sprinkle both sides of the bread with a little olive oil, turn over and bake again for 15 minutes.

(4) To serve, pour the soup into a bowl and place a croûte and some grated cheese on top.

Ratatouille Niçoise

This recipe comes from Michel Guillon, a Niçois man living in London: 'Everyone makes ratatouille a different way - this is my favourite.'

INGREDIENTS

450 g (1 lb) aubergine
450 g (1 lb) courgettes
450 g (1 lb) red or green peppers
450 g (1 lb) onions
750 g (1½ lb) tomatoes
2 cloves garlic
½ bunch parsley
10 leaves basil
½ bunch thyme
flour
olive oil
salt/pepper

METHOD

(1) Cut the aubergines and courgettes in approximately 1 cm (¼") thick slices and sprinkle with flour

(2) Cut open the peppers, remove the centre and pips and slice in thin wedges. Peel and cut the onions. Peel the tomatoes and remove the centre and pips.

(3) Cook separately, in a frying pan with a small amount of olive oil, the aubergines, courgettes, peppers and onions until tender. Do not forget to add salt for each.

(4) Once cooked, first reserve each ingredient individually in a sieve to avoid excess oil, then reserve together in a casserole.

(5) In a pan, squash the tomatoes, add the olive oil, garlic (optional), parsley, basil and thyme and simmer until the sauce thickens.

(6) In the casserole where the aubergines, courgettes, peppers and onions are reserved, add the tomato sauce and stir with a wooden spoon. Cook on a low heat for 20 minutes. Serve with bread, wine and a green salad.

GHANA

Ghana lies on the west coast of Africa, in an area that used to be called the 'Slave coast'. It was from this part of Africa that millions of people were taken to work as slaves in the Americas, so West African cooking styles and ingredients have strongly influenced the cooking of countries like Brazil. South America has in return provided West Africa with the now vital staples of cassava, corn, yams and of course, chilli. Ghana even has yam feasts on special occasions where they are eaten and prepared in many different ways.

An everyday meal in Ghana would normally consist of a starchy carbohydrate such as cassava, millet, corn, yams, rice served with a thick stew made with palm oil, vegetables, pulses, spices, fish and a little meat if available. Generally, animals are used for their milk not their meat. Milk, curds and whey are eaten across the region. A bottle of their favourite chilli sauce, piri piri, is served with every meal. Piri piri is very hot and is made of chillies, onions, garlic, lemon juice, tomatoes and horeseradish.

When meat is available for the pot, it is usually quite tough and requires long cooking times. Stews are an ideal method for cooking tough meat and marinating is another technique used in Ghana to tenderise and flavour meat. In the dish Jollof Chicken, popular all over West Africa, the chicken is marinated in a mixture of lemon, salt and garlic.

Peanuts are a staple food in Ghana, either chewed as a snack or used in soups and stews. They are a cheap and readily available source of protein used across the whole of West Africa and add a delicious flavour to many meals, such as the Peanut Stew below.

Peanut Stew

Akua Pinaman Adjei was born in Ghana and now lives outside Glasgow with her family. She comes from a family of 16 and learnt to cook when she was a child by practising on her brothers and sisters. In Ghana it is expected that a girl can cook by the time she is 14 years old. Akua describes an unusual piece of kitchen etiquette: in Ghana it is frowned on to sniff food in the kitchen. You only smell something which is bad, not the food you eat.

INGREDIENTS

Serves 8

1.75 kg (4 lb) chicken, skinned and cut into 8 pieces
225 g (8 oz) onions, chopped
110 g (4 oz) tin butter beans, mashed
400 g (14 oz) tin tomatoes, mashed
110 g (4 oz) smooth peanut butter without added sugar
225 g (8 oz) okra, topped and tailed
salt

METHOD

(1) Put the chicken and onion in a casserole without any oil and brown slightly. Cover with water, bring to the boil and skim the chicken fat from the surface. Add the butter beans and tomatoes and simmer for 45 minutes.

(2) Add enough of the stock from the casserole to the peanut butter to make a soupy mix. Return this to the casserole and continue to simmer for another 15 minutes.

(3) Add the okra and salt to taste and cook for a further 15 minutes. Serve with rice.

Mafe

A different flavour with every mouthful.

INGREDIENTS

4 tablespoons olive oil
450 g (1 lb) onions, finely chopped
2 green chillies, finely chopped
3 cloves garlic, minced
225 g (8 oz) potatoes, cut into large chunks
3 small turnips, cut into large chunks
225 g (8 oz) carrots, sliced
450 g (1 lb) sweet potatoes, cut into large chunks
450 g (1 lb) pumpkin, cut into large chunks
600 ml (1 pt) water
2 tablespoons tomato purée
400 g (14 oz) tin tomatoes
450 g (1 lb) mixed greens (cabbage, spinach, etc.)
110 g (4 oz) smooth peanut butter (without added sugar)
salt and pepper

METHOD

(1) Heat the oil in a casserole then sauté the onions until soft.

(2) Add the chillies and garlic and cook for a few more minutes.

(3) Add the potatoes and turnips and cook for a further 15 minutes before adding the carrots, pumpkin and sweet potatoes. Cook for 10 minutes.

(4) Mix the water with the tomato purée and add to the pot together with the tomatoes. Bring to the boil and then simmer slowly until the vegetables are nearly cooked.

(5) Finally, add the greens and then the peanut butter, mixed with a cup of the broth to make it smooth and runny. Stir and simmer for 15 minutes.

(6) Add salt and pepper to taste. Serve with rice.

Fufu

'Yam balls': good enough for any yam feast.

INGREDIENTS

675 g (1½ lb) yam, peeled and chopped
1 teaspoon salt

METHOD

(1) Put yam and salt in a saucepan and cover with water. Bring to the boil, turn heat to low, cover and cook until tender.

(2) Drain, put the yam in a blender and blend until you have a smooth paste. With wet hands, scoop up enough yam paste to form into 5 cm (2") inch balls.

(3) Serve with Peanut Stew or Mafe.

IRAN

One of Iran's favourite epic poems is the Shah-Nama or Book of Kings. It traces the history of Persia back to its earliest legendary rulers, the first of whom is credited with the invention of cookery. Whether this is true or not, Iranian cuisine belongs to a very ancient Middle Eastern tradition that has influenced the eating habits of the rest of the world. In around 10,000 BC, it was in the area which we now know as the Middle East that humans first became farmers rather than hunters. They kept sheep and goats and grew crops and fruit such as barley, wheat, figs and pomegranates.

During our Middle Ages, the Islamic Empire was in its Golden Age with one of the most advanced civilisations in the world. The art of gastronomy was highly prized and even if Christian Europe looked upon the Islamic peoples as infidels, the Crusaders came back with their cooking methods and ingredients. Nuts, dried fruits and rice all came back to Britain during the Middle Ages and recipes considered to be so traditionally English, like Christmas pudding, rice puddings and mince pies, all in fact have their roots in Middle Eastern cuisine.

There are many similarities between the cuisines of most Middle Eastern countries and they share many common recipes and ingredients, but one thing that sets Iran apart from its culinary neighbours is the range and sophistication of its rice dishes. Rice is Iran's staple food and it is eaten in quantity at every meal. The country grows many different varieties and has a wealth of different rice recipes within its culinary repertoire. One of the basic cooking methods is the Chelow. Rice is first parboiled, then mixed with butter before being cooked a second time, usually by steaming slowly on top of the stove until a golden crust forms at the bottom of the dish. Achieving a perfect crust, called the 'tah dig', is a valued skill as it is considered a great delicacy.

Chelow will most often be eaten with a Koresh, an Iranian stew that can be made from a wide variety of ingredients such as meat, poultry, vegetables, fruits, nuts and spices, often using the best of seasonal produce. The combination of meat and fruit is extremely popular and a common characteristic of Middle Eastern cuisine.

Borani
(Spinach and Yogurt Salad)

Spinach and yogurt make a great combination. Yogurt has been eaten for centuries in Iran and there is a strong belief in its health-giving properties. It is said to confer long life and good looks and, mixed with some garlic, can apparently be used as a cure for malaria.

INGREDIENTS
225 g (½ lb) fresh spinach, washed and destemmed
juice of a lemon
1 clove garlic, minced
300 ml (10 fl oz) yogurt
salt and pepper to taste
mint, finely chopped

METHOD
(1) Place the undried spinach in a pot, cover and cook over a low heat until it is a mush (for about 10 minutes).

(2) Drain the spinach in a sieve, let it cool, then squeeze dry. Chop finely.

(3) Mix the spinach, lemon juice, garlic, salt and pepper in a bowl, then stir in the yogurt.

(4) Refrigerate for an hour, then garnish with the mint.

Coucou Sabsi (Herb Omelette)

Iranians are particularly fond of Coucous, a sort of omelette or tortilla. They are often served as appetisers or side dishes, either hot or cold. A light and extremely flavourful dish, this is traditionally eaten at New Year because of the green colour, promising the birth of a new year.

INGREDIENTS
4 spring onions, finely chopped
1 leek, finely chopped
40 g (1 ½ oz) flat leaf parsley, finely chopped
20 g (¾ oz) chives, finely chopped
20 g (¾ oz) mint, finely chopped
2 sprigs fresh oregano, finely chopped
6 eggs
salt and pepper
5 tablespoons olive oil

METHOD
(1) Put all the vegetables and herbs in a large bowl.

(2) Beat the eggs in 1 tablespoon of olive oil in another bowl. Add this to the vegetables and herbs and mix in. Season with salt and pepper.

(3) Heat the remaining 4 tablespoons of olive oil in a large heavy frying pan over a medium heat until a haze forms. Pour the mixture into the frying pan, spreading it evenly.

(4) Turn heat to low and cover. Cook for 8-10 minutes or until the top is set.

(5) Turn grill to high.

(6) Run a spatula around the rim of the frying pan to release the omelette. Place under grill for 2 minutes.

(7) Serve as a side dish or as an appetiser with Borani.

Fesenjan

Made with pomegranates, this dish is a typical example of the Iranian fondness for combining meats with fruit.

INGREDIENTS

4 pomegranates
juice of 2 lemons
1 tablespoon sugar
3 tablespoons sunflower oil
1.4 kg (3 lb) chicken, quartered
2 medium onions, sliced
200 g (7 oz) walnuts, coarsely chopped

METHOD

(1) Scoop out the flesh and seeds from the pomegranates, and place them in a blender. Blend for a few seconds and then strain through a sieve, extracting as much juice as you can with the back of a spoon. Add the lemon juice and sugar and make up to a pint with water.

(2) In a heavy casserole pot heat the oil and then brown the chicken quarters. Remove and reserve.

(3) Fry the onions in the pot until browned, for approximately 8-10 minutes.

(4) Add the walnuts and fry for 2 minutes.

(5) Add the pomegranate juice and chicken, bring to boil. Reduce the heat to low and simmer covered for 1 - 2 hours. Serve with Chelow rice.

Chelow (Iranian rice)

INGREDIENTS

350 g (12 oz) Basmati rice
salt
55 g (2 oz) butter

METHOD

(1) Wash and rinse the rice 5 times. Put in a bowl and cover with water and add a teaspoon of salt. Leave to soak, overnight if possible.

(2) In a large saucepan, put 1½ l (2½ pt) cold water and a tablespoon salt. Bring to the boil.

(3) Meanwhile, drain the soaking rice, add slowly to the boiling water, then boil vigorously for 5 minutes. Drain, then rinse with warm water.

(4) Melt half the butter in a saucepan, add the rinsed rice, stir, then dot with the remaining butter. Turn heat to low, cover tightly and cook for approximately 30 minutes. You should have a golden crust at the bottom of the pan.

ITALY

Italian food is really the food of many different regions which, before 1861, were separate states in their own right, sharing neither the same language nor climate, let alone food. The wide varieties of ingredients and cooking styles therefore make an exploration into Italian food a delicious journey of gastronomic discovery.

Different regions have given their names to foods and dishes which have become instantly recognizable: Bolognese sauce from the eastern side of Italy, one of the richest gastronomic areas, Parma ham, Parmesan cheese, Milanese sauce and all the varieties of pizzas. The Italians were the first to recognise the potential of the tomato in making delicious sauces: the pomo d'oro or golden apple was brought to Italy from Peru by explorers in the sixteenth century. It was thought to be poisonous and it was 200 years before its true qualities were discovered.

Known as the Mother of European Cuisine, Italian food is the food of the people. Recent research suggests that the nutritional properties of the food of southern Italy are second to none in Europe. This is the home of the so-called Mediterranean diet (See A-Z); with its high carbohydrate content and wealth of fruit and vegetables, all washed down with the local red wine, it is good for the heart as well as the soul.

Many of the essential ingredients in Italian cooking such as extra virgin olive oil, balsamic vinegar, and many different varieties of beans and pasta, are now widely available in UK supermarkets or delicatessens.

The following dishes were prepared for a special dinner in celebration of the Duttons' eight-week Mediterranean diet, featured in the first series of Food File, by Italian chef Franco Taruschio, owner of The Walnut Tree Inn near Abergavenny, Gwent.

Chelso Bean Soup

INGREDIENTS

Serves four

225 g (8 oz) haricot beans
2½l (4 pt) water
1 white onion, quartered
generous few leaves of fresh basil
generous few parsley or celery leaves
85 g (3 oz) fresh tomato sauce or passata
60 ml (4 tablespoons) extra virgin olive oil (plain olive oil can be substituted)
salt to taste

METHOD

(1) Soak the haricot beans in water overnight, then boil them in the soaking water for 1½ hours. Drain, rinse in cold water and return to the pot. Add the 2½ ltr (4 pts) of water, the quartered onion, herbs, tomato sauce and olive oil. Season with salt. Cover and simmer gently for 30 minutes.

(2) Serve over hard, crusty bread; a stale loaf of wholemeal, perhaps warmed in the bottom of the oven so that it crusts up, would be a good alternative to the crusty Chelso bread with which the Italians eat it.

Fettucini and Seafood Sauce

INGREDIENTS

Fettucini pasta (preferably home-made) sufficient for 4 people.

The sauce:
4 scallops, cleaned and cut in half (coral can be used)
225 g (½ lb) prawns, peeled
225 g (½ lb) mussels, boiled and shelled
2 garlic cloves, crushed
pinch of freshly ground chilli
45 ml (3 tablespoons) chopped parsley
olive oil
½ glass of white wine
salt and pepper

METHOD

(1) Cook and drain the pasta.

(2) In a separate pan, fry the garlic, chilli and parsley in some olive oil for a few minutes.

(3) Quickly add the prepared seafood and fry on high heat for 3-4 minutes. Add the wine and reduce the sauce until a glaze appears. Season the mixture and pour over the pasta.

Supreme of Chicken Pizzaiola

INGREDIENTS
4 breasts of chicken
extra virgin olive oil
salt and pepper to taste
2 garlic cloves, chopped finely
1½ ripe tomatoes, peeled, deseeded and chopped
good pinch of oregano or basil

METHOD
(1) Preheat the oven to 170°C/325°F/gas mark 3.

(2) Fry the chicken breasts in a heavy pan previously brushed with olive oil over a high heat for a few minutes, turning once to seal them.

(3) Remove the breasts, place on a baking tray and put in the oven for approximately 7-8 minutes, testing with a skewer or fork to check if cooked through. Season with salt and pepper.

(4) Prepare the sauce by heating a little olive oil in a frying pan. Fry the garlic. Add the tomatoes and quickly fry. Add salt, pepper and herb of choice to taste. Pour the sauce over the chicken, then serve.

(5) Divide the sauce between four plates and place the chicken breasts on top.

KOREA

Many characteristics of Korean food are shared with other Asian cuisines, especially those of China and Japan. The popularity of chillies, garlic, rice and noodles, the predominance of soups and seafood and the use of chopsticks are common themes found in most Far Eastern cooking.

Along with almost every other nation in the Orient, China and Japan have frequently invaded their geographical neighbours over the centuries and Korean cooking is rich with their influence. For example, the principle of five flavours (sweet, sour, hot, salty and bitter), on which much Korean food is based, has been learnt from the Chinese.

But Korea does have distinctive aspects to its culinary repertoire. Its most famous dish is Kimchee, a fermented vegetable pickle served as a side dish at every meal from breakfast to dinner. It is something of a national institution and even has a museum devoted to it in Seoul, which documents its 160 varieties. Kimchee is made with a range of different vegetables, but the most common is Chinese cabbage. It is prepared by every household in the autumn after the cabbage harvest. The vegetables are salted and then stuffed with a potent mixture of ginger, garlic, chillies and spring onions before being packed into earthenware vats where they will be left to ferment until they become sour. Kimchee can be a bit of a shock to the taste buds when first eaten, but Koreans tell you that once you have eaten it twice, you'll be addicted.

As well as pickles, the everyday Korean diet is based on fish, rice and beancurd and is extremely low in fat. The annual rice consumption per head in Korea is one of the highest in the world and, as in most other parts of Asia, it is the basic foodstuff. Like the Japanese, Koreans prefer short-grain, sticky rice.

Beancurd, or 'tubu' as it is called in Korea, is an immensely popular food and although some packaged forms are now available, it is mainly bought daily and consumed on the day of purchase. It is most frequently cooked in soups or tchiges. A tchige stew will be eaten at every meal in Korea and range from a basic mixture of bean paste and water to the more elaborate combinations such as Saeng Sun Tchige made with fish, shellfish, beancurd and lots of vegetables.

Traditionally, Koreans eat sitting at low tables surrounded by cushions. All the food and drink is served in one course which can range from a simple meal of rice, one main dish and a helping of Kimchee, to more elaborate ones which can include up to 20 different side dishes. Side dishes are seen as a sign of wealth: the wealthier the family, the more side dishes are served.

Saeng Sun Tchige

Mr CJ Kim cooked this dish for the third series of *Food File*. He described it as a luxury tchige and one that would be served on special occasions. In the past, Mr Kim explained, it would have been served for breakfast:

'In the days gone by, Korea was basically a farming country and people used to get up very early to go out into the fields to work. They would come back to the house for their breakfast but usually a good four hours had passed and these workers were very hungry and needed a lot of food. So breakfast became the main meal of the day and even when guests were invited to the family home, they were invited not for dinner but for breakfast.'

The Koreans not only eat well but they care very much about presentation and this dish, with its little parcels, is no exception.

INGREDIENTS

1 lb (450 g) cod fillet
450 g (1 lb) mussels, carefully scrubbed and debearded
110 g (4 oz) prawns, cooked and finely chopped
3 cloves garlic, finely chopped
black pepper
1 teaspoon sesame oil
300g (10 oz) beancurd, chopped into 1 cm x 7 cm x 4 cm (½" x 3" x 1½") pieces
1 tablespoon sunflower oil
6 spring onions
1 clove garlic, bruised and coarsely chopped
½ mooli (white radish), peeled and sliced
1 medium onion, sliced
110 g (4 oz) mushrooms, sliced
2 Chinese leaves, coarsely chopped
salt
2 tablespoons fish sauce (Nuom Plak) or anchovy essence
4 fresh chillies, deseeded and sliced into long strips
watercress
2.4 ltr (4 pt) water

METHOD

(1) Put prawns, garlic, pepper and sesame oil in a small bowl, mix and leave to marinate.

(2) Put the tablespoon of sunflower oil in a frying pan over a moderate heat, brown the beancurd slices in it and set them aside.

(3) Heat the water to boiling point in a saucepan, add the spring onions and blanch for 2 minutes. Remove and set aside. Remove water from heat.

(4) Slice spring onions lengthways. Make little sandwiches using the beancurd and prawn/garlic mixture and tie up with the strips of spring onion.

(5) Bring water back to boil, add garlic, mooli and mussels and then bring back to boil again.

(6) Add onions, mushrooms, Chinese leaves, salt and fish sauce.

(7) When the stock is boiling again, add the cod and then the parcels and skin off any scum. Add the chopped chillies and simmer for 15 minutes.

(8) Garnish with watercress and serve with rice.

Pajon (Spring Onion Pancakes)

This is often eaten as a snack by Koreans, bought from street vendors.

INGREDIENTS

Makes 2 pancakes

For the batter:
1 egg, beaten lightly
110 g (4 oz) plain flour
½ tablespoon peanut oil
150 ml (½ pt) water

5 spring onions, split lengthwise and chopped into 4" pieces
1 small courgette, chopped into 10 cm (4") matchsticks
1 small carrot
55 g (2 oz) peeled prawns
fresh chives
2 eggs, lightly beaten
peanut oil

METHOD

(1) Mix the egg, flour, oil and enough water to make a medium batter. Leave to rest for 30 minutes.
(2) Heat a large frying pan with just enough oil to cover the bottom. Put in half the batter.

(3) Place half the spring onions, courgette, carrot, prawns and fresh chives evenly over the batter.

(4) Spoon half the egg over the pancake and cook for 5-7 minutes over a medium heat.

(5) When the bottom of the pancake is well browned, turn over and cook for a further 5 minutes.

(6) To make the second pancake, repeat steps 2 - 5.

(7) Cut each pancake into pieces and serve with Chojang Dipping sauce.

Chojang Dipping Sauce

INGREDIENTS

3 tablespoons soy sauce
½ tablespoon cider vinegar
1 teaspoon sesame oil
1 teaspoon sugar
1 teaspoon toasted sesame seeds
1 spring onion, finely chopped
1 teaspoon garlic, finely chopped
1 teaspoon ginger, finely chopped

METHOD

(1) Mix together and stir well.

Pulgogi (Marinated beef strips)

Beef is being eaten more and more in Korea and Pulgogi is the most popular way of eating it. This dish tends to be addictive.

INGREDIENTS

450 g (1 lb) sirloin steak

Marinade
3 tablespoons soy sauce
2 cloves garlic, minced
1 tablespoon sesame oil
1 teaspoon sugar
2 spring onions, chopped
1 teaspoon roasted sesame seeds
ground black pepper

METHOD

(1) Trim the steak of all fat and slice the meat into thin strips.

(2) Mix the marinade ingredients together in a bowl and add the meat.

(3) Work the marinade into the meat with your hands and leave to marinate for at least an hour.

(4) Turn on the grill to warm it up. Put the marinated beef strips on to a baking sheet, place under the grill and grill for 4 minutes, then turn over and grill for a further 3 minutes.

(5) To serve, place a few strips of beef and some rice on a lettuce leaf, and, if you like, some chilli sauce, and roll up and eat.

MALAYSIA

Malaysia is a multicultural society with Malay, Chinese, Indian, and Arabic influences. Situated in the heart of the tropics, its generous rainfalls and fertile soil enable it to harvest two rice crops a year. A rich bounty of seafoods, vegetables, fruits and coconuts, combined with the diverse culinary influences of its people, have given rise to many of the world's great dishes.

Until the development of a comprehensive road network, most Malaysians lived on the western coast of the Malay Peninsula, on the strait of Malacca, a calm ocean passage joining the South China Sea to the Indian Ocean. Malaysia has been called the crossroads of Asia. For 2000 years Arab, Persian, and Indian traders took advantage of the ocean corridor by setting up trade and resting posts on the route between the West and the Moluccas or 'Spice Islands' over a thousand miles east of Indonesia.

Since the nineteenth century, colonialism, the development of the city of Singapore and Malaysia's tin and rubber industries have brought thousands of people from China and India to work and live in Malaysia.

Intermarrying between Chinese and Malaysians has resulted in a clearly-definable people known as the Noyan. Today the Noyan people are in many respects Chinese. Noyan cooking, however, is a unique combination of Chinese and Malaysian ingredients and techniques.

Zaharah Othman and her friend Hamida prepared a classic Malay Noyan dish called Johore Laksa for us. Zaharah works as a journalist in London and didn't start cooking until she came to Britain. She says that she missed Malaysian home cooking so much that she was forever telephoning Malaysia to ask her mother for advice. It cost a fortune but was definitely worth it.

Meals in Malaysia usually consist of several side dishes served with rice. Johore Laksa is an unusual dish as it makes a complete meal in itself when served with noodles or spaghetti. There are many different kinds of laksas. Johore Laksa reflects Malay, Chinese and Indian influences: the noodles were brought from China, the curry powder from India and the coconut is native to Malaysia.

This Laksa recipe is cheap, easy to prepare and nutritious: the curry powder provides iron, the garnishes, vitamin C and fibre, and the noodles or spaghetti provide starchy carbohydrate. Mackerel, an oily fish, is rich in protein, vitamin D and an essential fatty acid which is now thought to prevent heart disease. Recent research in the UK has led to the recommendation that we should aim to eat at least three portions of oily fish a week.

Johore Laksa

An exciting and different way to cook mackerel.

INGREDIENTS

900 g (2 lb) fresh mackerel
15 little dried red chillies deseeded, soaked and chopped (see recipe for Gado Gado sauce)
2 x 50 g (2 oz) tins anchovies (drained of oil)
350 g (12 oz) onions
2 cm (1") of ginger (chopped)
2 cloves of garlic
2 teaspoons treacle
2 teaspoons lemon juice
bunch of mint leaves
bunch of basil leaves
3 stalks of lemon grass (bruised)
salt to taste

METHOD

(1) Put mackerel in pot, cover amply with water and simmer for 20 minutes.

(2) Separate flesh from bones, discard the bones and blend the flesh in a food processor.

(3) Blend chillies, anchovies, onions, ginger and garlic in the processor, add blended fish and then return to fish stock with some more water.

(4) Add basil and mint leaves, lemon grass, treacle and lemon juice and simmer for an hour or so.

(5) Serve with rice noodles or spaghetti. Be sure not to overcook them by carefully following the instructions on the packet.

Gado-gado Salad

A cooked vegetable salad popular all over Malaysia and Indonesia.

A mixed vegetable salad, served with Gado-Gado Sauce. To blanch the vegetables, cook them briefly in boiling water (see below), then dip them quickly in cold water to cool them.

INGREDIENTS

450 g (1 lb) small new potatoes, boiled and sliced
110 g (4 oz) French green beans, boiled and refreshed in cold water
225 g (8 oz) shredded white cabbage, blanched
110 g (4 oz) beansprouts, blanched
110 g (4 oz) spring onions, sliced longways, or 110 g (4 oz) onions, sliced
225 g (8 oz) tomatoes, quartered
½ cucumber (cut in 2 cm (1") slices and quartered)
1 lettuce (leaves separated)

Garnishes:
2 sliced hard-boiled eggs
pineapple chunks

METHOD

Mix all the ingredients in a large salad bowl. Serve the Gado-Gado Sauce and garnishes separately.

Gado-Gado Sauce

INGREDIENTS

8 dried little red chillies
1 onion, grated
2 cloves garlic, minced
2 tablespoons peanut oil
45 g (1½ oz) creamed coconut mixed with 375 ml (13 fl oz) boiling water to make coconut milk
170g (6 oz) crunchy peanut butter (without added sugar)
1 teaspoon brown sugar
2 teaspoons lemon juice

METHOD

(1) Cut chillies in half with a sharp knife and remove the small seeds. Soak them in a little hot water for 30 minutes.

(2) Drain and chop chillies finely, mix with onion, garlic and 1 tablespoon of the peanut oil.

(3) Heat the remainder of the oil in a heavy frying pan over a medium heat and fry the chilli mixture for 5 minutes stirring occasionally.

(4) Add the coconut milk gradually, stirring constantly.

(5) Add the remaining ingredients and mix until smooth.

POLAND

The cuisine of Poland is the direct result of the country's climate and local ingredients. Juniper berries, wild game and forest mushrooms, honey, soured cream, pork and herrings, preserved vegetables, cereals like rye, wheat or buckwheat and ice-cold vodka are the basics of traditional Polish life.

Bigos or Hunter's Stew is Poland's national dish, an ancient Polish stew served with rye bread. Looking at some of its ingredients tells us a lot about traditional life in Poland.

Sauerkraut: because of the fiercely cold winters, preserved vegetables played a vital role in the survival of the Polish people. Sauerkraut is made in November after the cabbage harvest. The cabbage is first shredded and then packed with salt into large wooden barrels. After washing their feet, the men would stand in the barrels, packing the cabbage down until they were completely full. The barrels were then sealed for use later in the winter. Many people think that the sour taste of Sauerkraut is caused by adding vinegar, but this is wrong. When foods are preserved in salt a fermentation process begins, giving the food its distinctive sour taste. The Poles have developed a great liking for preserved foods of all kinds and, despite modern refrigeration and canning methods, preserved foods are still very much part of their diet.

Smoked meats: smoking is another method of preserving food and the Poles are renowned for their smoked hams and sausages. Polish pigs were tradionally raised with great care, fattened up on potatoes, milk and cereals so the pork is almost white and very tender. Canned ham is one of Poland's major exports, but in Poland itself the smoked sausage reigns supreme.

Wild game and mushrooms: foods from the forest have always played an important role in the Polish diet. Wild game was a staple food of the wealthy and any peasant lucky enough to live near the great forests. Wild boar, partridges, pheasants and stags all feature on Poland's tables. Bigos is called 'Hunter's Stew' because it was the perfect meal to take on long hunts in the forest. It will last for up two weeks, needing only to be heated each day.

Wild mushrooms are the other major forest food: morels, chanterelles and brown-capped boletus are just a few of the delicious mushrooms found on the forest floors. Poland has a great tradition of mushroom cooking and dried mushrooms are another popular Polish export. As it is a Catholic country, eating meat and animal products was not allowed on Fridays and other fast days; mushrooms made an excellent substitute.

Polish food differs from that of neighbouring Russia through the influence of Italian, French and Jewish food. In the fifteenth and sixteenth centuries Polish kings married Italian and French women. These women brought with them their chefs, who created such Polish classics as Pierogi, a kind of Polish ravioli. The Jewish influences are said to have started during the fourteenth century when a Polish king, Casimir the Great, fell in love with a Jewish woman. To prove his love to her he made Poland a safe haven for Jews from all over Europe.

Since the second world war, food has been scarce and many traditional ingredients are hard to come by, but Polish cooks are very good at making the most of whatever is available.

Bigos (Hunter's Stew)

Barbara Buczek has been living in London, home to a thriving Polish community, since 1946. She often prepares Bigos after Christmas, using up the left-over turkey and smoked meats. It is a simple meal to prepare but takes three days to cook: every day the stew is cooked for 30 minutes until the flavours are well combined and mellow. Don't be put off - it is well worth the wait.

INGREDIENTS

Serves 8

1 kg (2 lb) jar sauerkraut
450 g (1 lb) green cabbage, shredded
caraway seeds
225 g (8 oz) onion, chopped
1 tablespoon olive oil
225 g (8 oz) leftover beef
225 g (8 oz) leftover chicken, turkey or game
225 g (8 oz) Polish sausage
225 g (8 oz) smoked bacon or ham in largish pieces
6 prunes, pre-soaked
1 bay leaf
salt to taste

METHOD

(1) Cover the sauerkraut with water and cook for 30 minutes until soft. In a separate saucepan, cover the green cabbage and caraway seeds with water and simmer for about 15 minutes. Drain both and reserve the cabbage water.

(2) In a frying pan, sauté the onion in the olive oil until the onion is soft.

(3) Mix the cabbage, sauerkraut, onions and all the meats in a large pot. Add the prunes, bay leaf and 600 ml (1 pt) cabbage water (or leftover stock) and reduce slowly over a low heat for an hour or so. Add salt to taste.

(4) The next day, bring to the boil and simmer for 30 minutes, then repeat the following day. While you can eat the Bigos after the first day, it does improve over time and will keep for up to 2 weeks, since the sour cabbage preserves the meat. Serve with brown bread or mashed potatoes.

Borscht

Borscht with Pierogi is traditionally served on Christmas Eve, with stunning colour.

INGREDIENTS

15 g (½ oz) dried porcini mushrooms
500 ml (18 fl oz) boiling water
450 g (1 lb) beetroot, peeled and grated coarsely
500 ml (18 fl oz) water
1 stick celery, halved
1 clove garlic, crushed

METHOD

(1) Soak the mushrooms in the boiling water for 30 minutes then cook covered for 10 minutes. Strain, and reserve both the stock and the mushrooms. (The mushrooms are used in Pierogi.)

(2) Put the beetroot, water, celery and garlic in a stainless steel pan, bring to the boil, reduce heat and cook covered for 30 minutes.

(3) Remove the celery and garlic and strain the stock through a fine sieve, extracting as much stock as possible by pressing down hard with the back of a spoon.

(4) Put the mushroom and beetroot stocks back into the stainless steel pan together and heat to simmering point. Salt to taste.

(5) To serve, place some Pierogi in a bowl then add the Borscht.

Pierogi (Mushroom Dumplings)

'Best with Borscht'

INGREDIENTS

1 small onion, finely chopped
15 g (½ oz) butter
leftover mushroom (see Borscht recipe), finely chopped
1 egg white
a little fresh dill
1 tablespoon fresh breadcrumbs
170 g (6 oz) plain flour
2 egg yolks
½ teaspoon salt
3-4 tablespoons water

(1) Fry the onion in the butter until it starts to colour.

(2) Mix the onion, mushroom, egg white, dill and breadcrumbs together.

(3) Mix the flour, egg yolks, salt and as much water as is needed to make a stiff dough.

(4) Roll the dough out on a floured board until 3 mm (1/8") thick, cut in 5 cm (2") squares.

(5) Put a little of the mushroom mixture into each square, fold into triangles and press the edges together, dipping your fingers into some water if the dough starts sticking to them.

(6) Lower into boiling water and cook for 5 minutes.

PORTUGAL

Although Portugal is not actually a Mediterranean country, the Portuguese diet has many of the ingredients which we associate with Mediterranean food, such as seafood and olive oil (Portugal is the fourth largest producer of olive oil in the world). Portugal in fact lies on the Atlantic and for centuries formed a gateway to the Americas. The Portuguese were famed as navigators and their intrepid sailors brought back coffee, tea and cocoa to Europe, as well as new seeds and plants which they learned to cultivate in a European climate.

Fish is the staple food in Portugal: 40% of their protein comes from the sea and will often be served in the form of a stew or Caldeirada, the best known of Portuguese dishes. But even though fresh fish is widely available, the most popular fish dishes are made from Bacalhau - dried salted cod. The Portuguese have been preserving fish since at least 1000BC and traditional Portuguese cookery contains a vast number of salt cod dishes. To be properly enjoyed, Bacalhau does need careful preparation. It must be washed and soaked in clean cold water for at least twelve hours before use, and ideally, the water should be changed two or three times during this period.

The Portuguese dry not only cod, but their meats as well. They have raised the curing of ham and sausages to an art form, the apex of which is Chourico, a highly seasoned salami-like sausage that can be eaten on its own with bread, or added to stews and soups.

There are a huge number of soup recipes in Portugal. Soup is eaten at least once daily and is usually served at the start of every meal, although farm workers will often have a hearty bowl made with beans or chickpeas for breakfast before venturing into the fields. Fish and shellfish are also popular ingredients for soup, as indeed is bread.

Portugal's bread consumption is extremely high and it is served not just as an accompaniment to every meal, but is also found in many main dishes. Although practically unknown outside Portugal, there are a whole collection of bread recipes known as the Acordas which are eaten throughout the country, a style of dry bready soups made with vegetables, shellfish, chicken or pork. The main ingredient is boiled in water to form a flavoursome stock to which a soft pappy mixture of bread, olive oil and garlic is added.

Acorda de Bacalhau

(Bread and Salt Cod Soup)

There is said to be a different Bacalhau recipe in Portugal for every day of the year. Bread and salt cod combine for this very typically Portuguese dish.

INGREDIENTS

400 g (14 oz) loaf stale bread, thinly sliced
450 g (1 lb) salted cod, soaked for 24 hours changing the water three times
2 tomatoes, peeled, seeded and chopped
2 cloves garlic, finely chopped
2 onions, thinly sliced
75 ml (3 fl oz) olive oil
bay leaf
salt and pepper to taste
600 ml (1 pt) water
3 eggs, beaten

METHOD

(1) Put the olive oil in a heavy frying pan over moderate heat. Add the onion and sauté for a few minutes until soft. Add the tomatoes, garlic and bay leaf, cover and turn heat to low and cook for 15 minutes.

(2) Meanwhile, rinse the cod, place in a saucepan with the water, bring to the boil then turn heat to low, cover and cook for 15 minutes.

(3) Skin and bone the cod and return to the pan. Add the onion and tomato mixture, add the bread ripped up into pieces and cook for a further 10 minutes covered over a low heat. Season with salt and pepper to taste.

(4) Remove from the heat and stir in the beaten eggs. Serve garnished with olives.

Caldo Verde

Originally from the Northern Province of Minho, this soup is now eaten all over the country.

INGREDIENTS

225 g (½ lb) fresh kale, washed, destemmed and very finely shredded
450 g (1 lb) potatoes, peeled and quartered
1½ l (2½ pt) water
2 teaspoons salt
50 ml (2 fl oz) olive oil
1 link of chourico (chorizo) sausage, thinly sliced
black pepper

METHOD

(1) Put the potatoes, salt and water in a large saucepan, bring to the boil over a high heat. Reduce the heat to medium and cook uncovered for 15 minutes.

(2) Remove the potatoes from the water and mash them to a puree. Return them to the water, and add the oil, chourico and some black pepper.

(3) Bring back to the boil over a high heat and add the kale. Boil uncovered for 4 minutes. Serve with Portuguese cornbread.

Broa (Portuguese Cornbread)

INGREDIENTS

170 g (6 oz) fine yellow cornmeal
1 teaspoon salt
250 ml (9 fl oz) boiling water
1 tablespoon olive oil
a sachet of dried yeast
1 teaspoon sugar
50 ml (2 fl oz) tepid water
225 g (8 oz) plain flour

METHOD

(1) Put half the cornmeal, salt and boiling water in a large mixing bowl and blend until smooth. Stir in the olive oil, then set aside.

(2) Put the yeast, sugar and tepid water in a small bowl, stir and leave to ferment for 10 minutes.

(3) Stir the yeast into the cornmeal mixture, add the rest of the cornmeal and half the flour whilst stirring continuously.

(4) Gather the dough into a ball, leave in the bowl, cover with a tea towel and leave to rise for 30 minutes.

(5) Meanwhile, grease a 22 cm (9") round flan tin.

(6) Place the dough on a floured surface and knead, adding as much of the remaining 110 g (4 oz) flour as is needed (no pun intended) to make a firm dough. The kneading process should go on for 5 minutes, then make the dough into a flat round shape, place on a baking tray, cover and leave for another 30 minutes.

(7) Preheat the oven to 180°C/350°F/gas mark 4.

(8) Bake for 40 minutes in the middle of the oven.

SCOTLAND

Many of Scotland's traditional foods reflect their origins in a harsher, less accommodating world than today. The haggis, for example, thought of as Scotland's national dish, is made from parts of the animal that nowadays we are far more likely to discard. The prevalence of oats as a staple food in the Scots' diet is in common with other areas in the British Isles with difficult, hard terrain. Dr Johnson disparagingly described the Scots as a nation of oats eaters. The English, with their warmer climes more appropriate to growing wheat, thought oats were only fit to be fed to horses. But Dr Johnson, despite his reputation as a man of knowledge, was presumably ignorant of the fact that oats are much richer in protein, iron, calcium and calories than the English staple cereal of the time. Potatoes are now an established part of the Scottish diet but this versatile root crop that will flourish in many conditions was regarded with some suspicion in Scotland until the early part of the nineteenth century although they were first brought to Europe from the New World in the sixteenth century.

Although many Scottish recipes are the product of an earlier, rural lifestyle dominated by a necessary frugality, there are many dishes that reveal Scotland's aristocratic French ancestry. The so-called 'Auld Alliance' of Scotland and France has certainly left its mark on the Scottish kitchen. A plate is often called an ashet, from the French assiette, a leg of lamb is known as a jigget, like the French gigot. In the time of Mary Queen of Scots, so much money was spent on foreign sweetmeats that Parliament had to pass a law forbidding all but the rich to have anything on their table that was not made in Scotland. Later, the French Revolution played its part in influencing not just the tables of Scottish lairds, but upper-class British cuisine as a whole, when many French refugees, a number of whom were chefs, fled their home country and established themselves in the houses of the British aristocracy.

Scotland has a very long coastline, but its fish-rich diet is not just a product of superabundant seas. Scotland is famous for some of the best fishing rivers in the world, and their salmon, especially smoked, now has an international reputation. The smoking of fish in Scotland was a tradition born from necessity, to preserve the seasonal surplus for times when fresh fish was difficult to come by, but the Finnan haddock and Arbroath smokie are now equally enjoyed for their flavour and remain a regular feature of Scottish cuisine.

Cock-a-Leekie

A regular feature of Burns' Night suppers, Cock-a-Leekie would originally have been made with tougher, older boiling fowls and usually with an old rooster, rather than a hen, as she would have been saved for her eggs.

INGREDIENTS

Serves four with leftovers

1.75 kg (4 lb) boiling fowl, skinned
1.75 kg (4 lb) leeks, well washed and chopped
12 prunes
2 tablespoons coarse oatmeal
salt to taste
1.2 l (2 pt) beef stock

METHOD

(1) Put skinned boiling fowl in a large pot and cover with the stock and extra water if necessary. Bring to boil, cover, turn heat to low and simmer for 1½ hours.

(2) When boiling fowl is well cooked, remove the flesh from the carcass and save it.

(3) Add half the chopped leeks to the stock and simmer until they become a thick mass of leeks in the pot (about 1 hour).

(4) About half an hour before you are going to eat, add the rest of the sliced leeks and 2 tablespoons of oatmeal to thicken the soup. Simmer for a final 25 minutes.

(5) Just before serving, add the prunes and the chicken cut from the carcass, and salt to taste. Serve with fresh brown bread.

Mussel Brose

Scotland has some of the largest and tastiest mussels in the world. It is vital that the mussels are fresh and properly prepared. Never eat any that remain closed once they have been cooked.

INGREDIENTS

1 kg (2½ lb) mussels, scrubbed and debearded
1 leek, washed and finely chopped
1 stick celery, finely chopped
1 onion, finely chopped
a few sprigs parsley, finely chopped
300 ml (½ pt) dry cider
40 g (1½ oz) butter
30 g (1 oz) flour
450 ml (1 pt) milk
salt and pepper
nutmeg, freshly grated

METHOD

(1) Put leek, celery, onion, parsley and cider in a large, non-ferrous saucepan, bring to boil, turn heat to low, add mussels, cover and cook for 10 minutes.

(2) Remove mussels and reserve, discarding any that have stayed closed. Strain the broth through a sieve and reserve it. Discard the vegetables.

(3) Melt the butter in a small saucepan, add the flour and mix thoroughly. Add the milk slowly, stirring continuously, and bring to the boil. Turn the heat to low, add the strained broth, nutmeg, and salt and pepper to taste. Bring back to simmering point, add the reserved mussels and cook for a few minutes to warm mussels through.
(4) Serve with chunks of bread.

Cullen Skink

This should be made with a floury potato such as Golden Wonder. The waxy varieties don't achieve the right consistency.

INGREDIENTS

1 Finnan haddock
1 medium onion, finely chopped
600 ml (1 pt) milk
450 g (1 lb) potatoes, peeled and quartered
30 g (1 oz) butter
salt and pepper
parsley

METHOD

(1) Place the haddock in a pan with enough water to cover. Bring to the boil and simmer for 10 minutes. Remove the fish.

(2) Add the onion and potatoes to the water and boil for 15 minutes. Meanwhile, remove the skin and bones from the haddock and flake the fish. Reserve.

(3) Drain and mash the potatoes and onions, add the milk, the flaked fish, butter and salt and pepper to taste. Bring back to the boil, then serve.

SOUTHERN INDIA

Although Indian restaurants and takeaways are a common feature of most British high streets, the overriding perception of Indian food in this country is restricted to what is known as 'curry'. But curry - or kari - simply means 'sauce' in the Tamil language, spoken in parts of Southern India, and certainly doesn't reflect the huge variety and range of dishes that make up the cooking of this huge continent.

Indian cuisine varies from region to region, but the most obvious differences in the eating habits of India's 600 million people are between the north and the south. Northern Indian food is chiefly meat-based. It is a cuisine that has been profoundly influenced by the Moguls, India's sixteenth century Muslim conquerors, whose fondness for meat-eating inspired a wealth of rich and lavish lamb dishes.

In contrast, the cooking of southern India is predominantly vegetarian. The south was much less affected by Moghul rule, partly due to its geographical distance from Delhi, the Moghul seat of power. But it is also much less affluent than the north and through economic necessity, the diet is much simpler.

Most southern Indian meals are based on a combination of rice, pulses and vegetables. Rice is a vital component of every meal both to provide bulk and to absorb the spicy liquid dhals that it is always served with. An invaluable source of protein, dhal is the name for split peas, but also applies to all pulse dishes of this type. Chutneys or pickles also play a part in most meals, not just in the south, but all over the country. They can stimulate even the most jaded of palates and offer an astonishing variety of flavours, ranging from sweet, fruity preserves made from mangos or green tomatoes, to the fresh coconut chutneys made with chillies and tamarind that are so popular in the south. Chutneys originated in India and although the West has long been used to preserves such as jams and jellies, chutneys were only introduced to Britain in the nineteenth century by returning colonials.

India is renowned as the source of a range of precious spices which play an essential part in the country's history as well as its cuisine. The lure of spice riches drew explorers and traders to India's shores, and the Malabar coast in the south ranked as one of the Old World's most important trading centres. Valued the world over for their flavours and their important role in food preservation, in India spices have always been especially prized for their medicinal properties. The ancient Sanskrit treatise on Ayurveda, the Hindu science of medicine, describes the curative characteristics of many of India's best known spices: turmeric for its antiseptic qualities; ginger for liver complaints; cardamom for headaches, fevers and eye diseases; coriander for constipation and insomnia.

Indian supermarkets are the best place to buy any unusual ingredients. Ghee and vegetarian ghee are available.

Lali Nayar was brought up in Hyderabad in southern India. She is an excellent cook and won the Indian Cook of the Year Award in 1993. She feels the secret of her success lies in her emphasis on home cooking and she is critical of the quality of many Indian fast food outlets, feeling that it misrepresents Indian cooking:

'I find many of the dishes monotonous and drab . . . Indian food is not fast food, it needs a lot of care and every dish has its individual characteristics . . . it is in ordinary homes and ordinary kitchens that the true taste of India lies.'

Lali has kindly provided us with all the recipes in this section.

Kabuli

A one-pot Indian meal of rice, vegetables, dahl and whole spices. This recipe comes from Lali's home town of Hyderabad and she always serves it with Dahi Chutney.

INGREDIENTS

350 g (12 oz) rice (basmati)
125 g (4 oz) channa dhal (split yellow peas)
150 g (5 oz) mixed diced vegetables (combination of beans, carrots, corn)
125 ml (4 fl oz) ghee or cooking oil
125 ml (4 fl oz) yoghurt
3 tomatoes, chopped
1 medium onion finely sliced
1 teaspoon grated garlic
1 teaspoon grated ginger
6 green chillies, finely chopped
1 tablespoon lemon juice
1 tablespoon mint leaves, finely chopped
2 tablespoons coriander leaves, finely chopped

Whole spices:
½ teaspoon black cumin seeds
2 green cardamoms
6 cloves
5 cm (2") cinnamon
pinch saffron strands, mixed with 125 ml (4½fl oz) milk
salt to taste
½teaspoon turmeric powder
pinch of tomato red colouring

METHOD

(1) Pressure-cook the split yellow peas with just enough water to cook them without breaking the lentils, keep aside.

(2) Boil rice until it is nearly done (do not cook fully) drain any excess water left and keep rice aside.

(3) Fry the onion until golden in colour. Keep aside half for later use. To the rest add all the whole spices and fry for a few seconds.

(4) Add grated garlic and ginger, turmeric and salt and fry further for 1 minute.

(5) Add green chillies, tomatoes and yoghurt and fry till a homogenous mixture is formed, then add mint, coriander leaves and lemon juice. Stir for a while, remove from heat and add to the cooked dhal. Mix gently and keep aside.

(6) Cook mixed diced vegetables with a little water and salt (defrost if frozen). Add a little (1 tablespoon) ghee and keep separate.

To assemble Kabuli:

(1) In a large pan/baking dish put a teaspoon of ghee, spread a layer of nearly cooked rice, then a layer of the cooked lentils, then another layer of rice. Now add all the vegetables on one layer followed by a thin layer of rice, and a second layer of the lentils, finishing off with another layer of rice on the top.

(2) Sprinkle the fried onions which were kept aside over the rice and gently pour the milk and saffron mixture all over: if wanted, a little more ghee can be sprinkled on top as well as a few sliced and toasted almonds.

(3) If cooking on top of cooker: cover the pan (must be with a heavy base), with a large piece of foil and then put a tightly fitting lid on and simmer on low heat for a further 15-20 minutes.

(4) If baking in the oven, cover dish completely with foil and bake slowly for 15-20 minutes. Remove foil and serve hot with Dahi chutney (below), Pappad (poppadoms) and salad.

Dahi Chutney

INGREDIENTS

300 ml (10 fl oz) carton natural yogurt
3-4 tablespoons grated coconut, fresh (preferably) or dessiccated
2 tablespoons finely chopped onions or spring onions
2 green chillies, finely cut
salt to taste

Seasoning:
1 tablespoon cooking oil
½ tablespoon mustard seeds
a few curry leaves
2 whole small red chillies

METHOD

(1) Whisk yogurt in a serving bowl and add coconut, onions, green chillies and salt. Mix gently and keep ready.

(2) Heat oil in a small frying pan. Add mustard seeds, curry leaves and red chillies. When seeds begin to splutter, quickly pour this mixture over the yogurt and immediately cover with a plate or lid to infuse the flavour into the yogurt. After a few (2-3) minutes, remove lid and serve the Dahi Chutney immediately with Kabuli.

Also serve Pappad (poppadoms) and salad. The salad is usually a combination of chopped cucumber and tomatoes.

Kebab ka Korma (Kebab Curry)

INGREDIENTS

For kebabs
500 g (1 lb 2 oz) minced lamb (twice minced)
55 g (2 oz) grated onions
2 cloves finely chopped garlic
2 cm (1") piece finely chopped ginger
2 green chillies, finely chopped
1 tablespoon finely chopped mint leaves
1 tablespoon finely chopped green coriander leaves
1 tablespoon garam masala
1 teaspoon salt or to taste

2 teaspoons mustard oil
1 teaspoon lemon juice
1 egg - lightly beaten

For korma sauce:
200 g (7 oz) grated onions
30 g (1 oz) fresh ginger (grind together with a little water)
4 cloves garlic
30 g (1 oz) almond powder (mix together and keep)
1 large cup coconut milk
110 g (4 oz) ghee

Spices:
6 cloves
3 green cardamoms
5 cm (2") piece of cinnamon
20 peppercorns
4 small whole red chillies
2 silver leaves for decoration

METHOD

To make the kebabs:
(1) In a big bowl, combine all above ingredients and mix well.

(2) Put this mixture through an electric grinder/food processor and mix further to blend all ingredients. Leave to stand for 15-20 minutes.

(3) Divide mixture into 16-20 parts and shape them into small sausage-like kebabs. Place the shaped kebabs on a greased baking tray and cook them in a very hot oven for 15-20 minutes. Turn them once in between to brown them all over.

(6) Remove from oven and set aside to cool.

To make the sauce:
(7) In a large pan heat the ghee and fry the onions until golden brown in colour. Add ginger and garlic and fry further for a minute or so. Grind the cloves, cardamoms, cinnamon, peppercorns and chillies together with 1 cup of water. Add the ground spices to the pan and fry on low heat for another few seconds. Add salt to taste. Slowly add the coconut milk and almonds and let the mixture cook for a while - do not let it thicken.

(8) Gently add the cooked kebabs to the sauce. Let them simmer for a while until the gravy turns thick and creamy (a few minutes). Serve hot, decorated with silver leaves.

Double ka Mitha
(Bread and Milk Pudding)

I feel this is one of the nicest and tastiest of Indian puddings. Don't let its simple ingredients put you off: it truly gives a grand result with very little effort.

INGREDIENTS

12 slices (medium) white bread, preferably a day or two old
1 ltr (36 fl oz) milk
300 ml (½pt) sweetened condensed milk
6 green cardamoms (shelled and crushed)
few drops rose essence or 1 tablespoon rose water
2 tablespoons sultanas
2 tablespoons coarsely chopped almonds with their skins
2 tablespoons coarsely chopped cashew nuts
vegetable oil for deep frying

METHOD

(1) Cut bread slices diagonally into halves and deep fry on medium heat in batches until crisp and deep golden in colour. Remove and keep aside.

(2) In the same oil fry the almonds and cashew nuts lightly. Drain well and keep aside.

(3) Bring the milk to boil. Lower heat and slowly add condensed milk to it. Let the mixture simmer for 1-2 minutes. Add the fried bread pieces - gently mixing them and soaking them completely in the milk mixture. Add the crushed cardamoms, rose essence and the sultanas. Stir occasionally, but very slowly and with care - as it is nice for the pieces to retain their shape. Cook on a medium heat until the bread soaks up all the liquid and acquires a semi-dry appearance.

(4) Remove from heat, transfer to a serving dish and garnish with fried almonds and cashew nuts. Serve hot or cold.

HANDY HINT: A chocolate flavour can be produced by adding 1 tablespoon cocoa powder along with the milk mixture before adding the fried bread. Try it, it makes a lovely change!

SWEDEN

Sweden's extreme climate with its long, cold winters, has had a huge effect on the country's cuisine. In medieval times, produce from the summer months had to be preserved for winter consumption when it was almost impossible to get hold of fresh foods. As a result, there is a predominance of smoked, salted and pickled dishes in the Swedish diet. Though these methods of preservation were once a method of life insurance and all-important to survival, they have remained central to the country's cooking through sheer enjoyment of their flavours.

Preserved dishes are an essential part of the Swedish Smorgasbord, that huge array of different foods that is crucial to any Swedish celebration. The Swedes invented the Smorgasbord and it is an immense source of national pride. It can contain a staggering number of dishes which can seem daunting for the first-timer, but they are always eaten in the same order: a variety of herrings to start, which might be pickled, smoked or served in sour cream, then other cold fish and cold meats, and finally the hot dishes, such as Jansson's Temptation.

Aquavit is Sweden's most popular tipple and is almost always served with Smorgasbord. A colourless, potent spirit made from potatoes and flavoured with caraway seeds, its name comes from the Latin ***aqua vitae*** meaning water of life.

Swedish-born Anna Hegarty has been running her restaurant, Anna's Place, in North London for the last 20 years. Anna made this dish for World in a Stew in the third series of Food File, and explained where its name comes from:

'Jansson was a rather pompous opera singer who fancied himself as being an excellent cook. One night he was descended upon by lots of his friends who challenged him to cook something for them. He opened his larder and all he had in it was anchovies, potatoes, onions and cream, so this was the dish he designed. Everyone applauded probably more loudly than they ever applauded his singing.'

The anchovies Anna uses in this dish are Swedish cured anchovies. These can be found in specialist shops, but the dish can also be made with the tinned Mediterranean anchovies, although they should be soaked in milk first.

Jansson's Temptation

This is a mouthwatering combination of potatoes, onions, anchovies and cream, baked together in the oven. Jansson's Temptation is traditionally eaten in Sweden on feast days as part of a Smorgasbord. Modern Swedes still enjoy this dish with just a green salad and bread.

INGREDIENTS

3 x 55 g (2 oz) tins anchovies
900 g (2 lb) potatoes, grated
75 g (2½ oz) unsalted butter
1 tablespoon oil
4 medium onions, thinly sliced
300 ml (½ pt) single cream
150 ml (¼ pt) milk
black pepper

METHOD

(1) Soak anchovies in some milk for an hour or so to remove some of the salt. The milk is then discarded.

(2) Cover grated potatoes with water to prevent discolouring.

(3) Preheat oven to 200°C/400°F/gas mark 6.

(4) Sauté the onions in 30 g (1 oz) of the butter and the tablespoon of oil until they are golden and soft, but not brown.

(5) Grease an ovenproof dish with 15 g (½ oz) of the butter. Drain and dry the grated potatoes. Add a layer of potatoes followed by layers of onions and anchovies, sprinkling each layer with a little ground black pepper. Continue the layers, ending with a layer of potatoes. Dot with the remaining 30 g (1 oz) of butter.

(6) Heat the milk and cream to barely simmering and pour over the dish. Place dish in the middle of the oven and cook for 45 minutes.

Swedish Meatballs

Another traditional Smorgasbord speciality, a light creamy change from the normal meatball.

INGREDIENTS

15 g (½ oz) butter
1 medium onion, finely chopped
225 g (½ lb) boiled potato, mashed
4 tablespoons dry breadcrumbs
450 g (1 lb) ground beef (lean mince)
60 ml (2½ fl oz) single cream
1 teaspoon salt
1 egg

For the sauce:
30 g (1 oz) butter
2 tablespoons sunflower oil
1 tablespoon plain flour
150 ml (½ pt) single cream

METHOD

(1) Melt the butter in a frying pan over a medium heat. When the foam subsides add the onions and sauté for 5 minutes until they are soft but not browned.

(2) Put the onions, potato, breadcrumbs, beef, cream, salt and egg in a mixing bowl. Mix until all the ingredients are blended. Shape into 2 cm (1") balls. Arrange on a baking tray, cover with plastic film and refrigerate for an hour.

(3) Remove plastic film and place the meatballs under grill for 4-5 minutes, then turn over and cook for a further 4-5 minutes.

(4) To make the sauce: put butter and oil in a frying pan, melt over a medium heat, stir in the flour, then add the cream and continue cooking for a few minutes stirring constantly until you have a thick smooth sauce.

(5) Place the meatballs on a dish, and pour the sauce over them. Serve with pasta or potatoes.

Gravadlax

A Swedish delicacy and a must on any Smorgasbord. The name means 'buried salmon' from the time when the curing of the fish would be done by burying it under the freezing ground. It is cheaper than smoked salmon and often tastier. Serve with the mustard sauce.

INGREDIENTS

675 g (1½ lb) salmon, split down the centre, boned, cleaned and scaled
1 bunch dill, coarsely chopped
2 tablespoons coarse sea salt
2 tablespoons sugar
1 tablespoon crushed white peppercorns

METHOD

(1) Put half of the fish skin side down in a shallow glass bowl and place the dill on top.

(2) Mix salt, sugar and peppercorns together in a bowl and put this mixture on top of the dill and place the other half of salmon over it, skin side up. Cover with foil.

(3) Place a plate on top of the foil and add some weights.

(4) Refrigerate for 48 hours turning the fish over every 12 hours and basting both the inside and outside of the salmon with the marinade that accumulates.

(5) To serve, remove the marinade and dill and dry the fish with a paper towel. Place the salmon skin side down and carve thinly and diagonally. Serve the slices with a mustard and dill sauce.

Mustard and Dill Sauce

INGREDIENTS

2 tablespoons Dijon mustard
½ teaspoon dry mustard
1 tablespoon white wine vinegar
1½ tablespoons sugar
45 ml (3 tablespoons) olive oil
1 tablespoon fresh dill, chopped

METHOD

(1) Mix the mustards, vinegar and sugar in a bowl.

(2) Slowly beat in the oil until the mixture is the consistency of mayonnaise and finally stir in the dill.

(3) Serve with Gravadlax.

TUNISIA

Tunisia lies in the Maghreb region of northwest Africa and is a country with a fantastic culinary tradition. Couscous, mint tea with rose water, Merguez sausages and harrissa, a hot spicy sauce served with every meal, are the backbone of Tunisian life. Mix this with a wealth of seafoods, a love of lamb and street markets overflowing with vegetables and pulses, and the results are some of North Africa's favourite dishes.

The Tunisian people are mainly Muslim, preferring tea or lemonade to alcohol and never eating pork. Lamb has a special significance in Tunisia. During 'Aiyda', the main feast of the Muslim calendar, every family slaughters a lamb to be eaten during the three days of celebration. The significance of the lamb dates back to the Old Testament story of Abraham. Abraham was asked to prove his love of God by sacrificing his only son. Of course Abraham obeyed, but at the last minute God produced a lamb which was sacrificed instead of the boy.

Wheat is the staple grain of this region and is used to make Tunisia's favourite ingredient, couscous. The dish Couscous uses this semolina-like grain served with a spicy stew made with lamb, beef, or fish with vegetables.

Lamb Couscous

Tunisian-born Abdul Boukraa and his English wife Frances, run 'Adam's Cafe' in West London. A 'greasy spoon' cafe by day, by night it is magically transformed into a restaurant serving traditional Tunisian dishes to its ever-growing clientele. Abdul was taught to prepare this couscous recipe by his mother when he was a child. He remembers that they would always cook too much couscous so that in the morning they could heat the grains on a charcoal grill until crispy and eat them for breakfast.

Because of the long cooking time, cheaper cuts of meat like the shoulder or neck of lamb are always used for making Couscous. According to Abdul, they actually taste better than the more expensive cuts like the leg.

'Ras-el-hanout' is the name of the main spice mix used in Tunisia. A mix of over twenty different spices, Ras-el-hanout literally means 'top of the shop' or 'grocers' own mix'. As it is not readily available in this country, Abdul has specified the basic ingredients so that we can mix our own.

Traditionally, Couscous is made in a couscousier, a two-tiered pot where the stew is cooked in the bottom with the couscous grains steaming in the top. You can always substitute a rice steamer or a metal colander with a lid.

INGREDIENTS

Serves 6

8 tablespoons olive oil
1 onion, chopped
2 cloves garlic, chopped
3 tablespoons tomato purée
450 g (1 lb) lamb (neck or shoulder), cut into pieces
salt
1 teaspoon black pepper
1 teaspoon turmeric
2 teaspoons paprika
½ teaspoon each powdered cumin, coriander and ginger
harissa or any other chilli sauce
600 ml (1 pt) water
450 g (1 lb) couscous
3 carrots, chopped
2 potatoes, chopped
2 turnips, diced
4 courgettes, sliced
2 tomatoes, chopped
110 g (4 oz) chickpeas, soaked overnight, or 400 g (14 oz) can chickpeas

To garnish:
sliced hard-boiled eggs
black olives
sultanas

METHOD

(1) Pour the olive oil into the bottom of a steamer or couscousier and heat. Add the onion and garlic to the oil and cook over a low heat until just browned.

(2) Add the tomato purée and the meat, with a little water. Then add the salt, black pepper, turmeric, paprika, cumin, coriander and ginger. Finally add the harissa or chilli sauce to taste. Pour in the water, bring to the boil, cover, and cook for 30 minutes.

(3) Meanwhile, prepare the couscous. Put it in a sieve and then put the sieve in a bowl filled with cold water. Keep it there for about 30 seconds, no longer. Pour the couscous on to a large dish and let it fluff out. After 10 minutes separate the couscous grains from each other with your hands. Every grain needs to be separated or it will go lumpy when cooked.

(4) Add the carrots, potatoes, turnips and chickpeas, if using dried, to the meat. Put the couscous into the top of the couscousier and cover. After 30 minutes take the couscous out and separate the grains again. Sprinkle with a little water and oil to help the grains separate.

(5) Add the courgettes, chopped tomatoes and chickpeas, if using tinned, to the meat stew. Put the couscous back on top of the couscousier and cook for a further 30 minutes until cooked.

(6) To serve, put the couscous in a large bowl, pour the stew over it and serve, garnished with hard-boiled eggs, olives or sultanas.

Harira

This traditional soup breaks the fast at sunset during the Muslim month of Ramadan

INGREDIENTS

30 g (1 oz) butter
2 chicken thighs, skinned
1 onion, sliced
1 celery stick, chopped
a handful chopped, fresh coriander
1 teaspoon ground turmeric
1 teaspoon black pepper
1 teaspoon chilli powder
7cm (3") cinnamon stick
1 green chilli, deseeded and chopped
1 tablespoon tomato purée
1.8 l (3 pt water)
400 g (14 oz) can chick peas, drained
110 g (4 oz) long grain rice, rinsed
1 tablespoon cornflour mixed with a little water
1 egg, beaten

METHOD

(1) Place all ingredients up to and including the water, in a large saucepan and simmer covered for 45 minutes.

(2) Shred the cooked chicken meat, remove the bones and return to the pan.

(3) Add the chick peas and rice and simmer covered for 15 minutes.

(4) Add the cornflour mixture and simmer for a further 5 minutes.

(5) Just before serving add the beaten egg.

(6) Serve with wedges of lemon.

Tfina

This tasty lamb stew was eaten by the Jews of North Africa. It would always be prepared on a Friday to be eaten on the Sabbath (Saturday) when cooking was not allowed.

INGREDIENTS

Serves 8

25 g (1 oz) butter
2 tablespoons palm oil
1.5 kg (3 lb) lamb, shoulder of mutton or beef (or a mixture) cut into large cubes
4 l (6 pt) water
4 cloves garlic, finely chopped
1 round red chilli, finely chopped (optional)
3 green chillies, finely chopped
3 medium onions, finely chopped
450 g (1 lb) potatoes, peeled and cut into 5 cm (2") chunks
¼ teaspoon each: ground black pepper, ground mixed spice, ground turmeric, ground coriander, ground cumin
225 g (8 oz) carrots, thinly sliced
5 cm (2") cinnamon stick
110 g (4 oz) chickpeas, soaked and drained
55 g (2 oz) prunes, pre-soaked, stoned and chopped
55 g (2 oz) dried apricots, soaked and chopped
55 g (2 oz) sultanas
2 tablespoons fresh coriander, finely chopped
juice of 1 lemon
selection of whole dried fruits (55 g (2 oz) in total)

METHOD

(1) In a large frying pan, heat the butter and palm oil and brown the meat pieces, in several batches if necessary.

(2) Place the browned meat pieces and the remainder of the ingredients, (except the coriander, lemon juice and whole dried fruits), in a large casserole, using

some of the water to rinse out the oil and meat juices for the frying pan. Stir and bring to a slow simmer, then cover and cook over a very low heat so that the stew simmers gently for at least 2 hours.

(3) Fifteen minutes before serving, stir in the whole dried fruits, coriander and lemon juice. Serve with boiled long-grain rice.

WALES

Traditional Welsh cooking has very ancient roots and dates back to a time when early Celtic tribesmen worked hard to make this bleak, primitive land yield enough food for its people.

Unlike England, Wales' traditional cuisine did not develop through wealthy manor-house kitchens, but rather through the life of rural Wales. The rich didn't eat the foods of the country, preferring to ape their English counterparts across the border, so the culinary history of Wales belongs to its farming folk and peasantry.

Consequently, many Welsh recipes have evolved to satisfy hardworking, outdoor appetites and are based on produce that could thrive in Wales's often forbidding and inaccesible landscape. The harsh mountain regions could support few cereal crops other than oats and in common with other Celtic countries, they appear in many Welsh dishes, both sweet and savoury.

These mountainous areas of the principality are now home to the very best Welsh lamb. Lamb is regarded as a national speciality and is gaining something of a reputation in Europe, but in the past it was more usually saved for special occasions as it was the lowly pig, mainly in the form of salty bacon, that formed the backbone of the Welsh diet.

Pigs have always been the animals of the poor because they can survive in the leanest of conditions. Even in the earlier years of this century, most Welsh families would keep a couple of pigs, not just in rural areas, but in the semi-urban parts of the mining valleys where they would be kept at the bottom of the garden throughout the year until they were killed to keep the family fed. As all the pig couldn't be eaten at once, most of it was salted and hung from the beams in the kitchen. Pieces would be cut off as and when it was needed.

Cockles continue to provide a source of inexpensive protein along Wales's Gower peninsula and local cocklemen and women continue to gather these humble shellfish by hand today in the same way as they have for centuries. This part of South Wales is also home to laver, an edible seaweed that grows naturally along the coast. Sea vegetables were a regular feature of the British diet in early times, especially in northern and western Britain, but it was only the Welsh who kept a taste for this vitamin and mineral-rich food. Laverbread is always sold ready prepared in the numerous markets throughout South Wales. Traditionally enjoyed warmed through in a little bacon fat and served with bacon and eggs, laver is now being adapted by some contemporary Welsh cookery writers into more modern recipes and is often served as a sauce with Welsh salmon.

Wales has some extremely good salmon rivers but they are now much less abundant than they once were. But then salmon has not always been the delicacy it is today: apprentices once petitioned for a special clause in their indentures, to stipulate that they should not be made to eat fresh salmon more than twice a week.

All the recipes in this section were kindly provided by Anne Llewellyn.

Cawl

Cawl was once the mainstay of the Welsh diet and would have been eaten every day by people living in rural areas for their main meal. This hearty, soupy stew made from a mixture of meat and vegetables is still eaten regularly in Wales, although these days it probably contains slightly more meat and rather less fat than it once did. There are no strict rules for making Cawl - it is a dish made out of whatever is to hand. The meat can be lamb, beef or hock end of bacon. Whatever vegetables are in season can be used, although leeks always form part of the recipe. In particularly hard times, if people couldn't afford any meat then the cawl would be made just with the vegetables and cooked with a wooden spoon in it to add flavour.

Cawl can be eaten either as a meal in itself, or as was more common in the past, in two courses, the broth eaten on its own with bread, and the meat and vegetables afterwards or even the following day. This is very similar to the French way of eating Pot-au-feu, another dish with Celtic connections.

Mair ap Mervyn, from west Wales, makes Cawl regularly for herself and her son, Llywelyn. Mair makes her Cawl with lamb, and is lucky enough to get her vegetables from her sister's organic farm.

INGREDIENTS

900 g (2lb) lamb, such as best end of neck cutlets
5 large potatoes, cut into chunks
2 large carrots, cut into small chunks
3-4 leeks, carefully washed and chopped
1 large onion, chopped
1 small swede, chopped
bunch of parsley

METHOD

(1) Cover the meat in cold water in saucepan. Bring to the boil and simmer for an hour. Cool overnight and remove all the fat that has risen to the surface.

(2) Bring the meat back to the boil. Add all the vegetables, but keep back a third of the leeks and all of the parsley. Simmer for 45 minutes.

(3) Five minutes before serving, add the rest of the leeks and the parsley.

Leek and Bacon Tart

Leeks are the national emblem of Wales, probably because they are eaten so regularly. This is another recipe that Wales shares with France.

INGREDIENTS

170 g (6 oz) shortcrust pastry
450 g (1 lb) leeks
1 tablespoon butter
3 rashers bacon, chopped
2 well-beaten eggs
300 ml (½ pt) milk or single cream
salt and pepper

METHOD

(1) Line a 20 cm (8") flan tin with pastry and leave in a cool place.

(2) Wash the leeks thoroughly and chop into 2 cm (1") pieces, using as much of the green part as possible (depending on the age of the leeks).

(3) Cook the leeks gently in butter until soft, then spread them in the flan case, sprinkle over chopped bacon and season to taste.

(4) Beat eggs with the milk or single cream and pour over leeks.

(5) Cook in oven at approximately 180°C/350°F/gas mark 4 for 30 - 35 minutes, until the filling is set.

Glamorgan Sausages

Glamorgan sausages are meat free. Caerphilly is ideal for this dish, but any hard Cheddar-style cheese can be used. Serve for breakfast with bacon and eggs.

INGREDIENTS

170 g (6 oz) grated hard cheese (e.g. Caerphilly)
255 g (9 oz) fresh breadcrumbs
1 tablespoon grated onion
1 tablespoon mixed fresh herbs (parsley, chives, etc.)
good pinch mustard powder
salt and pepper
2 eggs (1 separated)
flour
oil and butter

METHOD

(1) Mix together cheese, breadcrumbs, mustard powder, herbs and onion and season well.

(2) Add 1 whole egg and 1 yolk and mix thoroughly. If mix is too dry, add a little milk.

(3) Whip up remaining egg white until frothy. Form mix into sausage shapes, roll in egg white and then in flour.

(4) Fry sausages in frying pan a few at a time in butter and oil, until golden brown.

Addresses

Please send a large, stamped self-addressed envelope for further information from any of the following groups.

Age Concern England, Distribution Department, 1268 London Road, London SW16 4ER
Age Concern produce a booklet, *Eat Well, Age Well*

Baby Milk Action, 23 St Andrew's Street, Cambridge CB2 3AX
Baby Milk Action is a non-profit making organization which aims to halt the commercial promotion of bottle feeding and to protect and promote good and appropriate infant nutrition. It is a member of the International Baby Food Action Network (IBFAN), which has over 140 groups in more than 70 countries.

British Dietetic Association, 7th Floor, Elizabeth House, Suffolk Street, Queensway, Birmingham B1 1LF
The British Dietetic Association provides information about state-registered dietitians.

British Heart Foundation, 14 Fitzharding Street, London W1 4DH
The British Heart Foundation is a charity which funds vital research into the causes, treatment and prevention of heart disease. It publishes leaflets and other publications on food for a healthy heart.

'Chuck Sweets off the Checkout' Campaign, c/o Community Nutrition Group, Health Promotion Unit, Wilson Hospital, Cranmer Road, Mitcham, Surrey CR4 4TP

Compassion in World Farming, 20 Lavant Street, Petersfield, Hampshire GU32 3EW
Compassion in World Farming is Britain's leading farm animal welfare organization campaigning for the end of factory farming and the live animal export trade.

Consumers Association, 2 Marylebone Road, London NW1 RDF
The Consumers Association are producers of the 'Which?' publications.

The Cool Chile Company, 34 Basset Road, London W10 6JL

Coronary Prevention Group, Plantation House, Suites 5/4 D&M, 31/35 Fenchurch Street, London EC3M 3NN
The Coronary Prevention Group is the only UK charity solely concerned with the prevention of coronary heart disease. Its target is to contribute to a reduction in deaths from coronary heart disease by 30% by the year 2000.

Diet Breakers, Church Cottage, Barford Saint Michael, Oxon OX15 0UA
Diet Breakers are running a national anti-diet campaign which aims to unite people of all sizes, backgrounds and professions to fight the tyranny of thinness.

Eating Disorders Association, Sackville Place, 44 Magdalen Street, Norwich NR3 1JU
The Eating Disorders Association provides details of counsellors, NHS programmes and self-help groups for those concerned about anorexia and bulimia. They run a helpline on (0603) 621414 (Monday - Friday, 9am - 6pm) and a youth helpline for anyone under 18 on (0603) 765050
(Monday - Wednesday, 4 - 6pm).

Food Commission, 3rd Floor, 5-11 Worship Street, London EC21 2BH
The Food Commission is one of the leading consumer watchdogs on food. It aims to provide independently-researched information on the food we eat and to ensure good-quality food for all.

Food Safety Advisory Centre, Collier House, 163-169 Brompton Road, London SW3 1PY
The Food Safey Advisory Centre provides the consumer with impartial information about food safety, through leaflets, books and Food Line
(Freephone (0800) 282407).

The Migraine Trust, 45 Great Ormond Street, London WC1N 3HA
The Migraine Trust provides a booklist and publishes information on how to find your trigger factors.

National Food Alliance (including the 'Get Cooking' project), 3rd Floor, 5-11 Worship Street, London EC2A 2BH
The National Food Alliance is an association of national voluntary, professional, helath, consumer and other public-interest organisations. Contact the NFA for details of the 'Get Cooking' project and also the NFA Campaign for healthier food advertising for children.

Pesticides Trust, Eurolink Centre, 49 Effra Road, London SW2 1BZ
The Pesticides Trust is a charity closely concerned with health and the environmental effects of pesticides. It was established as an independent body to provide a forum for discussion on pesticide issues, and to help co-ordinate action and information dissemination about pesticides.

RSPCA, Causeway, Horsham, West Sussex RH12 1HG

School Meals Campaign, c/o National Forum for CHD Prevention, Hamilton House, Mabledon Place, London WC1
The School Meals Campaign publishes an action pack for parents, governors and anyone else wanting to improve school meals.

Soil Association, Organic Food and Farming Centre, 86-88 Colston Street, Bristol BS1 5BB
The Soil Association's purpose is to research, develop and promote sustainable relationships between the soil, plants, animals, people and the biosphere, in order to produce healthy food and other products while protecting and enhancing the environment. Their handbook on animal welfare is available from the above address.

Vegetarian Society, Parkdale, Dunham Road, Altrincham, Cheshire WA14 4OJ
The aim of the Vegetarian Society is to increase the number of vegetarians in the UK in order to save animals, benefit human health and protect the environment and world food resources.

World Cancer Research Fund, 11-12 Buckingham Gate, London SW1E 6LB
The World Cancer Research Fund aims to educate consumers about the relationship between the foods they choose and cancer risk. The WCRF also provides funding for cancer research at universities and hospitals to help further understanding of the relationship between diet and cancer.

Index of recipes